Oct 2023

Jim,

Thanks for your many years of friendship & all the memories,

[signature]

STICKS 'n' STONES

OFFICIAL ENDORSEMENT OF KEVIN MARTIN

IN STICKS 'N' STONES Warren Hansen outlines in detail the struggle for over 10 years that the sport of curling went through to become an Olympic medal sport. It is fascinating to read about the challenges the sport faced to become medal considering curling is now such an important part of the Winter Olympics television coverage. Warren was very involved with getting curling into Calgary as a demonstration sport in 1988 and then assumed a key role with the organizing committee to effectively stage curling at the Games.

I can honestly say that I loved competing at the Winter Olympic's each of the three times I had the honour.

The 1992 Winter Olympics in Albertville, France was my first Olympic experience. Curling was a demonstration sport at that 1992 Winter Games and I enjoyed the pleasure of representing Canada. It was such a joy to be part of the much larger Canadian Olympic Team and being able to cheer on teammates in the various sport disciplines. We failed to medal at the 1992 Olympics but the seed was planted and later that year, when it was announced that curling would be an official medal sport, I started my quest to return. My love of the Olympic Games was deeply engrained forever.

My next opportunity to compete at the Olympics was in 2002 at Salt Lake City, Utah. Curling had full medal status by now and as a result we stayed at the Olympic Village which quickly became my favourite place to be.

It was fantastic to meet and make friends with athletes from all over the world, enjoy massive television coverage and experience the overwhelming pressure during the competition. It was a thrill to win the silver medal although we were within inches of capturing the gold.

In 2010 I was fortunate enough to be a member of the Canadian contingent in Vancouver where we were part of the home team at the Winter Olympics! I will never forget the thrill of walking into the loud and proud B.C. Place Stadium at the opening ceremonies which set the stage for the weeks ahead. Incredibly loud crowds and boisterous Canadian fans gives me chills still when I think about the 2010 Olympics. To be at the top of the podium after recording Canada's 13th gold medal of the Vancouver Games (tying Russia for the record) is a moment that will never be erased from my memory. Of course, we all remember Sid Crosby scoring to win gold the next day and Canada breaking the tie with that 14th gold medal. It brought all of my Olympic memories to a crowning moment to experience being part of the larger Canadian team and the accomplishment it was for the nation.

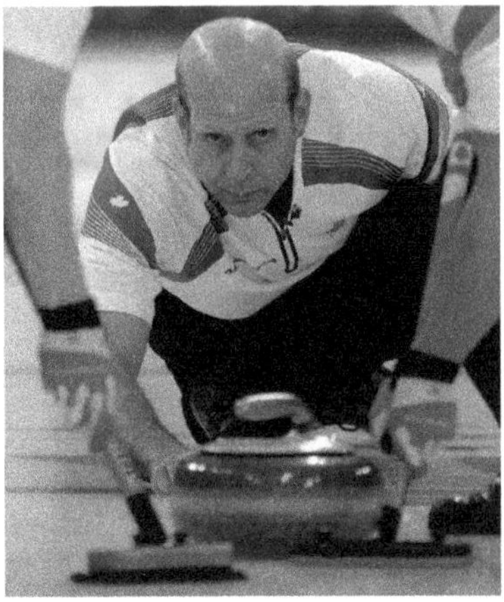

Kevin Martin
Olympic Silver Medalist 2002
Olympic Gold Medalist 2010

STICKS 'n' STONES

The Battle for Curling to be an Olympic Sport

WARREN HANSEN

FriesenPress
One Printers Way
Altona, MB, R0G 0B0
Canada

www.friesenpress.com

First Edition — 2021

www.warrenhansenauthor.com

Photographs by Michael Burns

ISBN
978-1-03-911791-4 (Hardcover)
978-1-03-911790-7 (Paperback)
978-1-03-911792-1 (eBook)

1. SPORTS & RECREATION, WINTER SPORTS, CURLING

Distributed to the trade by The Ingram Book Company

TABLE OF CONTENTS

FOREWORD BY TERRY JONES

NOBODY IN THE entire history of curling did more for the sport than Warren Hansen, who took it from being viewed as a highly social winter recreation to a high-performance sport deserving of a spot in the Olympic Winter Games.

And it's highly unlikely that anybody was presented with more obstacles in trying to do so, especially from the very athletes that ended up becoming the biggest benefactors. This is that story.

Warren Hansen's fingerprints are on almost everything that happened to drive the sport into the Olympics, turn it into a significant television property, and fill NHL buildings with fans.

A three-time Little Grey Cup winner with the football Edmonton Huskies, who won the 1974 Brier playing second for the legendary Hec Gervais, Hansen was inducted into the World Curling Hall of Fame, the Canadian Curling Hall of Fame, and Alberta Sports Hall of Fame at the conclusion of his full-time career as Director of Event Operations for Curling Canada in 2015.

Hansen was the first-ever person to be paid on an annual basis by the Canadian Curling Association way back in 1974, when the business was being transferred from one president's kitchen table to the next.

Hansen was the man most responsible for taking the cigarettes out of the mouths of the curlers, forcefully teaching them how to dress and conduct themselves, and otherwise making them presentable enough to go into the Olympics and for curling to develop into the major TV property it has become.

He's the man who, when told it was going to be the biggest flop in the history of Canadian sport, took the Brier into NHL buildings in Western Canada and developed the event and other properties into the attractions that drew over 1.1 million fans in five visits to Edmonton's Rexall Place in a fourteen-year span.

Hansen created the mixed doubles event that has become an Olympic sport, created the Canada Cup and Continental Cup and Season of Champions, went to four sheets of ice from five, adopted the Page playoff format, and added officiating and scorekeeping systems and dozens of other tweaks and innovations.

It began in Namao, Alberta (just north of Edmonton), for Hansen. He went to a small school that had three grades in one room and no sports programs. When he was just a youngster, he often tagged along with his parents as they travelled to Edmonton to curl at the Thistle Club, and he quickly fell in love with the sport.

Hansen became an Edmonton Huskies football player, one of eight who played on all three of the title teams: 1963, 1964, and 1965. The team was enshrined in the Alberta Sports Hall of Fame and, eventually, in the Edmonton Sports Hall of Fame.

During the seventies, Hansen was a curling broom representative in Alberta, ran the Silver Broom Curling School on both sides of the Atlantic, and made trips to Sweden, Denmark, Germany, Japan, and the USA. In 1974, he started the coaches/instructors' program that became known as Curl Canada and was part of the National Coaching Certification program, which continues today. He even did radio reports from the Brier and other major events for a string of radio stations around the country for seventeen years. In addition to directing all of curling's major championships, he was also media relations director throughout most of his career.

He partnered with Ray Kingsmith of Calgary in getting curling into the Olympics as a demonstration sport at the 1988 Winter Olympics and was the main force, at the same time, in trying to make it presentable. Probably Hansen's most significant contribution to the sport worldwide was the work he initiated that eventually ended in curling becoming an Olympic sport in 1992.

Curling, arguably second only to hockey in Canada, grew to reach its full potential because of one man more than any other.

Terry Jones is a member of the Canadian Curling Hall of Fame and columnist of the Edmonton Sun *and the* Edmonton Journal, *with more than a half century covering sports in the City of Champions and championships for either one or the other, and now both newspapers. In addition to a dozen other books, Jones authored the highly acclaimed* World Capital of Curling *and* The Ferbey Four *books on curling. He's also in the Hockey Hall of Fame, Canadian Football Hall of Fame, Alberta Sports Hall of Fame, Edmonton Sports Hall of Fame, and was honoured with the Canadian Sports Media Lifetime Achievement Award.*

ACKNOWLEDGEMENTS

THIS STORY STARTED about forty-five years ago, so many of the people that played an important role in making it possible to unfold are no longer with us. Many of these people and others helped in so many ways to get curling on the Olympic podium.

I will start with my old friend Ray Kingsmith, whom I shared the vision and desire for curling to be more than it was, and together, we laid the foundation for curling to be accepted as a demonstration sport in the 1988 Winter Olympics in Calgary. Ray left us a way too soon in May of 1988. Ray introduced me to Herb Millham at the 1974 Brier shortly after he was elected as the third vice president of the Canadian Curling Association (CCA). Millham was given the task of developing a program within curling in Canada that involved teaching people to instruct the sport. Herb hired me and provided the green light to start curling in Canada down a whole new exciting path that would play a major role in gaining acceptance as an Olympic sport. Sadly, before curling even made it to Calgary in 1988, Herb was taken from us in August of 1985. I will mention two other former presidents of the CCA, Cec Watt and Tim fisher, who also played a major role in helping me advance a number of new ideas forward in the early eighties. I will always be indebted to these two gentlemen who are also no longer with us for their never wavering support and vision.

Gerry Peckham and Garry DeBlonde worked hand in hand with me in the operation of the Silver Broom Curling School and the development of the Curl Canada program, which advanced a teaching standard for curling. Since 1974, curling in Canada has had only three people responsible for high performance: Warren Hansen, Garry DeBlonde, and Gerry Peckham. I thank both Gerry and Garry for all of their support over the many years. When Canada was facing the task of selecting and training teams for the 1988 Olympics, Garry was the person chosen to perform that task. Garry and I, along with Vera Pezer, Art Quinney, and Ron Anton, formed the National Team Program Committee (NTPC) that determined the process and selected the teams for the 1988 Olympics. A special thank-you to the original NTPC for your ongoing support and contribution to the development of curling and playing an important role in moving the sport closer to Olympic medal status. I also want to thank Neil Houston for his contribution and support through the period of 1995 until present. Neil became a world junior champion with Paul Gowsell in 1976 and a world champion in 1986 with Ed Lukowich. Neil worked with me at the CCA from 1995 to 2007, and then Neil became the director of curling at the 2010 Olympics in Vancouver before returning to an event manager position at the CCA. Neil worked with me on many projects, but one of the most important was the development of mixed doubles in 2001 that eventually became an Olympic sport.

When curling did not gain medal status following the 1988 Olympics, three gentlemen appointed by the World Curling Federation (WCF) picked up the torch and led the charge to increase the membership of the WCF from eighteen nations to twenty-five. Gunther Hummelt, Jack Lynch, and Franz Tanner were very involved in taking things to the next plateau. Both Gunther and Jack passed away a number of years ago, but Franz is still with us. Few people in curling have probably heard of Hiroshi Kobayashi, but Hiroshi played a very important role in pulling the right people together in Japan that were influential in directing the final proposal to the IOC Executive Committee in June of 1992 that led to medal status. Hiroshi also passed away just a few years ago.

Michael Burns Photography has pretty much been the official photographer of curling worldwide since the first Scotch Cup was held in 1959. Michael Burns Sr. was there in Scotland in 1959, and

Michael Burns Jr. continues to carry on the company's involvement as the official photographer of Curling Canada today. A number of the photos in this book were taken by Michael Burns Photography, and for that, we are grateful.

Larry Wood was a writer and sports editor for the *Calgary Herald.* Larry was also one of the leading curling writers in Canada for many years and worked with me on the production of numerous curling publications over a period of thirty plus years. Larry was my mentor and writing teacher over those years, and for all of his assistance, I say thank you. Terry Jones of the *Edmonton Sun* has also been a huge supporter of curling for many years and another writer who has helped me in so many ways. Terry read the first rough manuscript of *Sticks 'n' Stones* and gave the book a much appreciated thumbs up. Al Cameron, another old friend from the media world, helped a great deal with the final editing.

Finally, a thank-you to my wife, Irene, who was there as my sounding board when I started to put this entire book together and the first litmus test for each and every chapter I wrote.

PREFACE

WHEN I WAS only eleven years old, I witnessed the great Matt Baldwin win the Brier in my home town of Edmonton in 1954. I had little knowledge of curling or the Brier, but as I reached the age of thirteen, I had an opportunity to step on the ice and attempt to throw a curling stone for the first time. I instantly fell in love with the sport.

I grew up in a small farming community just north of Edmonton. My parents were curlers, which is how I initially became interested in the sport. I suffered heartbreak early in curling when our high school team, skipped by Tom Kroeger, who had actually won the Canadian high school championship two years earlier, failed to win Alberta to play in the National Schoolboy Championship in Halifax. We had to win one out of two games to advance but lost two straight to a team we were sure we could beat.

When you subject yourself to be part of any sport at the top level, you will enjoy many moments of gleeful success, but you will also be forced to endure at least a certain amount of dejected defeat—and that was the story of my involvement with competitive curling for most of my twenties. When I was thirty-one, I finally reached the pinnacle of achievement for a male curling in Canada: the Brier. We won the Brier and went onto a world championship in Berne, Switzerland, where we lost in the semi-final. The whole experience left a bad taste in my mouth and ignited a fire inside to start the process of making curling better and more universally accepted as a sport.

I had always felt that curling did not receive the respect it should, but to a large degree, it was because the sport was its own worst enemy. Many curlers did little to help improve the image and, in fact at times, seemed to enjoy the quirky aspects of the sport that made those on the outside suggest it really wasn't a sport. To a very large degree, it was always an old boys' club, and in certain regions, that was still very prevalent even as late as the seventies. From my early beginnings, I always wanted more for curling, and after my experience with the 1974 Brier and world championship, I became driven to initiate change.

Ray Kingsmith from Calgary was about fifteen years older than me, and he also felt the sport deserved to be more than it was. During a late-night chat in a Paris hotel room, about a week after the 1974 world men's curling championship, Ray and I agreed to do everything within our power to move curling to a new level. We agreed to take two separate routes in an attempt to take curling to where we felt it could be with far more recognition and respect. Ray would attempt to become a member of the Canadian Curling Association (CCA) board of directors, and I would try to get the top players in the game united and working from the same page.

In sort of a coincidence series of events, I became involved with the CCA in the fall of 1974 and was contracted to research and develop a teaching standard for Canada. During the same period, I was instrumental in getting the top male curlers in the nation organized into a group that became known as the Association of Competitive Curlers. A couple of years later, Ray was elected to the board of directors of the CCA. During this same period, there were many other things that became obvious that had to change if curling was to ever become more legitimate, which included proper officiating, game statistics, dress codes, no smoking on the ice, proper warm-up, and, overall, a greater concern for fitness. In the back of my mind, I saw the sport gaining Olympic status, but all of the above and more would need to change for that to even be a distant dream.

Macdonald Tobacco had been the sponsor of the Brier since 1927, but at the 1977 Brier opening day, the president, David Stewart, announced that following the 1979 Brier (the 50th Macdonald Brier), the tobacco giant would be stepping back as the title of the event. The old guard were in shock, but in the back corner of the room, I was quietly cheering, because with Macdonald's out of the way, I knew change would be possible. When the new sponsor, Labatt Brewing Company, stepped on the stage in March of 1980, numerous changes were already in place, including officiating, statistics, and no more smoking on the ice, with more in the works. It was the beginning of a change, but many didn't like it!

On September 30, 1981, in Baden Baden, West Germany, Calgary, Alberta, won the right to play host to the Winter Olympics from February 13 to 28, 1988. This got my attention, but it was sometime later when I started to muse about the possibility of curling getting demonstration status at the 1988 Winter Games. In September, I called Ray Kingsmith in Calgary, asking what he thought the possibilities might be of curling getting demonstration-sport status in the 1988 Winter Games. Ray suggested he had the same question on his mind and would investigate the situation. The result was a breakfast meeting on December 7, 1982, at the Westin Calgary with Kingsmith and Brian Murphy, vice president of sports from the Calgary Committee (OCO).

Murphy was friendly and informative, and the points that Ray and I needed to know were laid on the table. In addition to curling, ski orienteering, freestyle skiing, short track speed skating, dog sled racing, and ballroom dancing were being considered for demonstration status. Only three would be selected, and Murphy agreed that he would advise us as soon as he was aware of the procedure to be followed for acceptance. He did, however, indicate that the facility situation would be difficult for curling and the acceptance of the proposal might have to be based on the event being held at the Calgary Curling Club. It was also strongly recommended that the approach should include both men's and women's curling as part of the demonstration.

On June 6, 1983, Ray received a letter from Murphy that asked for a detailed questionnaire on curling to be answered, and on August 22, 1983, we would be called upon to make a presentation to the executive board of OCO. We were advised that the presentation would be verbal and should outline why curling should be a demonstration sport, what it would do for the Games locally and internationally, and would the financial returns from curling in the Olympics be significant? I contacted Bob Moir at CBC television, and he put together a presentation video, along with written documentation that answered the three questions and a lot more. August 22 was an anxious moment, as Ray was called away at the last minute on business and I had to do the presentation by myself. I sat like a school kid waiting my turn to do my "stuff."

In early September, Ray was informed by Murphy that OCO had officially accepted curling, along with short track and freestyle skiing. However, it was also communicated that International Olympic Committee (IOC) President Juan Antonio Samaranch had endorsed curling and freestyle, while IOC Director of Sports Marc Hodler recommended curling and ski orienteering. Ray was "unofficially" assured that curling was in. The only question still to be answered was, which of the other sports would be chosen? OCO advised at the same time that curling had been recently recognized by the IOC at an executive committee meeting. In late October of 1983, it was officially announced by the IOC that curling, short track speed skating, and freestyle skiing would be the three demonstration sports at the 1988 Winter Games.

On March 29, 1984, Murphy wrote Kingsmith a letter suggesting the International Curling Federation would have to provide the event with its blessing while the demonstration would be operated by OCO in conjunction with the CCA. In March 1986, at the ICF annual meeting in Toronto, an Olympic Committee was established within the ICF that consisted of President Phillip Dawson of Scotland, Harvey Mazinke of Regina, representing North America, Pierre Thuring of Switzerland, representing Europe, and Ina Light of Winnipeg, representing women's curling.

The key decision made by the committee at the first meeting was that Canada plus the top seven nations from the 1987 world curling championships would be the participants in the demonstration.

Over the next twenty-four months, there were many anxious moments as curling felt its way along the process of becoming first a proper demonstration sport in 1988 and, hopefully, a full medal sport in future Winter Games. A crisis took place with the Calgary Organizing Committee in the fall of 1986, when an attempt was made to move curling from the Calgary Curling Club to the Max Bell Arena. It was finally agreed that the necessary funds required to bring the arena in line to host not only curling but also short track speed skating would be approved and curling would be demonstrated in a venue where it could really put its best foot forward.

But along the way, the lack of understanding of protocol in dealing with the IOC cost curling some precious points when more emphasis was placed on how the sport would appear to the IOC and the world rather than making all the back-room deals required for acceptance. The key item ignored by the ICF was the fundamental IOC medal requirement calling for twenty-five member nations on three continents. It seemed the message sent to curling officials was incorrect when it was suggested that lobbying IOC members and putting on a good demonstration would be all that was necessary.

I was part of the National Team Program Committee that was formed by the Canadian Curling Association to develop the process that would determine Canada's representatives for the Olympics. It was decided there would be two ways to become a participant in the eight women's and eight men's teams Canadian Trials. Four of the teams would be selected the conventional way of winning in the major events leading up to the trials, and the other new unknown approach that would involve the assessment of individuals after which a selection committee would construct a number of teams. Needless to say, a number of issues that developed around the new selection process led to a lot of public criticism and much of it was done in such a way as to paint curling in a less than favourable light, which did not go unnoticed. Ideas put forward by the CCA that suggested that to be in the Olympics, a curler needed to display a level of physical fitness was, to the Canadian media, laughable. A world curling scandal in 1984 that saw Air Canada removed as the title sponsor of the men's world championships for really no reason also attracted a lot of press in

Canada. These distractions and others did not go unnoticed by at least Canada's representatives to the IOC.

Nevertheless, Ray and I, along with all the others involved in putting on the show in Calgary, did our jobs well as curling grabbed its share of media and public attention. However, the high profile established by curling as a demonstration sport did not receive a favourable nod from one of the key people: IOC Director of Sport Walter Troeger of Germany made it very clear he wasn't pleased with the status of curling in Calgary and thought the demo sport would never enjoy such a notable position again.

To add to the confusion, a ticket fiasco created by OCO saw the strange scenario of numerous people wanting to get into Max Bell but, with no tickets available, could not, and yet the arena was nearly empty. To this day, the reason for the confusion has not been disclosed; however, it is obvious that corporate sponsors and Olympic insiders sat with bundles of the 2,500 plus tickets available unused somewhere in office closets and desks.

By the end of the Games, most of us close to the scene knew there were many problems and it seemed the probability of curling becoming a medal sport in 1992 was slight. Nevertheless, we had a glimmer of hope. However, Ray fell ill shortly after the Games, and the curling world was shocked when, on May 3, 1988, he passed away after a very brief struggle with cancer.

The IOC advised that a decision on all demo sports from the Calgary Games would be made at the Summer Games in Seoul, and on September 19, 1988, the following statement was made by Vitaly Smirnov, IOC program commission chairman, and Walter Troeger: "Curling will not be a medal sport at Albertville in 1992 or included on the 1994 Games agenda at Lillehammer, Norway. It will, however, be a demonstration sport again at Albertville. Curling did not meet the basic criteria in Calgary, which states that a sport must be practiced by at least 25 nations on at least three continents. Possibly in five or six years, curling can start again to put a medal sport request before the IOC."

During the same media conference, Canadian Olympic Committee member Dick Pound also passed on comments for digestion: "The ticket confusion in Calgary, when the event was sold out but nevertheless had many empty seats, had no bearing on the final IOC decision. The best way for curling to get IOC recognition is to qualify under the existing criteria, which is available as an excuse for its failure to merit recognition."

And so in the fall of 1988, the torch was passed to retiring COA Technical Director Jack Lynch and then Austrian President Gunther Hummelt to gain the necessary twenty-five member nations and the proper representation from three continents.

Without question the mistake made by curling officials going into the Olympics in 1988 was to assume that the IOC requirement of the sport having participation in at least twenty-five countries was not important.

In the fall of 1988, a group of Canadian officials, under the guiding eye of former COA technical director Jack Lynch, developed a strategy for obtaining Olympic status for curling. Following the meeting, the CCA sent a proposal to the ICF semi-annual meeting in Perth, Scotland, with comprehensive proposals to:

- form an international development committee of the ICF;
- build the ICF membership to twenty-five or more countries;
- get automatic entry into the world championships for the Pacific championships; and
- join the General Assembly of International Sports Federation (GAISF).

By the summer of 1989, the international development committee had been formed, with Gunther Hummelt as its chairman. Later that year, the ICF joined GAISF, which promoted a request for a name change since both canoeing and carting used the initials ICF. Curling complied and, thereafter, was identified as the World Curling Federation (WCF).

Jack Lynch, working with Gunther Hummelt, established an operational plan, with three specific goals to be reached prior to the 1991 session (General Assembly) of the IOC, when the host city for the 1998 Olympic Winter Games would be selected, which were to:

- bring the WCF membership up to twenty-five countries or more;
- revise the World Curling Championship format to ensure that three continents will always be represented; and
- lobby the program commission and executive board of the IOC and all cities bidding to host the 1998 Games to be favourable to curling.

The first objective to be tackled was the second one, and at the 1989 semi-annual meeting of the WCF, the initial proposals for a system of zonal qualification for the world championships were tabled. Keeping to the ten-team format, any proposal to guarantee one entry to the Pacific would automatically reduce either North America or European entry by one. Hence, the debate was long and complex. It culminated in Winnipeg about three years later, when the new system was passed. It gave seven or eight entries to Europe, one or two to America, and a solitary entry to the Pacific. The system was in place in time to provide the Pacific, with entries in both the men's and women's demonstration events in Albertville. The system was updated again in 2005, when the men's and women's world championships were split into separate entities.

In 1990, Gunther Hummelt, now the WCF president, went to work with a vengeance on the recruitment of new curling countries. He personally did all the spadework to bring Czechoslovakia, Hungry, Bulgaria, and Belgium into the fold and negotiated furiously with Romania, Yugoslavia, Argentina, Turkey, and Russia among others. He also made some preliminary overtures to Korea.

The basic strategy was to find a curling "attaché" resident in the target country, who could remain on site to coordinate the introduction of the game and guide existing sports federations toward the addition of a curling branch. A WCF novice clinic would follow for thirty-two or more people, and two or three sets of curling stones used for the clinic were usually left with the new curling group on a renewable loan basis. Through this process, countries like Czechoslovakia and New Zealand were brought into the fold.

By March of 1991, the addition of New Zealand, Andorra. Liechtenstein, Iceland, and Mexico brought the WCF membership to twenty-five countries (counting Scotland, England, and Wales as only one: Great Britain). A group from the Virgin Islands applied in the summer of 1991, and Russia wasn't far behind.

The most daunting task facing a sport seeking medal status is to convince the IOC to accept it. The IOC has set the minimum guidelines to be met before it will consider the addition of a sport to the program of the Games, but acceptance rests on the free vote of its ninety-odd individual members. All applications are first filtered through a commission for the program to the executive board before the general membership ever sees them.

The program commission consists of about a half-dozen IOC members, supplemented with an appointee from each of the International Federations, the National Olympic Committees, and the Athletes Commission.

After finally reaching the twenty-five-country, three-continent participation target in 1991, the WCF had the harrowing and unique distinction of having its application for Olympic status rejected twice by the program commission, only to have that recommendation reversed each time by the executive board.

In 1991, the commission met in Barcelona, a few short days after the WCF annual meeting in Winnipeg. Attempts were made to circulate the WCF application to the members, but no personal interventions were possible. The commission, chaired at that time by Vitaly Smirnov of Russia, came out with the conclusion that curling wasn't really a sport but a pastime requiring little if any athletic skill. At the executive board, this conclusion was shot down by Canadian Dick Pound, son of a past-president of the Montreal Thistle Curling Club. Pound, who was at that time first vice president of the IOC, was able to force the file back to the program commission for further study.

A little over a year later, on June 16, 1992, in Paris, the program commission met once again to consider several applications for the Winter Games. The WCF application, which had always emphasized equality of the sexes and the fact that it would be the first team sport for women in the Winter Olympics, had also been updated to show its ever-increasing membership.

However, the WCF application was again rejected. Interesting enough, the most influential voice against curling was Canadian ski great, former "Crazy Canuck," Ken Read, the athletes' representative on the commission.

"I am there to express my opinion, not follow some party line," he said after the meeting. "There are too many 'paper federations' on the WCF list of members. Curling may be ready by 2002 or 2006, but I feel strongly that it does not yet meet the 'widely practiced' requirements of the IOC."

To add insult to injury, women's ice hockey, with twenty participating countries and only two world championships behind it, was recommended for inclusion, starting in 1998. The people that were close to the scene made swift and instant contact with all members of the executive board. Curling, interesting enough, was supported as being a sport that was more deserving than ice hockey in becoming the first team sport for women at the Winter Olympics; the membership list was defended and the fact that there was a split vote among the program commission members was emphasized.

Phone calls went out from the CCA to COA representative Dick Pound and WCF Gunther Hummelt, who were on the scene in Barcelona, Spain, and were making last minute pleas to the appropriate IOC people before the final decision was made on curling's future Olympic status.

In the meantime, there were things happening in other parts of the world. On July 7, 1992, I received a phone call from my good friend Hiroshi Kobayashi in Tokyo and he suggested that the Japanese Olympic Committee (JOC) were also upset about the decision made by the program commission about curling. He also asked who Ken Reed was and as a Canadian how could he lead such a charge against curling.

I went to Tokyo on two occasions in the late eighties to instruct curling and, at that time, had established contact with Hiroshi, who was the driving force behind curling in the Tokyo area. Hiroshi and some very key figures in the Japanese sporting community were very supportive of curling being part of the 1998 Olympics in Nagano.

I had to reassure Hiroshi that Canada was very much on side and Ken Reed was sitting on the program commission as an athlete representative and not a Canadian delegate. Reed was in fact forwarding his own agenda, and while many had opinions with regard to his position, no one really understood why he was launching such a personal attack against a sport that was so strong in his native land.

So, on July 10, 1992, a letter went from the JOC to IOC President Juan Antonio Samaranch with a direct plea for curling to be included as part of the medal program for the 1998 Winter Games in Nagano, Japan. In this letter, it was made clear to the IOC that Nagano was not really prepared to host women's hockey because of lack of venues. However, a venue did exist in nearby Karuizawa that could host curling, and if the IOC considered including curling, then Nagano would make things work for women's hockey.

Everything that could be done was completed, and now all everyone could do was wait.

It was July 18, 1992, and it was an average Saturday morning, which found me sitting by Jericho Beach, not far from my Vancouver home, reading the morning paper.

I was more than aware that a meeting of the IOC executive committee had taken place on July 17, in Barcelona, at which time the future of curling as a medal sport was to be determined, but I really didn't expect to hear the result for a few days.

I came to the sport section and started to scan the second page when a headline caught my eye, "Canada's Medal Hopes Improve with New Events."

I zeroed in on the story and the first item that jumped out was the inclusion of two more short track and freestyle events for 1994. What I expected in the next paragraph was the usual, that curling didn't make it. I couldn't believe my eyes when the other paragraph lead said quote, "Curling was also granted full medal status and will be included by 2002—earlier if a rink is built for the 1994 Games or the 1998 Games in Nagano, Japan."

Emotion came over my body that was somewhere between disbelief and great joy. This was unbelievable! In the latter part of June, we had learned that the program commission of the IOC had for the third time failed to provide a positive recommendation of curling as a medal sport. All of us who had worked on the project for the previous ten years were anything but positive for future Olympic possibilities. I immediately thought of Ray Kingsmith and how proud he would be of what had finally been accomplished from our humble beginnings back in 1983.

But the final official announcement from Barcelona and the 99th session of the IOC General Assembly stated as follows: "Men's and women's curling will be definitely included on the program of the Olympic Winter Games in 2002, and negotiations will be undertaken with the Nagano Organizing Committee to stage the sport in 1998 as well." Since the Nagano people, along with all of the 1998 bidding cities, had promised to include curling even before they won the right to host the Games, this meant curling would be medal in 1998. Of course, the rest is history and we know Japan did not go back on its promise.

In the pages that follow, you will read the details of how this entire scenario unfolded over a period of roughly ten years between 1982 and 1992.

INTRODUCTION
The Lightning Bolt in Paris

THE EVENING OF March 29, 1974, in Paris, France, three Canadians from different cities—Ray Kingsmith, Terry Begin, and yours truly—sat around a dingy, smoky hotel room somewhere in the centre of the city, finishing the dregs of three weeks in Europe. Earlier in the evening, the conversation had been fairly calm, but as the night progressed, the alcohol kicked in and the speech, without question, became more spirited.

I had been on a roller-coaster ride for about three weeks. The first week of March, I played in the Brier at London, Ontario, representing Alberta, and on Saturday, March 9, our team *won* the Brier. On Sunday, we travelled back to Edmonton, and then the whirlwind started. Three days later, on Thursday, March 14, we left Canada for Berne, Switzerland, and the men's world curling championships, the Air Canada Silver Broom. On Monday, March 18, we were on the ice playing and everything seemed to be a blur. In just a slim ten days, after winning the Brier, we had gone home, quickly regrouped, and were now in Europe, representing Canada at the world men's championships. No one from the Canadian Curling Association (CCA) had helped us in any way, and all final arrangements and preparation were left to us.

The ice in Berne was crazy, and the stones were like throwing plates with draws that travelled an unbelievable twenty-eight to thirty seconds (normal speed would be around twenty-four seconds) from hog to tee. The field wasn't strong, but two teams concerned us—Switzerland and the USA. Yet, I knew neither would be a match for our team under normal conditions, but these were not normal conditions. In addition, we were still in a time when smoking was allowed on the ice, and our skip, Hec Gervais, was a chain smoker when he curled. The day before the event, the International Curling Federation (ICF) announced that Swiss Curling would appreciate it if no one smoked on the ice because of the concern of selling curling as a sport in what was a relatively new curling market. Gervais was no shrinking violet and said, "Screw you. I'm smoking." The result was that the Swiss press crucified us, and so did the fans. Yet, through all of this, we received no help or defence from the CCA, who were invisible. Most of the competitive curlers in Canada had been disenchanted with the CCA and the administration, or lack of it, for the sport overall, and this was the final straw for me. In the end, we lost the semifinal to Sweden, and in an instant, it was over. I had worked my butt off for ten years to reach the Brier, win it, and hopefully capture the world title, but in a moment, it was snuffed. I was numb, upset, and desperately wanted a whole bunch of things in the sport of curling to change.

Terry Begin, Ray Kingsmith and Warren Hansen

Ray Kingsmith and I had known each other for a number of years but had really got to know each other a lot better at the 1972 Silver Broom in Garmisch-Partenkirchen, Germany. He was there as a radio reporter, and I had travelled to the alpine resort as a curious guest of Air Canada, seeking to create and establish a curling school project under the guidance and name of the Canadian airline. Ray had attempted to promote a major curling event in Calgary during the mid-sixties called the Masters of Curling. It went pretty well for a couple of years but faded because of the lack of a major sponsor. He also worked as the secretary-manager of the Southern Alberta Curling Association for a number of years and was one of the few people on the CCA side of the table who saw the need for change. It was rare for a citizen of Calgary to agree with a native of Edmonton on anything, but on curling's need for a huge shake-up we agreed.

The spring night in Paris grew late, and as more of the alcohol leftovers were consumed, the discussion got louder, more pronounced, and filled with passion. Ray and I agreed that something had to be done, but what and how? Although Terry Begin (another curling reporter from Ottawa) was somewhat on the outside of the conversation, he also believed that the direction of curling had to change if it was to grow. When the evening finally ended, Ray and I had agreed on a plan of attack. He was going to work down the line in an attempt to become part of the CCA executive and eventually the president, while I would work with the players and try to get as many as I could onside to possibly form a players' association. Between us, we knew the curling world had to change if curling was to ever have any credibility in the sporting world, never mind the wild dream of it becoming an Olympic medal sport.

CHAPTER 1
The Beginning

IT IS PROBABLY difficult to say where this story really starts, but for the sake of argument, I will pick December 1971.

I was living somewhat of a normal life working for Alberta Government Telephones as an associate engineer in toll system design (primarily a specification writer) while other facets of my life were going through a bit of a change. My marriage of six years had ended in August 1971, and I was contemplating leaving my role as head coach of the Edmonton Wildcat Football team after a twelve-year career as player/coach in Edmonton junior football. I had been a player on the Edmonton Huskies when we won three Canadian championships in a row back in the early sixties, an assistant coach for the Huskies, then assistant for the Cats, and finally two years as head coach of the Cats.

I wanted something new in the sporting world, and I really wanted to find a way to make a living from sport. I was also tired of the telecommunications world and found the work to be boring, for the most part. I was a good curler but had struggled to make my mark on the sport in a meaningful way, although our current team—with Ron Anton as skip and yours truly throwing third rocks—had done a lot of winning during the past twelve months. Yet, we had not even been able to win a City of Edmonton zone spot in the Brier playdowns. Anton had blue-blood credentials in curling, having won the Brier in 1961 with Hector Gervais when he was only nineteen, then losing the final in 1962 to Ernie Richardson. My greatest Brier accomplishment to date had been three Northern Alberta zone berths with the trip to the Northern playdowns in 1968 (Wayne McElroy at skip with me throwing third) nearly turning into a trip to the four-team Alberta playoffs. Possibly it would have been for naught. Who knows? Those were the glory days of Ron Northcott, and he easily won the provincial, second Canadian, and second world titles in 1968.

The curling business had caught my eye to some degree, but it was a tough one in those days to find a way to actually making a living from. I had found a Rockmaster broom in a shop around 1966 and discovered that no one represented the Saskatoon manufacturer, Midwestern Broom in Northern Alberta. Through a series of communications with the owner-president, Joe Semenchuk, I eventually became the northern Alberta representative. While the sideline was doing okay, it would never become something that would allow me to quit my day job.

In early December 1971, our team of Ron Anton, Rich Twa, and Bruce Ferguson was scheduled to participate in the Canadian Open Carspiel, which was an annual event

Ron Anton won the Brier in 1961 and again in 1974. He was only 19 years old in 1961 and is still the youngest man to ever win the event. *Photo credit – Michael Burns Photography.*

held in Edmonton and operated by the lead for Hec Gervais's 1961 world championship, Wally Ursuliak. This was always an important event for us and, in 1971, probably especially so since we had made the final the year prior. The event usually had about sixty-four teams entered, including most of the best from Winnipeg west.

Earlier in November, our team had travelled to Prince George to participate in and win the first major cashspiel ever staged in Canada, where the first money was $3,000. Ron Anton, a teacher, had taken off more days than planned for the Prince George event and found out only a few days before the start of the Canadian Open that he would not be able to play. So, we were without a skip, and while I did not mind assuming that role, there was really no one available whom we might consider an adequate third for a major competition. Ron contacted Wally Ursuliak and suggested that our team would probably withdraw from the competition because we did not have a skip. Ursuliak did not want a hole in the draw in the eleventh hour, so he told Ron that he might have an idea.

During the sixties and early seventies, CBC television Edmonton did an annual series known as *Keen Ice*. This was a series of thirty-minute shows shot over one weekend that involved using a number of the shots from the old Scottish game of points curling. CBC Edmonton then showed the series once a week for over fifteen weeks and sold it to a few other stations across Canada. The prize was cash. It involved two players curling together and featured the big name curlers of the day from across western Canada. I had first played in the series in 1969 with Dr. Bill Mitchell when he was the defending Canadian mixed champion. Anton and I were in the event in 1971 as a result of our successes over the previous year (winning two of the largest bonspiels and finishing second in the other).

The world champions for the years 1970 and '71 were the Don Duguid team out of Winnipeg, and because of that success, Duguid had an automatic invite. However, early in the fall, Duguid announced his retirement from curling to assume the job of colour commentator on the CBC national curling telecasts with Don Chevrier. While Duguid was not invited, his third Rod Hunter and second Jim Pettapiece were.

The Hunter/Pettapiece combo did not do that well in the *Keen Ice* showdown; neither did Anton and I, so we were all eliminated on Saturday. Pettapiece and Hunter had booked flights back on Monday, assuming they would probably be in the Sunday playoffs. I did not know either Pettapiece or Hunter, but Wally Ursuliak did. Ron and Wally were good friends since they had won the 1961 Brier together, so Wally indicated he would attempt to get Rod Hunter to stay over for the week and replace Anton for the upcoming Canadian Open Carspiel that started on Monday.

On a side note, Wally and I were congenial to each other, but there was always some friction because we represented competing broom manufacturers—Wally with Curlmaster and yours truly with the upstart company from Saskatoon, Midwestern Broom. Remember, in those days, every competitive team swung broom corn, and broom companies wanted top sweepers, like Wally and I, representing them to other elite players.

On Sunday afternoon, Wally reported back to Ron that while he had been unsuccessful in getting Hunter to stay, Jim Pettapiece had agreed to stay after some lengthy discussions. While Pettapiece would only agree to play third, which meant I would have to step to the tee head and assume the role of skip, a position I had not played much at the top level since 1969. While we played pretty well as a team, we did not win enough games to qualify, and as a result, we were bounced out before the final round.

Much more did, however, result from the experience of playing with Jim (Jumbo) Pettapiece. We spent a fair amount of time together, and the discussion eventually turned to what both of us were looking at doing in life. I wanted out of the telecommunications industry, while Jim was doing some sales work with his friends company in Winnipeg, Sanford Evans Publishing. We quickly determined both of us wanted to head down a different path in life and would love to create a livelihood from curling, if that was somehow possible.

Anton and I had done some teaching work during the fall of 1970 and again in '71, largely based on Ron's analytical ability and his extensive knowledge about curling. I had honed some pretty good athletic skill-instructing techniques from my seven years as a junior football coach. Between Anton (who was a school teacher) and I, we put together some good teaching approaches to a sport that had never been analyzed or professionally instructed. Through this group of people—Wally Ursuliak, Ron Anton, and Jim Pettapiece—there were some other interesting connections. A group comprising Don Duguid, Ray Turnbull, and Wally Ursuliak had started a travelling professional curling instruction troop in 1968. Duguid was Pettapiece's old skip, Turnbull (also from Winnipeg) had at one point played with Pettapiece, and Anton had played for Hector Gervais, where Ursuliak was the team lead player. Anton had also been involved with Ursuliak in assisting with the teaching approach being used by the Duguid, Turnbull, Ursuliak (DTU) curling schools.

Jim Pettapiece was a world curling champion in 1970 and again in 1971. Pettapiece and Warren Hansen developed the concept of the Silver Broom Curling School.

It was just a matter of time until the conversation between Jim Pettapiece and me would turn to the potential of developing a professional curling school instruction operation. Jim quickly jumped to the idea of bringing in the sponsor of the world curling championship, Air Canada. He had just come off the experience of playing in two world championships and, as a result, had made connections with a number of key Air Canada people. He felt he could reach out to some of them and possibly get a hearing.

The main contact Jim mentioned was Pierre Jerome, who was the airline's director of public relations and one of the people responsible for the Silver Broom, although the key guy was the vice president of marketing, Don MacLeod. Early in 1972, Jim sent Jerome a letter, giving him a general idea of what we had discussed and our desire to make a presentation to Air Canada on the operation of a travelling curling school operation.

Early in the new year, we both got involved in our respective Brier playdowns in Manitoba and Alberta. Pettapiece and Hunter had picked up Danny Fink to skip their team, but their season in Manitoba ended about as quickly as ours did in Alberta. That was it for serious curling in '72.

In the meantime, Jim heard back from Jerome, who had swung our interests over to the marketing department and a guy by the name of Gary Lynch. Lynch communicated with Pettapiece and informed him that a person in his department by the name of Dave Giles would be in touch with us. Giles communicated quickly and suggested he would like a proposal from us, outlining how we saw Air Canada being involved with the curling school venture.

I had been having a lot of issues with my job at Alberta Government Telephones and applied for a leave of six weeks. I needed to put some distance between myself and the telecommunications industry, just to see how it would feel. The wish was granted, and I decided to travel to visit my relatives in Denmark and swing down to Garmisch-Partenkirchen, Germany, where the men's world curling championship, the Air Canada Silver Broom, was being played in late March.

I arranged my flights to land in Montreal on my way to Copenhagen, which would allow me to spend a few hours in the airport, where I would meet Dave Giles and discuss what our proposal to Air Canada might look like.

In the meantime, Joe Semenchuk of Midwestern Broom asked me to travel to Saskatoon for a meeting when the city was hosting the Macdonald Lassie (Canadian women's curling championship) in the middle of February. I did not know what Joe wanted to talk about, but I agreed to make the trip. Wally Ursuliak heard I was driving down to Saskatoon and asked if he could ride with me because he had a couple of meetings scheduled at the Lassie. Ray Turnbull and Don Duguid were flying in from Winnipeg, and the DTU Curling School was making a presentation to the Canadian Ladies Curling Association (CLCA) about a potential future agreement. During the trip to Saskatoon, Ursuliak and I talked about a number of things, including the curling school operation. Wally suggested the DTU operation was looking for new people to work with them and asked if I might be interested. I indicated I had an interest, and Wally suggested he would discuss it with Duguid and Turnbull.

The morning after arrival, I travelled over to the Midwestern office to meet with Semenchuk, who was about to make me an interesting offer. Joe had hoped that his eldest son Wade would work in and inherit the business. But after a couple of years, Wade moved to the West Coast to pursue his rock 'n' roll business interests. Joe made me an offer to become the manager of Midwestern Broom, slowly acquire stock, buy into the business, and, within ten years, own the operation. I was really surprised by the offer and indicated to Joe that I would think about it and get back to him by early spring. (Side note: After considering the idea, I decided it was not the direction I wanted to go, and I certainly did not have any interest in moving to Saskatoon.) Later, it proved to be one of the best decisions of my life because by the early eighties, the corn broom business was dead due to the increasing popularity of the brush as a sweeping device.

Ray Turnbull - Turnbull, Don Duguid and Wally Ursuliak were the creators of the DTU Curling Schools.

Don Duguid was the world champion skip in 1970 and 1971 and a CBC commentator on curling from 1972 until 2002.

I attended a couple of days of the Lassie, and it appeared the hometown team, skipped by Vera Pezer, was about to win its second Canadian title. I ended up having a chat with Ursuliak about the possibility of me working with DTU Curling School. Wally had brought up the topic with Duguid and Turnbull. While Duguid was okay with the idea, Turnbull wasn't, and he was sorry to advise me the DTU operation would not be able to hire me. Ironically, the eventual Silver Broom Curling School and Curl Canada clinics would grow to surpass the TU (Duguid left the operation in the middle seventies) School and eventually pretty much force them from the business.

Upon arrival in Montreal, on my way to Copenhagen, I was met by Dave Giles, who whisked me off to the Air Canada first-class lounge, where we spent a couple of hours discussing how our curling school proposal might fit into the marketing plans of Air Canada. Giles, a slender, tall, personable gent in his fifties, spoke well but knew little about curling and wasn't too sure how our idea and Air Canada might meld, but we both agreed to give it more thought and continue the dialogue in the weeks ahead. He indicated he told Pierre Jerome and Terry Denny that I would be in Garmisch, and he expected me to look them up. I thanked Dave for his time, he continued on his way home, and I prepared to catch my Scandinavian Airlines flight to Copenhagen.

I arrived in Copenhagen on Friday morning and spent the weekend with my cousin Mary-Anne before heading to Munich on Sunday morning via Hanover. When I arrived at the Munich airport, I ran into Edmonton sportscaster Wes Montgomery, who had also just arrived. I asked Wes how he was going to get to Garmisch, and he indicated there was a media bus and possibly no one would say anything if I just hopped on board. Wes said a number of Albertans would be in attendance for the event, including Al Williams and Ed Cancilla from the Northern Alberta Curling Association, as well as another Edmonton sports personality, Al McCann.

The bus trip into Garmisch was pleasant, and everyone was dropped off at the headquarters hotel to find out from that point where they would be located, as the accommodation in Garmisch was provided by a number of small local hotels, some of which only had a few rooms. At the Hotel Zugspitz, I found the Silver Broom office, where I chatted with some people from Doug Maxwell's office regarding my accommodation. After checking up and down, no one could find any record of my hotel and seemed very confused. When no one could determine what to do next, Maxwell was brought into the conversation, and for the first time, I met Doug Maxwell, who did not know who I was and didn't really give a damn. He said not to worry, and they would find a place for me to stay. Man, did they ever. While most of the people attending the event were housed in cozy little hotels in the central downtown area of Garmisch, I was banished to a hotel on the outskirts of the city that only had a community bathroom on each floor (something totally new to me). I will always remember how the lights in the hallways only came on with motion and would go out a few moments later. I was less than impressed with how Maxwell had taken care of me when it was he and his staff that had screwed up. This was only the start of what would prove to be a shaky relationship in the years ahead.

The week in Garmisch-Partenkirchen was wonderful, and I enjoyed learning more about international curling, the involvement of Air Canada, and how far behind Canada the rest of the curling world really was. I met and talked briefly with Pierre Jerome of Air Canada and actually had the opportunity to start what was a fourteen-year relationship with one of the younger guys on the Air Canada crew by the name of Terry Denny.

This was the first time I had ever witnessed European curling, and I was surprised at the poor quality of some teams. It was still the early days of world curling, and only eight nations competed for the world title. It seemed like Canadian champion Orest Meleschuk would breeze through the competition, but as the old saying goes, "Not so fast!"

History proved that I was unknowingly about to be a live witness to one of the most questionable conclusions to a world championship game in curling history.

In the final, Canada was playing a young American team skipped by Bob LaBonte. To everyone's surprise, going into the tenth and final end, Meleschuk was trailing by a score of 9–7, but with last stone. With his final stone of the game, Meleschuk attempted to remove the USA shot stone, roll slightly, and count two to force an extra-end. The stones hit, and the Canadian stone rolled and stopped. The Americans thought they had won, and skip LaBonte went airborne in celebration just as Canadian third Dave Romano was taking a closer look to see if the Americans had in fact won the world title.

But when LaBonte's feet hit the ice, he slipped and kicked the Canadian stone involved in the decision, and all of a sudden, no one knew who won. Fact is, by the rules of curling, the Americans were the ones who had made the mistake, so the two stones involved were no longer in question and the USA should have conceded the point, but this wasn't what happened. The head official was Doug Maxwell, and he asked LaBonte if he kicked the stone. (Which was bizarre because everyone in the arena and all the television viewers in Canada saw him kick it.) LaBonte said no, and so for the first and hopefully last time in world championship curling history, a stone that was kicked was actually measured. Fortunately, the Canadians won the measure because it would have been dead wrong for the win to go to the Americans.

In the extra end, Meleschuk made a last-rock come-around takeout which LaBonte was not able to follow giving the Canadians the win. The Americans were livid because they felt they had won in the tenth. The result was the famed "Curse of LaBonte," where the USA skip claimed Canada would not win another world title for seven years. And guess what? They didn't! The other spooky coincidence is the fact that I became part of Canada's seven-year dismal performance. Unfortunately, for all these years, Meleschuk has been called a cheater and accused of stealing the world championship from the Americans. It wasn't Meleschuk who did anything wrong—it was Maxwell and, to some degree, LaBonte because he did not understand the rule.

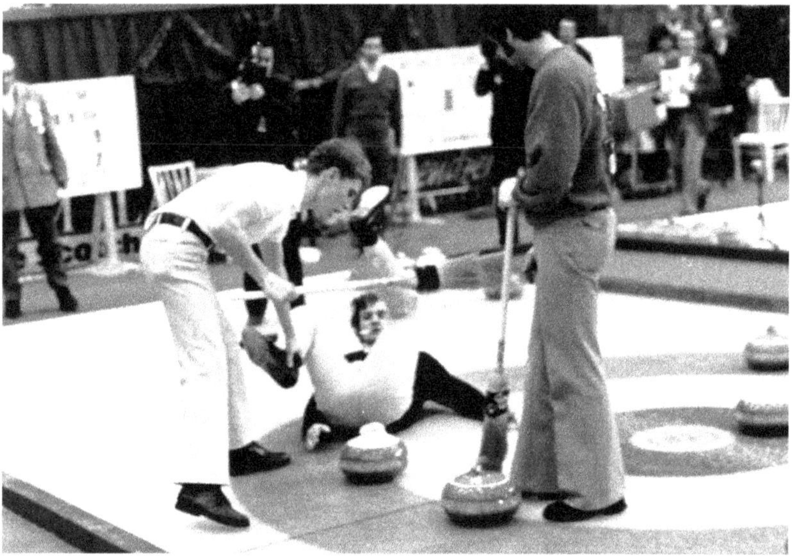

Labonte Boot - Canada's Orest Meleschuk had to score two points with his final stone of the 10th end to force the game to an extra-end. The Meleschuk shooter hit the LaBonte counter and seemed to have rolled too far for Canada to score two and tie the game. American skip Bob LaBonte thought he had won the game and leaped into the air in celebration. During the process of coming back to the ice he slipped and kicked the Canadian stone that seemed to have rolled too far. Canadian third Dave Romano was in the process of examining the two stones in question when the Canadian stone was moved by the LaBonte boot. The confusion that resulted still lives in curling folk lore today.
Photo credit – Michael Burns Photography.

The 1972 World Curling Champions from Winnipeg with the Air Canada Silver Broom. From the left Pat Hailley, John Hanesiak, Eves Pratt, President of Air Canada, Dave Romano and Orest Meleschuk.
Photo credit - Michael Burns Photography.

I was scheduled to fly back to Copenhagen on Sunday following the Silver Broom, but I teamed up with my buddies from Calgary, Ray Kingsmith and *Calgary Herald* curling writing legend, Larry Wood, along with another Calgarian, Gene Warwick, to play in a Bavarian bonspiel on the Silver Broom ice following the main event. The bonspiel lasted four days, and our Canadian contingent came in second, even though we hadn't lost a game. I had a crash course in European points curling, which I still did not fully understand after the bonspiel was over.

From there, Kingsmith, Wood, and I took a train to Copenhagen, and I finally made it home to Edmonton around the middle of April. It had been an interesting and rewarding experience that took my life in a new and totally different direction.

CHAPTER 2
The Next Steps

ONCE BACK IN Edmonton, it didn't take long for reality to set in as I headed back to the day job, which I hated, and my dreams of becoming a curling entrepreneur had to be put on hold. Through April and May, Jim Pettapiece and I stayed in constant communication as he continued to pursue the appropriate avenues in an attempt to at least get a personal hearing with someone at Air Canada about our curling school plan. Dave Giles had asked Jim to produce a proposal on the whole curling school idea, and while today it is something I would create in short order in 1972, it was a challenge.

I travelled to Winnipeg in early May, and while presentations and proposals were not Jim's strong suit, we sought the help of his friend Larry Wilson, general manager at Sanford Evans Publishing. By the middle of May, with Larry's help, we put together a paper that suggested a number of benefits the airline could acquire from an arrangement with Pettapiece/Hansen to operate clinics instructing curling throughout Europe, the USA, and Canada. The whole initial idea was for us to become ambassadors for the airline tasked with selling and raising the presence of curling around the world. The intent was for them to pay us a fee and all the bills, and yes, without question, unlimited air travel—first class, please!

The proposal went back to Dave Giles, and it wasn't long until we heard from Dave, who suggested we should come to Montreal for a meeting in the middle of June. Giles thought we should bring another curler with us because it looked like a potential involvement for three people rather than two if all of this came together. Danny Fink was now the skip of what was the Don Duguid two-time world-champion team of 1970 and 1971, so Jim thought it would be a good fit for Danny to become part of the crew. Toward the middle of June, we all headed to Montreal (first-class air, of course) for a meeting with Air Canada at its head office at 1 Place Ville Marie. We arrived there bright and early for the big meeting. The initial discussion was with Giles and his boss, Gary Lynch. While Giles was pretty enthusiastic about the game plan, Lynch wasn't so much. Lynch suggested the proposal really wasn't complete and that we should possibly retreat to our hotel room and discuss in more detail how this whole idea could work.

We spent all of Friday evening and most of Saturday attempting to massage the plan into a proposal that the airline would accept. Giles returned Saturday evening, took us to dinner, and completed a final review of our plan and potential budget. We departed on Sunday, and Giles indicated he would present the whole thing to Lynch on Monday to see if some steps forward could be made.

Doug Maxwell - Curling entrepeneur who had a major impact on the curling world for over 30 years.

June went into July, and finally, Jim got a call from Giles suggesting he thought they were ready to chat with us further and that a deal could possibly be made. From the phone call until our return to Montreal in early August, some things had happened that we were not aware of. We believed a deal was about to be made, but as everything became more apparent, it was not quite the deal we were expecting. We entered the Air Canada office at Place Ville Marie to find five people at the table: Dave Giles, Gary Lynch, Peter Jerome, and Doug Maxwell. Jim and I were both shocked to see Maxwell and did not know why he was there, but we soon found out. Maxwell had developed an agreement with Air Canada in 1968 that saw the airline become the sponsor of the world men's curling championship, known as the Air Canada Silver Broom. Part of the deal had Maxwell as the executive director of the championship. Remember my trip to Garmisch and Maxwell's screw-up with my hotel? To our surprise, we found out that part of Maxwell's agreement with Air Canada gave him the right of approval of any involvement that Air Canada might seek in any aspect of curling. We were puzzled that Pete Jerome was not aware of this when Jim initially contacted him, but soon realized this was because the original agreement was created by Maxwell and the VP of marketing, Don MacLeod.

Maxwell immediately started questioning the whole idea we had put forward. He suggested Air Canada should not hitch its star to our wagon because there were other people in the curling school business—mainly Ray Turnbull, from Winnipeg, who was a buddy of Maxwell's—who deserved the same consideration, even though no one else had thought to put a proposal such as this together. Little did I know at that time that this was the beginning of a twenty-five-year struggle between Maxwell and me. He was the old guard, wanting to hang onto the old boys' club and the old ideas, while I was the new kid on the block, who wanted to take the sport in a different direction.

While Maxwell was not able to completely derail the agreement, he did put it into a holding pattern, suggesting that he needed to have some separate discussions with Jim and me regarding how the school program might benefit everyone including him and his friends. We did not really buy what he was selling, but we had little choice except to go along with it.

We returned home after the meeting, somewhat disillusioned and started setting up a meeting with Maxwell at his office in Toronto. Maxwell owned a small agency that did a number of things, which included events, entertainment, and a division that managed athletes. Skier Nancy Greene and hockey star Dave Keon were his clients. In his book, *Behind the Superstars*, Gerry Patterson writes about meeting Maxwell at his office in the fall of 1971 to transfer Nancy Greene's account from Maxwell to Patterson.

We travelled to Toronto in the middle of August and arrived at Maxwell's office with a lot of skepticism that quickly proved to be warranted. In somewhat of an about-face, Maxwell thought the school idea could work if we hired him as our agent. This made little sense, but it was a way of attempting to claim 10–20% of everything we might receive from Air Canada. I did not want Maxwell involved, so I threw it back at him, suggesting his proposal would make some sense if Air Canada were to pay Maxwell. We did not want Maxwell as part of the deal, but we could maybe convince Giles and Lynch that paying Maxwell's commission would be a good idea that might prove helpful—even though this was not the way we felt at all. We left the Maxwell meeting with the understanding that we would both get back to Air Canada with suggestions on how to proceed.

August soon turned to September, and early in the month, we received a proposal from Air Canada, but it was nothing like we had originally planned. Maxwell had somewhat scuttled the deal we had proposed where Air Canada would hire us to operate the Silver Broom Curling School; however, what was presented to us was a licensing agreement. Air Canada was prepared to offer us a five-year agreement that would license us to operate the Silver Broom Curling School under the auspices of Air Canada and its agent. The airline would provide us a significant amount of free airline tickets, excess luggage, freight charges, and promotional support... with one catch: the person directing the promotion would be Maxwell. Nevertheless, we were ready to get the plane in the air (no pun intended), and on approximately September 15, 1972, the Silver Broom Curling School became a reality. On the same day, I left Alberta Government Telephones, where I was employed as an associate engineer in system design, to start down the road of being a curling entrepreneur. At this point in history, it was a path that could certainly be declared as the road less travelled.

CHAPTER 3

The Silver Broom School Gets Off the Ground

Silver Broom School logo

The original instructors of the Silver Broom Curling School, Warren Hansen, Bruce Ferguson and Jim Pettapiece.

THE SILVER BROOM School was out of the gate. Unfortunately, there weren't any schools booked. September was late to book schools for the fall of 1972, but we gave it a shot. The inaugural school was booked for the Balmoral Curling Club in Edmonton at the end of September, but because of lateness and lack of advertising, only about twenty-five people showed up, which did little for the break-even of the school.

A second school was booked for Grande Prairie, Alberta, at the end of October, so Jim Pettapiece and I, along with Bruce Ferguson, jumped in a rented station wagon with all of our equipment and headed for Grande Prairie. This clinic did not do well for the same reasons the Edmonton clinic did poorly. For a four-day school to make sense, we needed attendance to be around 100. We had a distance to go before those sorts of numbers became reality.

The 1973 Alberta Mixed champions from the left, Anne McGarvey, Warren Hansen, Gale Lee and Ron Anton.

Warren Hansen signs Jim Armstrong's cast at the 1973 Brier after the British Columbia second broke his wrist sweeping. Hansen went in and swept in Armstrong's place for the final seven games of the Brier. Hansen later played third for Armstrong in Vancouver for five years.

There was nothing else booked that fall. In late November, I travelled to Hamilton with Hec Gervais, Sam Richardson, and Jim McConnell to curl in the first-ever Grey Cup Bronco Spiel, where four new Ford Broncos were first prize. We did not do that great in the bonspiel, but being in the area gave me a chance to slip away for a meeting with Rick Hill at the St. Catharines, Ontario, Golf and Curling Club to see if there might be a chance of setting up a clinic at the club in early 1973. The dots connected. We would do a four-day session in early January, following another clinic that was scheduled for the Saint John, New Brunswick, Thistle Club on January 2. We weren't pulling in huge numbers, but we were up and running.

Following the clinic in St. Catharines, I returned home to Edmonton to play in the city of Edmonton Brier playdowns. It was our first attempt at a city zone position with Hector Gervais, and all of us on the team were feeling confident considering that Hector regularly won Edmonton zone positions and had done so the previous three years. But in 1973, it wasn't to be, as we were quickly bounced from the competition, which pretty much ended our team's competitive season. Ron Anton and I had entered the Edmonton mixed zone playdowns the previous year with former Canadian Women's Champion Gale Lee and Anne McGarvey. We had come within a whisker of making it to the provincial championship, so we gave it another shot. This time, we hit the right number and not only made it to the provincials in Lethbridge but managed to win the final and a trip to the first-ever Seagram-sponsored Canadian Mixed Championship in Charlottetown.

It was an unbelievable event, filled with former Canadian and provincial champions from men's and women's curling, most notably Sam Richardson representing Saskatchewan; Jim, Armstrong, BC; Doug Cameron, PEI; and Barry Fry, Manitoba. We played Fry the first game and beat him. While Fry went on to win his next nine games in a row, we dropped contests to New Brunswick and PEI, which left us in a second-place tie with Saskatchewan. This tie finally gave me some degree of notoriety to be matched with the two world championship titles held by Jim Pettapiece.

I also attended my first of forty-two consecutive Briers in Edmonton and started the week representing Midwestern Broom and attempting to get a Midwestern product in the hands of every curler in the '73 Brier. However, something unusual happened on Monday of the Brier that started another change in my life. BC second Jim Armstrong dislocated his wrist sweeping on Monday evening and, as a result, was sidelined for the balance of the Brier. In those days, there wasn't any substitution allowed at the Brier under any circumstances; however, a sweeper could be brought in from the local area to help with sweeping, but throwing stones wasn't allowed.

I was recommended to the BC team by the local host committee, so I ended up as a sweeper on the ice for BC for the last seven games of the Brier. Lead Gerry Peckham threw four rocks on every end, and I swept eight rocks for every end. It was tough, but I was now on the ice of the Brier for the first time. Maybe it was a good omen, but it gave me some special drive and desire to actually be in the Brier as an official competitor.

During the spring and summer of 1973, I travelled through many parts of Canada, meeting with curling clubs, individuals I knew, and various curling enthusiasts in an attempt to set up a sound schedule for the Silver Broom Curling School for the fall of 1973. I made the right connections, and by the fall, we were out of the gate running with our first school, set for Edmonton in late September and ending in Eastern Canada toward the end of November. The school still wasn't really at its full potential, but compared to the previous year's shallow schedule, things were reaching the point that could see us with a small profit. Our instruction crew of Gerry Peckham, Garry DeBlonde, Bruce Ferguson, Jim Pettapiece, and yours truly operated a total of about fifteen clinics that probably taught around 1,000 people

CHAPTER 4

The Curling Shoe Business

IN THE EARLY fifties, three-time Brier champion Ken Watson developed a curling shoe that pretty much became the accepted product for the fifties and sixties. The Watson shoe was more like a boot than a shoe and resembled something more equipped for a walk in the winter snow than curling. League curlers and those not taking the game that seriously wore the Watson boots, but the top competitive players of the day often resorted to street shoes with a Teflon sole glued to the sliding foot and a toe rubber on the opposite foot or with a grippy sole also glued on.

Don Duguid won the world championship in 1970 and, through his third, Rod Hunter, contacted Bauer athletic shoes. Hunter worked for Dominion Tanners in Winnipeg, which supplied Bauer with leather for its shoes. After some discussion, a new, very attractive shoe hit the market in a number of colours, including white, in 1971. The shoe looked good, but really did not provide any of the things a curling shoe needed, such as a proper slider, gripper, and overall support. It also had a heel, just like other street shoes, which did not provide the full slider opportunity that curlers needed. There was a view by some in the instruction business that the curler would ideally need just a slider on the sole of the shoe, retaining the rubber heel for a more stable position when moving on the ice. This assumed the curler would slide up on the toe only during the delivery of the stone, which is certainly not where things were going. While the Bauer shoe improved on what was out there, it was still a long way from what was really needed.

I wondered what might be possible with some other athletic shoe company. I did some research and found out the agent in Canada for Puma shoes was Peter Martin Agencies in Winnipeg. I told Jim Pettapiece and suggested we should possibly attempt a meeting with Martin Agencies on my next trip to Winnipeg.

The spring of 1972 provided me with the opportunity, and as a result, we had a meeting with Peter Martin and explained what I had in mind. Martin was receptive, and my idea was to develop a wedge heel shoe that would come equipped with the slider built into the sliding foot (left foot for right-handed throwers). The sliding product used until this point in time had pretty much been Teflon. While Teflon was fine, it quickly lost some of its sliding characteristics, and it marked very easily. I asked Martin if Puma decided to go ahead with the project if a slider made from a harder surface might be available. Martin agreed to take the entire idea to Puma in Europe and get back to us.

By early summer, Martin was back in touch with me and indicated that Puma was interested and would provide us with some prototypes for comment by early fall. The prototypes came through as promised, and I provided my comments, which Martin accepted and sent them back to the Puma factory. The next word I got was all my ideas had been accepted. Puma would produce about thirty sample pairs of the shoe that would be for distribution to a few players to use and provide feedback. I was using the shoes by late winter of 1973, and a number of high-profile curlers were also provided with a pair if they agreed to use them and provide us with feedback.

Some of us used the shoes through the '73–'74 curling season, and by chance, I played in and won the Brier, which provided the new Puma shoes with huge visibility. In the spring of 1974, Peter Martin and I had further discussions because everything was set to go, yet

Puma in Europe were hedging. Unfortunately, before the summer ended, word came from Europe that Puma was not prepared to put the shoe into full production. I was devastated because I saw the shoe as the future of curling footwear, as did 100% of the people I gave a pair to for trial wear.

The Bauer Professional shoe was designed by Warren Hansen and promoted through the Silver Broom School and the Curl Canada Clinics.

A couple of months later, I was talking to a friend of mine in Edmonton by the name of Rick Edgerton. Rick was the Alberta agent for CCM and Bauer, and we somehow got onto the subject of curling shoes. I told him about my idea and my experience with Puma, and he said he was going to Kitchener in a couple of weeks and would talk to Don Bauer about the situation and see if there was any interest. Frankly, I did not think it would go further than Rick, but what did I have to lose?

Two weeks later, I got a call from Rick. He had talked to Don Bauer, who told Rick he would like me to call him. I still wasn't totally convinced, but after talking to Don Bauer on the phone, I sensed a genuine interest in what I had to say. We set up a meeting in Kitchener–Waterloo for the spring of 1974, which was the start of a very interesting five-year relationship between the Bauer Division of Greb Shoes Inc. and me.

I immediately started working with Greb designers, and by early fall, we had a prototype produced of the Bauer Professional, which was the first-ever curling shoe with a hard KTX sole attached to the sliding foot and soft moulded gripper to the opposite sole. Fact was, between 1975 and 1980, well over 50,000 pairs of the shoes were sold across Canada. The idea led to the development of other similar shoes. The best-known one at the time, which is still manufactured today, is made by Arnold Asham.

The description of the shoe was as follows:

The Bauer "Professional"

The ideal curling shoe. The polyurethane coated long life upper is scuff resistant and water repellant. The fully padded leather lining provides maximum comfort. Speed lace system with Kraton moulded sole with attached PTX slider. Available in men's sizes 6–12, 13.65030 White with black trim.

CHAPTER 5

The Brier Finally Becomes a Reality

I DIDN'T CURL a lot in the fall of '73 because I was getting more involved with the business of curling, but the one event I did play in with Hector was the spiel in Prince George, which Ron Anton and I had won together a year earlier. It was the bonspiel of the day with the largest cash prize, which was top money of $3,000. The stars were aligned, and for the second year in a row, we took home the grand prize.

Otherwise, we did not do well on the bonspiel circuit, and Gervais' play was very inconsistent. In those days, the Yuletide Bonspiel at the Derrick Golf and Winter Club (in Edmonton) was used as a tune-up for the Brier playoffs. We did not do well at all and were one of the first teams to exit the scene.

Ron Anton and I talked on the phone a few days later and discussed whether we would even bother to enter the Brier playdowns because there seemed to be little hope. It was no big deal for me, but Anton had to book time off from teaching, which meant losing wages for probably the two to four days required to complete the playdowns. He believed we had little chance of making the Brier, so why bother going through the pain? We talked further and finally agreed that we had made a commitment to Hector and at least owed it to him to play out the season.

I will never forget our first game of the City of Edmonton playdowns was on sheet eight at the Shamrock Curling Club. Interestingly enough, it was against a guy named Ken Watson (no relation to the three-time Brier champion from Winnipeg). We were playing in a see-saw game, and into the third end, lead Darrel Sutton and I were standing at the hog line of the playing end and were gazing out across the other seven sheets of ice. All of a sudden, Gervais hollered at us from behind the sheet, "Hey, you guys. We're playing on this sheet of ice!"

My head jerked around so fast I almost got whiplash. This great curler, who had been playing with low interest—almost in hibernation—for most of the season, had suddenly come to play. This was what the great Hector Gervais had become: still an outstanding player, when motivated, but the challenge was to motivate him. For whatever reason, he had decided it was time to rise to the occasion and rise to the occasion he did. We swept the A side of the City of Edmonton playdowns and were now into the northern playdowns.

The northern playdowns were at the old Balmoral Curling Club by the University of Alberta farm in Edmonton. I had a special place in my heart for the Balmoral because it was there, over the Christmas holidays in 1960, that our ragtag team from Namao High School had ventured into the big city to play against the best junior curlers in the Edmonton area. To the surprise of everyone, including ourselves, we finished second in the second event. I still have a little bonbon dish with a curling stone in the middle of it that is engraved clearly, "Balmoral Curling Club, High School Bonspiel, 1960, 2nd—2nd."

The year 1974 marked a change in provincial Brier playoff structure. In previous years, the championship playoff to determine the team that would represent Alberta at the Brier involved only four teams: Southern Alberta, Northern Alberta, Peace Curling Association, and the Northwest Territories. That's right—NWT. The year 1974 was the last time NWT played off with Alberta because in 1975, NWT/Yukon had a direct entry to the Brier for the first time. But in 1974, there were two teams from the south, two from the north, two from the Peace Curling Association, and two from NWT. The championship was set as an eight-team round robin without a playoff, so the round-robin winner would be declared provincial champion for 1974.

This meant the northern playoff would, for the first time, have two champions instead of one. The sixteen-team playoff was still set as a double knock-out, but the A-side winner would become one of the teams going to the provincial and the B-side winner was the second team. We won our first three games with relative ease and were up against Stan Trout, a former Canadian High School (Junior) champion from 1967. Trout's team was good, but I felt confident going against them because it was the famous Hector Gervais playing against a much younger team. My assumption proved wrong because when the smoke cleared, it was Trout who came out the victor and team number one heading to the 1974 Provincial.

This meant we had to drop to the B side and win two more games to become the second team from Northern Alberta in the provincials. The first game was against Gil Svensen from Leduc, and I was pretty confident because I could not remember when had Hector lost to Svensen. It was just one of those teams that Hec had the number of, and it wasn't any different that day as we won the game easily. That set up the B-side final against the young Tom Reed team, who were also out of the St. Albert Curling Club. Interestingly enough, my old teammate and quarterback from the Edmonton Huskies, Tony Rankel, was the second player on the Reed team and was playing head-to-head against me.

We got out in front early, but difficult ice conditions caused by television lights made it necessary part way through the game to change the sheet of ice being used, which probably also allowed the young team from St. Albert to catch up and force an extra end, which would be a thirteenth end.

The winning shot of the 1974 Alberta Brier playdowns.
From the left Darrel Sutton, Mel Watchorn, Ron Anton and Warren Hansen

We had last rock, and Hector executed a perfect in-turn hit and stay for the 9–8 win and a trip to the Alberta provincial.

In addition to Stan Trout, the other notables playing in the Alberta provincial were three-time world champion Ron Northcott from Calgary and defending champion Mel Watchorn of Fairview, Alberta. We opened on Thursday evening against Fred Davies from NWT, and the game went in our favour, as pretty much expected. Game number two was on Friday afternoon, and again against a team we did not expect to have any problem with, Fred Davies of Fort St. John (teams from northeastern BC actually playoff with Alberta). However, Hector was anything but spectacular, and after eight ends, we were down four points. In the ninth, Davies wrecked on a front guard with his last, which allowed us to steal a single or we could have been down by eight. Thank God for twelve-end games, as we kept slugging, and in the end, Hector made his last one good in the twelfth for a win. That evening, we took on Ron Northcott, and although the game was close, we were pretty much in control all the way. I had played against Northcott on many occasions, but looking back at history, this was the last time I ever played against him.

Saturday was another good day for us as we easily took care of Howie Brazeau of NWT in the afternoon and the brush-wielding Bruce Stewart team from Calgary in the evening. Both games were done after ten ends. Sunday was going to be our tough day, as we were going against Stan Trout in the morning. Remember, he defeated us in the Northern Alberta playoff. In the afternoon, we would be playing the defending champion, Mel Watchorn. Watchorn had already lost to Ron Northcott, so if we beat Trout, we would be guaranteed at least a playoff, even if we lost to Watchorn. But the game against Trout seemed to be like a replay of the Northern A final, as nothing seemed to work, and we were down 3–0 after three ends. We battled back, but Trout made his last one good in the twelfth end for an 8–7 win.

In the afternoon game against Watchorn, it was all on the line... The winner would go to the Brier in London, Ontario, and Watchorn was looking for his third Alberta title in as many years. We were down 5–3, playing the seventh, and Watchorn had the hammer. With his last stone in the seventh, Mel had a come-around tap back to count three, which would have put us down 8–3, but his final stone wrecked on the front, and we stole a single to still be in the game and then came back with another steal of two in the eighth. The score went back and forth from that point, and finally we were up 8–7, going home with the hammer. With his final stone, Watchorn attempted to draw around a stone in the top of the 12-foot, but the rock did not bury and about two-thirds of it was sticking in the open.

The 1974 Alberta representatives for the Brier from the left, Warren Hansen, Macdonald hostess, Hector Gervais, Darrel Sutton, Ron Anton and representative of Macdonald Tobacco.

I turned and headed to the away end to get ready for Hector's shot, which I assumed would be a chip-out, but once at the other end, I saw Hector had placed the broom a way over by the divider. But that was Hector—never that confident of a pretty much open hit but with weight just a few feet more than draw, he was deadly. Hector seldom said a word to either Darrel Sutton or I prior to delivering his stone, but this time he looked up at me and said, "When I let this go, start sweeping like hell and don't stop unless I really yell." And sweep like hell we did, from the instant the stone left Hector's hand until it reached the Watchorn shot stone and moved it about a foot. We won the game 9–7 and were heading to the Brier!

I had never been to London, Ontario, so arriving there for the 1974 Brier was a whole new experience, from beginning to end. I was familiar with some of the teams and players either through playing against them in bonspiels or as a result of relationships I had developed, particularly in Atlantic Canada, through the Silver Broom Schools. Starting on the west side of the country, you might recall that I mentioned earlier in the book about being called in as a sweeper for BC in the 1973 Brier. Three members of that 1974 BC team—Bernie Sparkes, Jim Armstrong, and Gerry Peckham—had also played in '73. All of us knew Larry McGrath from Saskatchewan because he had played in Edmonton a number of times in the annual Canadian Open Carspiel. Team Ontario, skipped by Paul Savage, and Quebec, with former Manitoban Jim Ursel at the helm, were two of the teams we were concerned about, along with BC and Saskatchewan. From my involvement in the Silver Broom Schools, I was familiar with John Clarke from New Brunswick, Bob Dillion of PEI, and Fred Whyte from St. John's, Newfoundland. I knew we would have to play well against the teams from Atlantic Canada, but I did not expect to lose to any of them. But that should have been one of the first signs to say, "Beware."

The Hog-Line Rule

A couple of problems went on at the 1974 Brier, but before I get to those, I will expand on another sideshow. The hog-line rule of the day stated that the thrower's body had to come to a complete stop before reaching the first hog line. No part of the thrower's body or equipment could touch the line after the stone had been released. The rule had been creating a lot of issues, and while it wasn't being enforced, it still provided difficulty for many of the top players. The result was a lot of stones were fouled at the line.

The International Curling Federation (ICF) recognized the problem and made it known that starting with the 1974 Silver Broom in Berne, Switzerland, the hog-line rule would be changed to the rule still in use today, which simply states, "The stone shall be released before it reaches the hog line at the delivering end." However, the CCA had yet to make a similar move prior to the 1974 Brier in London. It also seemed unclear whether the CCA would follow the path laid out by the ICF.

The opening draw of the 1974 Brier.
The Alberta team is third from the left in the blue sweaters.

To make a point that the rule needed to be changed, a group led by George McCord of the Pacific Coast Curling Association and CCA Vice President Bill Leaman of Trail, BC, decided to force the umpires at the 1974 Brier to enforce the hog-line rule. Now, remember the CCA really had little to do with the operation of the Brier. Macdonald Tobacco usually recruited a group of local retired curlers to be "the official umpires." Fact is, the "official umpires" did little nor were they expected to, but all of a sudden, McCord and Leaman appeared in their world and demanded the hog-line rule be enforced. So, a bunch of old guys were forced into action to start pulling stones at the hog line. This went on for about two days, and I think Ontario skip Paul Savage was the victim twice and BC's Jim Armstrong maybe once.

The outcry from the curlers and the media was so loud there wasn't another stone removed for the balance of the Brier, and oh yes, the CCA AGM on Thursday morning voted in favour of changing the rule to what it is today.

Rock and Ice Problems

Then there were the issues with rocks and ice. The ice maker for the event being staged in the old London Gardens (about a 3,000-seat arena) was Marcel Dewitt. Marcel was known for being the best ice maker in the area, but he had never made ice for a major event like the Brier in his life. In those days, there was no one being sent in to assist or advise. Remember that during the time of Macdonald Tobacco, it was their show and the CCA had little to do with the operation. Time had caught up to Macdonald Tobacco with many things, and ice making was one of them. In the sixties and early seventies, a number of Brier ice surfaces had dealt with a heat problem, and in a couple of cases (Kelowna, BC, 1968 and Winnipeg 1970), the ice was nearly lost, so Marcel was going to make sure this did not happen. He drove the level of the brine refrigerant (temperature) so low, the ice surface had big cracks all over it. We were soon going to find out there was another consequence to ice being at such a low temperature: frost. With the humidity in the air, frost instantly started to collect on the surface. The frost was so heavy by the opening Monday of the Brier that a corn broom could be used for about two ends until it was so wet from absorbing the frost it had to be replaced with a dry broom. For the entire event, I had twelve corn brooms on the go: six on the ice for the game I was playing, and another six back at the hotel drying out.

The Brier started Monday with an afternoon and evening draw and day two was also a two-draw day, with a break Tuesday evening for the Macdonald Brier dinner. The frost was so bad that during the Tuesday evening break that Marcel Dewitt resurfaced the ice, which in those days meant giving it a flood. If you are old enough to remember the days when ice makers flooded the ice once a week (usually Sunday night), you will remember how difficult the "green ice" was for a day or so (in years gone by the ice was referred to as being "green" when the surface was freshly flooded). The result was day three of the Brier started on green ice, which set out another set of challenges.

There were also issues with the stones. In 1967, the Canadian Curling Association (CCA) had purchased a set of stones that were to be used for the Brier and nothing else. These were brand new stones and were the best of the day, made of Ailsa Craig granite from Scotland. However, using the stones only once a year for the Brier never really gave them a chance to be properly worn-in, and as a result, even after two or three Briers, the stones were still providing the inconsistency of newly sharpened stones, which is based on release sensitivity. The problem was enhanced when, somewhere along the way, the stones were put on the ice warm and the running edge of the stones filled with water, which when it froze expanded and took actual chips out of the running surface. This was so bad that after the 1972 Brier in St. John's, Newfoundland, rock expert Herb Olson actually sharpened the stones in an attempt to eliminate the "pitting," and while this was successful to a degree, it did not totally fix the problem. You might recall earlier that I had swept for Team BC for the final seven games of the '73 Brier after second Jim Armstrong broke his wrist and, as a result, swept on all five sheets of ice. The rocks had the actual sheet of ice engraved into the stone, so you knew for sure the rocks from sheet A in 1973 were also the rocks on sheet A in 1974. We played Saskatchewan's Larry McGrath in our first game on sheet A, and I remembered well that there were three stones on that sheet that would curl and then back up as the stone travelled down the ice. I told the boys about the situation, and by the conclusion of the first end, we knew Saskatchewan was throwing the rocks that looped their way down the sheet. Team McGrath figured the problem out by about the sixth end, but by then, we were up about three points and coasted to a fairly easy 8–4 win. Game two was against Bobby Dillion of PEI, but again, we were in control most of the way and grabbed a 5–3 victory, which ended day one.

The Alberta team with vigorous sweeping on Ron Anton's stone. Anton is following the stone while the sweepers are from the left Warren Hansen, Darrel Sutton and Hector Gervais.
Photo credit – Michael Burns Photography.

Day two had a morning draw and one in the afternoon, with the evening reserved for the annual Macdonald Brier dinner. While the banquet was unique and always had an interesting presentation by eccentric company President David Stewart, the curlers hated it because it broke the rhythm of the event. We played Chucker Ross of Northern Ontario in the morning draw and easily disposed of him by a score of 14–3.

The afternoon game was against John Clarke of Fredericton, New Brunswick, and John was a guy I knew from having done a couple of years of Silver Broom Schools in the New Brunswick capital. While I thought Clarke would give us a game, I did not expect it to be a game we could lose. Hector did not play his best, and as a result, the score was tied going into the twelfth end and Clarke had the final stone. The result was an 8–6 win for New Brunswick and our first loss.

Remember I mentioned earlier that the ice was flooded on Tuesday evening, so with the first draw on Wednesday, we were playing BC on green ice. Playing BC was like old home week because we all knew BC third Bernie Sparkes from his years as second for Ron Northcott in Alberta, and Gerry Peckham, Jim Armstrong, and I became well acquainted at the 1973 Brier in Edmonton. The BC game was fairly well played, but we remained in control for most of the game and ended with the score of a single in the twelfth end and a 9–7 win. On Wednesday, our second game was against Manitoba and a team from Glenboro, with Don Barr throwing the final stones, seeing his first Brier action ever. The boys from the buffalo province had come out of the gate fairly strong at the start of the Brier but had dropped their first game of the day to Paul Savage of Ontario.

We felt pretty confident going into the game and jumped in front by a score of 4–1 after three ends and coasted to a 10–6 victory. On Thursday, in game seven, we defeated Barry Shearer of Nova Scotia 7–5 and, later in the day, took care of Fred Whyte of Newfoundland by the same score. So, going into Friday and the second last day of the Brier, we were sitting in first place with a record of 7–1 and close on our heels were Jim Ursel of Quebec and Larry McGrath of Saskatchewan, each with a record of 5–2.

Herb Millham, the Canadian Curling Association board member who was responsible for making the Curl Canada development program a reality.

On Friday afternoon, we played host Ontario in a game where Hector struggled a lot, and opposition skip Paul Savage capitalized on every Gervais miscue to coast to a 12–5 win. This was our second-to-last game because with the eleven-team field and five sheets of ice, one team had a bye on each round and Friday night was our turn. We went out for dinner with our driver and were joined by *Edmonton Journal* sportswriter Don "Buckets" Fleming. Following the Friday evening draw, the stage was set for a very interesting final round on Saturday afternoon. We were tied on top with Saskatchewan, each of us with a record of 7–2, but right on our heels at 6–3 was Quebec's Jim Ursel. The final round would have us playing Ursel while McGrath was going against Savage. A win by us and a win by Savage, and we would be Brier champions, but if we lost and McGrath won, the Brier would belong to Saskatchewan. However, if we lost, and McGrath lost, there would be a three-team playoff to determine the 1974 Brier champion.

Before we could get into our Brier final draw, I spent an interesting Saturday morning that would in fact lead to my life being changed forever. My friend Ray Kingsmith of Calgary was the secretary-manager of the Southern Alberta Curling Association, so he attended all the meetings leading up to the AGM of the CCA on Friday morning. Kingsmith approached me on Wednesday and asked if I knew the CCA was planning on getting involved in some way with curling instruction and a possible program of training people on how to be instructors/coaches. I was surprised and indicated to Ray that I wasn't aware. I did, however, know the Canadian Ladies Curling Association (CLCA) were looking at something along this line and had been talking with my competitors, Duguid, Turnbull, and Ursuliak (DTU). Kingsmith advised me that newly elected third vice president, Herb Millham of Vancouver, was now the chair of the public relations committee, and the responsibility for this project was on his plate. Ray asked if I wanted to meet Millham, and I agreed it would be a good idea.

So, at ten a.m. Saturday morning, before going out to try to win a Brier, I met with Kingsmith and Millham for coffee at the headquarters hotel, the Holiday Inn, just a stone's throw from Highway 401. It was an interesting meeting as Millham gave me some idea of what the CCA was going to attempt to do. They had an idea of running a clinic in the fall of 1974 in twelve centres across Canada to teach people how to instruct curlers, but they only had a budget of $3,000. Even by 1974 standards, that was more than a little low. Herb also mentioned that an Ottawa PR firm headed up by a person named Norm

Shannon had been hired to do some preliminary work on various PR projects, and one was to develop a slogan and logo for this new arm of the CCA. The name was Curl Canada, and the logo was a stylized curling stone. We did not talk long, but Herb suggested it would be a good idea for me to travel to Ottawa and meet with Shannon as soon as possible. I laughingly suggested if we won the Brier, I could possibly drop into Ottawa on my way to Switzerland the following week. However, it was more than a passing comment because whether we won the Brier or not, I was still heading to Switzerland as a member of the curling media, since I had been working on curling reports all year with CHQT radio in Edmonton. I indicated I would contact Herb on Monday and see if it was possible for me to at least spend an afternoon in Ottawa before heading to Switzerland.

Shortly after the meeting with Millham and Kingsmith, it was time to head for the arena and the final round of the Brier. This was before the days of playoffs, so if we could finish the afternoon with a better win–loss record than anyone else, we would be the Brier champions. I had never played against Jim Ursel, but both Ron and Hector were in the 1962 Brier, where Ursel played third for Manitoba's Norm Houck. The game was very wide open, and Ursel was careful not to get into any sort of come-around game with Hector. We scored a single in the second end, and the next score was another single by Quebec in end six. The seventh was another blank, but the difference in the game was a deuce scored by our Alberta foursome in the eighth. Ursel came back with a single in the ninth, and we blanked ends ten and eleven to be one up going into the last with the hammer.

The end was again played pretty clean, but when Ursel went to deliver his last, we had a counter at the back of the tee line just behind the button. Ursel attempted to freeze to our shot stone, and while he did not weld it on, he stopped about six inches short of our stone to be counting one. This left Hector with a chip shot to remove the Quebec counter, to give us a score of one and a 4–2 win. But when Hector was throwing any sort of a takeout with his last, we were always nervous because he had a clear push on the stone at release, so variations were always possible. Had it been a draw required to the corner of the button, I would have felt a lot more confident.

Anyway, the chip shot it was, and as Hector, Darrel Sutton, and I headed down to the far end of the arena to complete the shot, no one said a word. Hector settled in the hack, started the backswing, and came forward in the slide. The instant he let the stone go, he started to scream for the sweep. I think I leaned on the Wildcat heavy-weight broom in my hand harder than at any time in my life and kept that pace right until inches before the moving stone and stationary stone made contact. The rocks made a chinking sound on contact, and the crowd went wild as the Quebec stone rolled past the front of our stationary stone to the left and our shooter went to the right side of the shot stone. To this day, I'm not sure how much of the Quebec stone we caught, but I can assure you it wasn't much. We had won the game by a score of 4–2, which stood for about the next twenty years as the lowest score ever in a Brier game.

The Alberta champions march to the dias to be awarded the Brier Tankard at the conclusion of the 1974 Brier. From the left skip Hector Gervais, third Ron Anton, second Warren Hansen and lead Darrel Sutton.
Photo credit – Michael Burns Photography.

The 1974 Brier champions with the Tankard
from the left Hec Gervais, Ron Anton, Warren Hansen and Darrel Sutton.
Photo credit – Michael Burns Photography.

While we had beaten Quebec, we had not yet won the Brier because over on sheet B, the game between Ontario and Saskatchewan was just finishing the tenth end, and to our delight, Ontario was up by four, but there were two ends to be played. In the eleventh, Saskatchewan took two points, so going into the twelfth, Ontario was up two with the hammer. I can still remember nearly every stone from that twelfth end, and without question, it was the longest end of curling I ever witnessed. If Savage could hold on to the lead and score a victory, we would win the Brier, but if McGrath could pull off a win, we would be into a playoff with Saskatchewan. Hector had been dealing with knee problems all week, and both Ron Anton and I knew if we had to face a playoff match, it could be too much for the Fat Man, which was our pet name for the big guy. Savage and his team did not play the end well, and when it came down to his final stone, Paul was looking at two Saskatchewan counters that were both partly behind cover. Savage calmly threw an out-turn (left-hander) down, and snuggled up to McGrath's shot to score a single and an 11–8 win... and with that, we won the Brier.

The next hour was a period of my life that I will never forget, which included the walk down centre ice to the prize table and the presentation of the Brier Tankard by David Stewart of Macdonald Tobacco. But soon, the crowd was gone and the media interviews were over, and now we wondered what was next. It was Saturday afternoon, we were in London, Ontario, and we would have to journey back to Edmonton on Sunday, travel back to Toronto and Berne, Switzerland, on Thursday. Who was going to help us do all of that? The answer was... no one. While we were standing around the home end of the arena and not knowing for sure what was happening, an old guy in a tam came out with a bag of CCA pins and some Canada back crests. He said, "Here you go, boys. Someone from Air Canada will get in touch with you about your plane tickets, and I think our second VP, Bill Leaman, will be in Berne, and he will see you there." There wasn't a Canadian uniform. All of our garments had "Alberta" all over them, amongst other things, and two of our guys didn't even have passports.

CHAPTER 6
The Air Canada Silver Broom—The Final Conquest Starts

THANK GOD FOR the local MLA back in St. Albert, Ernie Jamison, because he pulled some strings to get passports for Darrel and Ron.

I had some influence with a local tailor in Edmonton who had done all the garments for the Silver Broom School, so I was able to get all the Alberta crests on our garments replaced with Canada overnight, and by Tuesday morning, most things were ready to go. We were heading to a world championship wearing an Alberta uniform with the Alberta crests removed and replaced by "Canada" labelling. This was still at a time when there wasn't an official Canadian team uniform. It was most interesting wearing a dress blazer that was the Alberta tartan. I had Air Canada contacts through the Silver Broom School, so I got the airline tickets put in place. I actually left for Toronto on Wednesday morning, so I could travel to Ottawa on Thursday and spend the day with Norm Shannon, whom Herb Millham, from the CCA, had connected me.

I flew out of Edmonton to Toronto on Wednesday, and early Thursday morning, I was off to Ottawa, where Norm Shannon met me at the airport. By coincidence, the Canadian Schoolboy Championship was happening in Ottawa that week, and Shannon stopped by the HQ hotel, where we met CCA Secretary-Manager Charlie Scrymgeour. I knew who Charlie was but had never really met him before. He worked for the CCA pretty much as a volunteer but received a stipend for his efforts. Scrymgeour, a Brier champion with Ken Watson back in the forties, ran the CCA out of the basement office of his home in Winnipeg. There were no other employees of any sort working for the CCA.

Shannon and I had lunch, and he talked to me about some things he was attempting to do for the proposed Curl Canada curling instructor program. He had put in an application to the Carling O'Keefe Foundation for some potential support for the new initiative. The Canadian brewer's newly formed O'Keefe Foundation was created to contribute to the development of coaches in sport. Shannon drove me back to the airport, and we agreed I would touch base with Herb Millham as soon as I returned to Edmonton in early April.

I arrived at the Toronto airport from Ottawa and met the balance of my team in the Air Canada lounge. One of the nice perks for the North American curlers in those days was first-class airfare on Air Canada. The United States team, skipped by Bud Somerville, was also in the first-class cabin. The flight to Zurich was quite the party… oh, the good old days! We were all poured off the plane at the Zurich airport and met our two Swiss hosts, Rudy and Werner. We were swept off to our hotel, and for the balance of the day, we had some well-needed rest. In those days, while we arrived in Berne on Thursday, we were not allowed on the ice for practice until Sunday, just one day ahead of the opening draw. Friday was also a free day prior to the opening Air Canada party on Friday night.

The Friday night function was a pretty first-class affair, and the MC was Doug Maxwell, who performed his usual amazing act of introducing every player without the use of a script. When we were introduced, lo and behold, Bill Leaman from the CCA was there and stood up on stage with us when we were all presented with RADO watches with the Air Canada Silver Broom logo etched on the face. It was the first and pretty much last time we saw Leaman or anyone else representing the CCA. On Saturday, ten villages/towns throughout the area of Switzerland hosted a team for the day, and our host was the small city of Zug. It was a fun day, and the locals introduced us to the Swiss liqueur Kirsch, which was memorable for all of us.

The opening ceremony of the 1974 Air Canada Silver Broom at the Ice Stadium Allemend in Berne, Switzerland.
Photo credit – Michael Burns Photography.

Sunday was a practice day, and we were again dealing with a surface that was frozen so hard the ice was cracked. There was a lot of frost, and something seemed very strange about the stones. Draws were travelling at an unbelievable pace of twenty-eight to thirty seconds, and there was virtually no curl. To this day, we do not know if the stones were just really dull, or if they were actually an alpine outdoor rock that had a smaller than normal cup on the bottom of the stone. Whatever the case, it was a nightmare, and at some time during the week of the event, each of us on the team lost it to the extent of virtually being unable to make a draw to the rings. During the remaining eleven years of Air Canada's sponsorship, the rocks used for the Silver

Broom were flown in from Canada and, for the most part, were the stones owned by the Manitoba Curling Association.

The team meeting was held at noon on Sunday, and most things were sort of standard except for one. Remember, smoking was still allowed on the ice, and Hector Gervais chain-smoked for the entire game. However, at the team meeting, Doug Maxwell delivered a little speech about how Swiss Curling was attempting to sell curling as a sport in Switzerland and, as a result, suggested it would be appreciated if none of the curlers smoked on the ice, although there wasn't a rule in place that forbid it. Gervais said, "Screw you. I'm smoking." From that moment forward, our team became the target of the Swiss media, and a lot of it was nasty. Remember, we had just won the Brier ten days earlier, and that was sponsored by a tobacco company. Again, through it all, no one from the CCA said a word in our defence or even talked to us at any time about the issue. Adding to everything else was the strange, almost open-air arena, the Ice Stadium Allemend, which had glass covering both ends of the building. At midday, the sun actually shone on the ice and impacted it in many ways. Needless to say, there was no direction to the locals regarding ice making, stones, type of arena that should be considered, or anything else that could impact curling's technical elements.

The event finally got underway on Monday, and we were pitted against Norway in the first draw. We had noticed the Norwegian team a couple of times, and they were very young—when I say young, I mean kids. I guessed they were between fourteen and sixteen. Sjur Loen was the skip, and he went onto represent Norway in a couple of world juniors and then played third for Eigil Ramsfjell when they won world titles in 1984 and again in 1988. The boys knew little about the rules and repeatedly banged moving rocks with their brooms so hard you could hear it, yet they said nothing. We did not know what to do because they were kids, and how would it look if we called in an umpire? We let it go because we knew we would win regardless and chalked up our first victory by a score of 7–3. However, the conditions of the ice and stones made it clear this event would not be easy. Thankfully, the hog-line rule had been changed so you could slide over the line after letting go of the stone, or the majority of stones delivered would have been fouled at the line. The second game on Monday evening was against Denmark, and we easily won 11–2.

Warren Hansen delivers at the 1974 Air Canada Silver Broom. *Photo credit – Michael Burns Photography.*

Opening draw of the 1974 Silver Broom with Canada's very large Hec Gervais (in the back) playing Norway's 14 year old Sjur Leon. In later years Loen became a world champion twice playing third for Eigil Ramsfjell. *Photo credit – Michael Burns Photography.*

On Tuesday afternoon, we were against Pierre Duclos of France, who was playing in his first Silver Broom in place of Pierre Boan, who had skipped the French team at the worlds since 1968. We expected little resistance from France, and the game was 9–2 in our favour despite the continuing struggle with rocks and ice. Our first real test was going to be Tuesday evening against the USA, and it was more than a test. The American foursome, led by former world champ Bud Somerville, hit the ice with all guns blazing, and while we were still struggling with the ice and rocks, our USA counterparts seemed to have figured everything out. When the smoke cleared, we were defeated by a score of 7–3. This was at a time when Canadians travelling to the Silver Broom had been increasing every year, and in '74, with the event in Switzerland, over 3,000 Canucks crossed the Atlantic to be part of the event, so we had lots of people cheering for us, which helped but also added to the pressure since the expectations were high.

On Wednesday afternoon, we were drawn against Scotland, and while we did not expect to lose the game to James Waddell, we knew the Scots could give us a battle, and they did. When it ended we were the winners but only by a score of 3–2. We had all been struggling with draw weight on the strange surface with the unpredictable stones. Darrel Sutton and I had each gone through a game where we could not put a stone in the rings, and this game, it was Ron Anton's turn as he struggled from start to finish with his draws. The evening game was the one everyone had been waiting for, which had us pitted against the host nation, Switzerland. Peter Attinger's young team, with his brother Bernard playing third, was expected to be our toughest competition, and they were. In a game where the Swiss were in control most of the way, the final score was 5–3 in Attinger's favour.

But it was an interesting evening for a couple of other reasons. Curling was just making its mark on Switzerland, and the Swiss media had done a good job of selling the public on the idea that if Switzerland could defeat Canada, there was a good chance it could claim its first men's worlds title. We expected a crowd but had no idea when we stepped into the arena there would be 13,000 people there to greet us—so large was the crowd that it set a record for a curling game that wasn't broken until the 1997 Brier in Calgary. And the crowd was anything but friendly because the Swiss media had also done a number on Canada because of Gervais's smoking. Add to that the fact that every second person had a cowbell that rang loud and hard for every Swiss success but also for every shot we missed... and these were no ordinary cowbells that you would see around Betsy's neck in the pasture. These cowbells, in many cases, were the size of a bell you would find in a church steeple. No one had bothered to educate the Swiss fans that it was bad etiquette to cheer the opponents misses. I will swear I heard cowbells ringing in my head for at least a month after the experience in Berne.

Going into day four, we were now sporting a 4–2 record, with three games remaining and possibly in danger of missing the playoffs if we lost another game. On Thursday afternoon, we went against Renato Ghezze of Italy, and for the most part, the Italians did not take the game really seriously. Renato was a huge guy, and he spent a lot of time arguing with his much smaller third player, Lino Mariani. I thought it interesting that everyone was setting their hair on fire about Gervais smoking, but it was okay for the Italians to have a bottle of wine going behind the scoreboard at each end of the arena. Anyway, it was a relatively easy 8–4 win for us. The evening game was against Sweden, and the Swedes in 1973, with Kjell Oscarius at the helm, had won the nation its first world title. This year the Swedes were represented by a young skip by the name of Jan Ullsten, who would actually go on to win the world juniors in 1975 with second Anders Grahn. The Swedes, for certain, gave us a game, but Hector was clicking on all cylinders, so we won fairly easily by a score of 5–2.

Action in the round robin game between Canada and Switzerland. Ron Anton stands on the left while Warren Hansen and Darrel Sutton provide the sweep on a Hector Gervais stone.
Photo credit – Michael Burns Photography.

The final game of round-robin play was set for Friday afternoon, and we were against Manfred Raderer of Germany. We easily took the game 7–1. Playoffs were set for Saturday, with the team finishing first playing the fourth-place team while second place went against number three in a sudden-death showdown. Switzerland's Peter Attinger went undefeated with a 9–0 record, while we finished second with a mark of 7–2. The USA and Sweden both finished with a record of 6–3, with the Swedes ranked third because they beat the Americans in the round robin. This meant we would play Sweden in one semifinal game while Switzerland would go against the USA in the other. The two winners would play in the world championship final on Saturday evening. The closing party was held on Friday evening, and of course, we were expected to attend. It was held in a huge building known as the Kursaal, and it was packed to capacity. The huge Canadian contingent present offered us best wishes throughout the evening, but our Swiss hosts were not so gracious. Many wished we would lose because of Gervais smoking on the ice, and of course, they knew we were the team to beat if Switzerland was to win their first-ever world championship.

Hector Gervais played pretty well during the entire 1974 Silver Broom but in the semi-final game against Sweden Hector struggled and when the game ended Canada went down to defeat. Gervais however still went down in history as one of the greatest players of all time. *Photo credit – Michael Burns Photography.*

We arrived at the arena about forty-five minutes before the game on Saturday afternoon, just to get accustomed to the surroundings. This was before warm-up was allowed on the ice, so we could not place a foot on the surface before the start of the game. The building was packed, and at first glance, it looked to be as full as it was the night we played Switzerland in the round robin, which meant another day of cowbell torture. We were in the same dressing room as the Americans, and we chatted back and forth before the start of the game. Someone on Somerville's team suggested it was going to be pretty crazy in the arena with all the cowbells, and of course, it was the Americans who were against the Swiss. In response to the US comment, Gervais barked back, suggesting at least the Americans knew it would be quiet at the top of their backswing.

Ron Anton is not able to sweep the Swedish stone out of the house and the Swedes score two to defeat Canada in the semi-final. *Photo credit – Michael Burns Photography.*

The teams participating in the 1974 World Men's Curling Championship. Canada is in the right side of the front row in the dark sweaters. From the left Hec Gervais, Ron Anton, Warren Hansen and Darrel Sutton. *Photo credit – Michael Burns Photography.*

It was a bright day outside, so the sun shining in the open end of the arena made it very bright, and of course, warm, which seemed to cause a little melting on the ice. We were more or less in control of the game most of the way, but Hector was struggling. Each of us had experienced a game during the round robin where we virtually lost the feel of draw weight, but Hector had hung in well, for the most part. However, the semifinal was his day to lose it. The third end was huge, with the score tied 1–1, and we had last rock. Gervais had a chance to split the house to be sitting two when he went to throw his first. But he was heavy, and Sweden then removed our shot stone, which left Hector with a hit to blank the end. But he threw the shot a little wide, and it simply did not come up enough to hit the shot stone and Sweden stole a single to go up 2–1. We came back with three in the sixth and another deuce in the ninth to be up 7–6 heading into the last end but without last rock.

What happened next is one of those things you never forget. We decided to play everything clean and hopefully force the Swedes to take a single, which would send the game into an extra end, and we would have the hammer. Sweden put up guards with the first two stones. Darrel Sutton peeled off the first, and I killed the second one with my first shot. The Swedes put up a corner with their third shot to the in-turn side of the sheet. The way we had always peeled was to come into the rock, attempt to catch less than half of it and roll away to the left. I looked to the other end, and Hector motioned for me to throw across the face of the stone, cross it with the in-turn, and roll the shooter into the right side boards.

I paused for a moment. *This is not how we do this, and it is almost impossible on this ice, with these rocks, to throw a stone to make it go across the face.* I paused again and thought, *I guess if I make sure I turn it inside with big weight, it will surely move enough to roll off.* What I should have done was got up and gone down the ice to chat with Gervais, but this was something that simply never happened with Hector because you would be questioning him, which was a no-no. So… I took a deep breath, threw the stone as hard as I dared, and turned it inside as far as I dared. On release, I hollered, "Woa!" and Hector hollered, "Woa!" When contact was made, I hit the stone right on the nose. I couldn't believe what had just happened, and the immediate thought that went through my mind was, *It should be okay because with the rocks and ice that were in play, it was practically impossible for Sweden to draw a stone behind the guard.* But I was wrong. I do not know how he did it, but Sweden's second player, Anders Grahn, turned his stone enough to curl past the guard and stop the stone in front of the tee line, pretty much buried.

Today, there is little question of what the next play should have been, which was the straight run back on the front stone. But in those days, you did not try those types of shots very often. So, Ron Anton attempted to draw in behind the Swedish shot stone but was too heavy. The Swedes split the house to be sitting two, and Ron hit the Swedish counter with his final stone and stayed in the eight-foot.

Sweden hit the open stone and rolled out, and Hector attempted to draw behind the corner and the Swedish shot stone but was heavy. Sweden again attempted to split the house to be sitting two and barely did it, hanging on the back of the twelve-foot. Hector attempted to draw in front of the Swedish second shot stone but was again too heavy, and the Swedes did not have to throw their last. I was in a state of shock and could not believe what had just happened. We had just lost the world semifinal in a game that we'd had a chance to win at least four or five times, but because of the impossible stones and ice, we had blown the whole thing.

Meanwhile, over on sheet B, an equally bizarre game was taking place between Switzerland and the USA. After nine ends, the score was tied 2–2. In the final end, Switzerland had last stone, and although the USA only had a stone fully in the twelve-foot the Swiss decided to hit rather than draw. But again, because of the condition of the stones, you could hit as much as 80% of the stone and still roll out of the rings. That's exactly what Attinger did, so the game went into an extra end. In the extra, Attinger, looking at a similar shot, hit and rolled out again, forcing the game into its second extra end. In the twelfth, Attinger again played the hit rather than draw and rolled out, but this time the USA had a second stone in the rings, which allowed them to steal one and a berth in the final against Sweden.

I went back to the dressing room with Ron Anton, and we stared at the wall for at least half an hour. The final was played within about one hour of the semi, so by the time we made our way out of the dressing room, it was already underway. The USA had taken a commanding lead and won the game easily 11–4.

I remember sitting next to Somerville later that evening in a bar, and he could not believe what had happened and how he had won.

The next morning around noon, my friends Terry Begin and Ray Kingsmith rented a car and we started down the road toward Belgium. I sat in the back seat all the way and said very little. It was all like a nightmare. I had worked my butt off on a sheet of curling ice in an attempt to play in and win a world championship, and in a blink of an eye, it was gone. I knew the chances of getting back to that point again weren't good. I thought of many things, but the one thing that really burned me was the lack of support or direction we had received from the CCA. We had been thrown to the wolves, and while there was surely a time when Canada simply had to pretty much show up to win a world title, those days were gone.

By Wednesday, we had made our way to Paris, where we spent two days before finally heading home on Friday. In the opening paragraph of this book, I outlined in detail what happened that last night in Paris before we headed to the Charles de Gaulle Airport and our trip back to Canada.

CHAPTER 7
The Fight for Change Begins

WHEN I FINALLY landed in Edmonton, it was strange. There was one person there, Ken Hunka, whom I had asked to pick me up. Just about three short weeks earlier, when we arrived home from London, the airport had been full of people to greet us and every media outlet in Edmonton was part of the reception. I know I was a week behind the team, but it wasn't much better for the other three guys, with just family and a few friends there for the greeting. Oh, how quickly we fell from grace!

I spent the next few days trying to gather my thoughts and get my head back into the real world. I was still a sales rep for Midwestern Broom, so I needed to get around to all of my accounts before the end of April to accept orders for the 1975 season. And, yes, everywhere I went, people had the same question and comments, and the common theme was... what happened to you guys in Berne? Some even suggested that maybe we were partying too much. Right... I waited ten years to get to the Silver Broom and I was just going to drink it away?

The one thing I immediately did was call Herb Millham regarding the CCA instruction program I had spoken to him about in London. We agreed it would be a good idea if I could get out to Vancouver to meet with him ASAP, so we set a date for the latter part of April. When

I arrived in Vancouver, I headed to Herb's office, which was part of the law firm Davis and Company in downtown Vancouver. We chatted about the development of the Curl Canada program. I asked him if he knew the Canadian Ladies Association (CLCA) was looking at doing something similar, and he did not. I asked if anyone at the CCA ever talked to anyone at the CLCA. To the best of his knowledge, he said they did not, so sitting right there in his office, I suggested we call the CLCA president in Moncton, Mabel DeWare. I had Mabel's number, so Herb dialled it straight away, and Mabel answered. To the best of my knowledge, that was the day history was made, as it was the first call ever between the CCA and the CLCA. Mabel was to the point with Herb. She had been speaking with Don Duguid and Ray Turnbull about possibly doing some work for the CLCA in the instruction area, but she was open to other ideas if they made sense. Following the call, Herb said to leave it with him and he would get it straightened out. He did.

By early July, an agreement was reached between the CCA and CLCA to be partners in a new organization called Curl Canada that would basically look after matters common to both organizations. The first item of business was to start a Canada-wide program to teach people how to instruct curling. I completed negotiations with Millham by early July and soon after signed a one-year contract to start the operation of the Curl Canada clinics. One side of me was really excited, but I was also painfully aware if we taught a number of people across Canada how to instruct curling, it would eventually be the end of the Silver Broom Curling School, and for that matter, all the other professional teaching operations. However, I had little choice except to move forward because if I didn't do it, my competitors would. Better it be me than them.

CHAPTER 8
Curl Canada Program is Launched

THE NEXT CHALLENGE was the structure of the Curl Canada clinics. How many were going to be operated? How was the bill going to be paid? It was agreed that the clinics were going to be designed to teach curlers how to instruct curling, and the plan was to operate at least one in every province in Canada, but the money required to make it happen was another question. Both of the national associations—the CCA and the CLCA—had agreed to contribute $3,000 each for a total of $6,000, which wouldn't even scratch the paint on what was desired, even in 1974 values. I spoke to Norm Shannon, who indicated he had been in some discussions with the O'Keefe Foundation regarding funding. Shannon was informed that before any consideration would be given for financial assistance, a meeting would have to be held with the newly formed Coaching Association of Canada and its executive director, John Hudson.

This is the first time I would have contact with John Hudson, but over the next twenty years, we would cross paths many times. In 1976, Hudson became the head of CBC Television Sports, and he went from there in the early eighties to become the director of marketing for Labatt Breweries. When Labatt decided it was time for them to draw back as the title sponsor of the Brier in 1992, it was Hudson who delivered that message to the CCA.

I met with Hudson in August and found out about the National Coaching Certification Program (NCCP), which was relatively new but was quickly gaining momentum as more and more sports certified and trained coaches. The curling program that was being proposed was somewhat unique because it involved the training and certification of instructors, and in the initial plan, there was nothing being directed at coaching.

In my discussion with Hudson, it was agreed that if the green light were given to the O'Keefe Foundation to fund our plans for 1974–75, two things would need to happen. First, we would have to agree to appoint a national certification committee and begin the development of Level I Technical, but the following year, Level I Coaching would have to be part of the program. A totally new segment that was currently being developed by Sport Canada and various universities across Canada would be referred to as coaching theory. For each level of development, there would be a theory course presented that would be the same for all sports. For a coach/instructor to become certified at any level, three components would be necessary: Technical, Theory, and a period of practical experience. I agreed, and by late August, Norm Shannon was advised that $22,000 had been approved for the program of developing curling instructors by Curl Canada. We were now set to do something, but what that would be still wasn't totally clear. With the dollars approved by the CCA/CLCA ($6,000), we now had a total of $28,000, but with the task ahead, we were probably $50,000 short?

A fee of $10 would be charged to each person attending a clinic, which would help, but it was still going to be a difficult mountain to climb. A number of things needed to be put in place to get the program off the ground, including a complete set of instruction equipment, a uniform for the instructors, a manual (which would be provided to each course attendee), etc. I do not know how we got it all up and running, but by September 19, 1974, we offered the first session at the Balmoral Curling Club in Edmonton. Between then and the early part of December, sixteen clinics were operated between St. John's, Newfoundland, and Victoria, BC—Edmonton, Vancouver, Montreal, Quebec City, London, Ontario, Thunder Bay, Ontario, Toronto, Winnipeg, Ottawa, Halifax, St. John's, Saint John, New Brunswick, Moncton, Newe Brunswick, Charlottetown, and Kelowna, BC—and a total of 527 took the basic Level I Technical course.

Gerry Peckham, third from the left and Warren Hansen, far right provide instruction on the release of the stone at a Curl Canada Leve I Clinic.

However, this was all made possible in a very interesting way. As you can well imagine, even in 1974, $28,000 could not pay all the costs of operating sixteen clinics from coast to coast, producing a manual and support materials, and paying the instructors. The project was made possible by connecting it directly with the Silver Broom Curling School. The way it worked was that a Silver Broom School was scheduled into a city for four days, then for the two days following the Silver Broom session, a Curl Canada clinic was held, leaving a couple of the Silver Broom School instructors behind to complete the project. The Silver Broom School provided all the airfare required to operate the Curl Canada clinics from coast to coast through its agreement with Air Canada. Bottom line was, at the end of the day, the Curl Canada clinics were not charged a dime for airfare. In the end, it allowed the entire project to come in under budget and when the $10/person charged to each clinic attendee was taken into consideration, a profit of $3,000 was achieved. But what was interesting through this entire scenario was that never did the CCA/CLCA say even thank you to either Air Canada or myself for the support.

Once the clinics were up and running, the second challenge that faced us was to establish a certification committee of recognized experts who would be members of the committee provided with the responsibility of developing Levels I, II and III Technical. There were other problems that had to be overcome. There were three jurisdictions in Canada that already had an instruction program of sorts: the Ontario Curling Association (OCA), Saskatchewan Curling Association (SCA), and the Southern Alberta Curling Association (SACA). The OCA and SACA conditionally participated in the initial offering of clinics, but Saskatchewan did not. The condition that both SACA and the OCA participated under was a person appointed from both areas would have to be a member of the Curl Canada Certification Committee. When the committee was finally put together, Ray Lilly represented the OCA and Len Pasychny was appointed by SACA. Saskatchewan did not send anyone directly, although it was agreed that five-time Canadian champion, Joyce McKee, from Saskatoon, would be a member of the committee. In addition, the other two professional schools were asked to send a representative: the DTU School sent Don Duguid and the Canadian Curling Alliance was represented by Jim McConnell. I was appointed as the chair of the committee, and we were set to go.

The basics of the Silver Broom School were set down as technical starting points and the fight was on. I was confident that the techniques being taught by the Silver Broom School were as close to correct as could be, considering the more than competent people involved in establishing the Silver Broom School curriculum, which included Ron Anton, Gerry Peckham, and Garry DeBlonde to only mention a few. Between the fall of 1974 and the summer of 1975, three meetings were scheduled. By the last meeting, agreement was reached on Level I Technical, and the committee was now ready to wade into Level II. It wasn't easy, and I can remember declaring, after the first session, that it was the longest three days of my life.

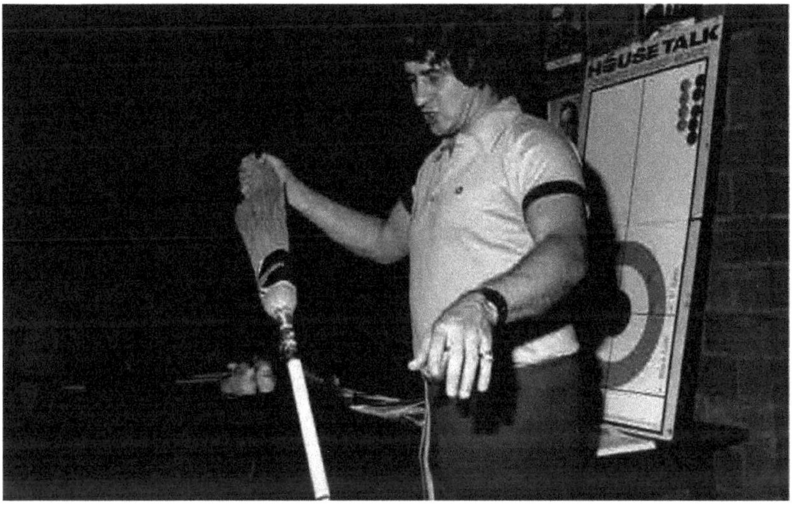

Warren Hansen directs a classroom session at a Curl Canada clinic.

Part of the National Coaching Certification Program outlined the structure of three aspects to every level: Technical, Theory, and Practical. So taking a Level I course was just the start to becoming a certified Level I Instructor-Coach. The Theory I course was common to all sports and was administered by the provincial governments, and the practical component was defined by the Curl Canada Certification Committee.

The fall of 1975 saw the start of year two, and it was set to be bigger and better than year one. Twenty-three Curl Canada Level I clinics were held with nearly 1,000 participants. The whole country was also now involved, except Saskatchewan. Two issues needed to be tackled by the certification committee prior to the fall of 1976: the introduction of Level II Technical and Level I Coaching.

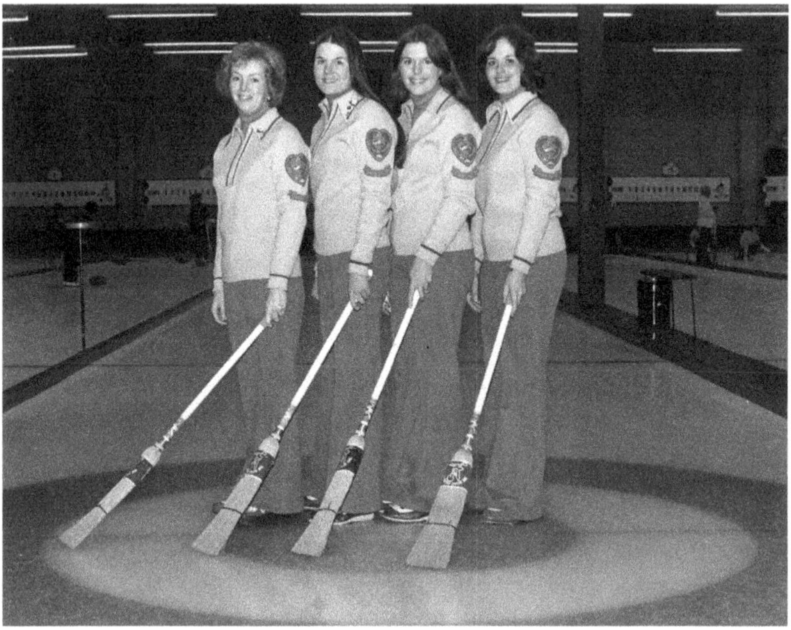

Warren Hansen developed a lot of the Curl Canada coaching program content when he coached the Lindsay Sparkes team to the Macdonald Lassie title in 1976. The team from left to right, Lindsay Sparkes, Dawn Knowles, Robin Wilson and Lorraine Bowles.

Coaching was a pretty new item to curling, and for the most part, it had never really existed except for junior men's curling (then known as the Canadian School Boys Championship). I had coached junior football for seven years in Edmonton, so I had coaching experience, but not in curling. In the fall of 1975, when I was in the process of moving to Vancouver, I decided to gain some first-hand experience in coaching curling by actually spending some time with a young women's team that I thought had the potential to possibly do great things. The team was out of the North Shore Winter Club in North Vancouver and was skipped by Lindsay Sparkes. Sisters Dawn Knowles and Robin Wilson filled the middle of the team, and Lorraine Bowles was the lead. They had been trying to get to the BC Women's Championship for a couple of years but had not made the grade. I started doing sessions with the team and applied a lot of my coaching knowledge from football and my curling technical knowledge from my own playing experience, plus my knowledge from the Silver Broom Curling School. Everything pulled together in the 1976 championship season, and when the smoke cleared, the team defeated former Canadian champion Gale Lee from Edmonton in a playoff at the Macdonald Lassie in Winnipeg. I continued to coach the team until the end of the 1979 season, when they won their second Canadian title and became the first Canadian team to play in the women's worlds in Perth, Scotland.

In the fall of 1976, after further discussions with the certification committee, the Level II Technical program was rolled out, along with Level I Coaching. The summer of '76 also brought forth another set of problems when the Carling O'Keefe Foundation suddenly withdrew its support, and at the same time, the involvement of both the CCA and the CLCA was reduced to a combined support of $6,000. For a moment, it looked like it was going to be the end of the clinics, but Sport Canada stepped up to the plate and produced a grant of $10,000. During the same time, we developed the Level I Novice Manual, which was a booklet the instructors we taught provided to their students. The manuals sold for $10 each, and that, along with an increase in the fees charged to participants by about another $10, allowed the program to get through the '76 season in the black. Things went so well in 1977 that financial support from the CCA/CLCA wasn't required at all. The '76 season saw a total of nineteen Level I clinics, five Level II clinics, and two senior instructor seminars, with every curling association involved in at least some phase of the program. By the end of the 1976 season and year three, 2,000 people had taken the Level I course, which reflected the popularity of the program; possibly as many as 80,000 curlers benefited from their teaching efforts.

In the meantime, there were activities happening on other fronts. The CCA/CLCA availed themselves of the grants and facilities offered by Sport Canada and took steps to hire an executive director for Curl Canada and set up executive offices in the National Sports and Recreation Centre in Ottawa. In June 1976, a committee consisting of senior CCA/CLCA executives hired John MacLeod as the executive director of Curl Canada, and he began his official duties on September 1, 1976.

The clinics continued to grow, and by 1978, in addition to the Level I and II Technical programs, Curl Canada was offering Level III Technical. Ice making was another one of my major concerns, and as a result, we brought together a group of master ice technicians in Calgary in the fall of 1977 to begin the formation of the Level I Ice Technician program.

The office end of things also took on a new look. The CCA had been operating its office in Winnipeg from the home of General Manager Charlie Scrymgeour. In May 1979, Charlie Scrymgeour moved from Winnipeg to Ottawa, and the office of the CCA was established next door to the Curl Canada office in Vanier City. I continued as the now-technical director of Curl Canada, under contract, but was still operating from my home office in Vancouver.

John MacLeod was hired as the Executive Director of Curl Canada by the CCA/CLCA in June of 1976.

Shortly after making the move to Ottawa, Charlie Scrymgeour decided to retire in late September 1979, and in December 1979, John MacLeod assumed the position of general manager of the CCA, as well as executive director of Curl Canada. In early 1980, Sport Canada decided if it was going to fund the position of technical director, it wanted that person to resident in the Sports and Recreation Centre in Ottawa. I resigned as technical director, and in the fall of 1980, Garry

Garry DeBlonde directs on-ice instruction at a Curl Canad clinic in Lahr, Germany.

DeBlonde moved to Ottawa and became the resident technical director of Curl Canada. In the spring of 1981, I assumed a new position with the CCA/CLCA that had the title of director of Corporate and Media Relations for both organizations, but I was still working under contract, which allowed me to pursue other opportunities, most of them within curling.

CHAPTER 9

Pre-Game Warm-up Becomes Part of Curling

LEADING INTO THE 1974–75 curling season, warm-up on the ice for any curling game at any level was not allowed. Prior to the first stone of the end being delivered, the players could not set foot on the ice. The only thing really possible was a single slide from the hack for each player just before the game commenced. This whole idea was contrary to every other sport and was another reason curling was looked upon by many as a pastime and not a sport. I knew if the sport were ever to have any credibility or even get a sniff of the Olympic flame, pre-game warm-up would have to be part of the routine for every high-performance curling game.

Dr. Art Quinney, PHD in exercise physiology at the University of Alberta designed a warm-up program for curling in 1975.

So, I knew I had to find someone with expertise in the field to provide the entire proposal some teeth. The person I sought to do just that was Dr. Art Quinney, a PhD in exercise physiology at the University of Alberta and, by coincidence, a curler. I approached Art with the challenge, and by February, he put together a detailed paper that spelled out clearly why curling needed to take a new direction that would allow time for a warm-up period.

I presented Art's paper at the CCA's AGM in Fredericton at the Brier, and it created a lot of discussion. Many of the old guard felt it just wasn't right because for anyone to set foot on the sheet of ice before the game was seen as an unfair advantage. In the end, I won a narrow victory, and the membership agreed that starting at all CCA events in 1976, a five-minute period would be allowed for each team to slide and stretch on the sheet of ice they were about to play, but rocks could not be thrown.

From there, it was on to the ICF meetings at the Air Canada Silver Broom in Perth, Scotland. Bob Picken was one of the Canadian delegates to the ICF AGM, and he agreed to do a presentation to the membership on the need for warm-up. It was apparently met with a mixed reaction, with nations such as Switzerland and Sweden being on side with the idea, while Scotland and many of the nations tied closely to Scotland were opposed. The result was the ICF AGM invited me to their General Assembly to make a presentation and to answer some questions.

I completed the presentation and asked for questions. From the back of the room, a hand was raised, and a distinguished Scottish gentleman by the name of Robin Welsh stood up. I knew who Welsh was and his reputation as an old guard hard nose. He was the secretary of the Scottish Association (Royal Caledonia Curling Club; RCCC) and the secretary of the ICF. Welsh did not mince his words, and what came forth was to the point. "I think it is all a pile of rubbish… Curling is a manly game." It wasn't quite the assurance I was looking for, but I took it in stride. Meanwhile, in the end, Sven Eklund (father of Swedish actress Britt Eklund) of the Swedish Federation stood up and provided some very supportive comments, as did the representative from Switzerland. In the end, it was agreed that the ICF would adopt the CCA position and allow curlers to slide for five minutes on the sheet of ice they were playing before the start of each game.

Following are the minutes provided by Robin Welsh on the issue of warm-up.

> *W. Hansen was invited to speak. He stated that research in Canada indicated that warming-up was important for physical reasons—not only for toning up the muscles but also for the heart, respiratory, and other areas. He recommended that warming-up should be permitted before games. The secretary stated (Robin Welsh) that curlers should be well prepared physically for World Championship play and that all this technical medical talk was a lot of hot air and should be totally disregarded by the Federation. Bob Picken disagreed and said that a form of calisthenics before any game was natural and beneficial. Views against throwing stones before the games were expressed and it was AGREED that, at the 1976 World Championship, a 5-minute warming-up session would be permitted prior to games but no stones would be thrown.*

Interesting enough, later that evening, Welsh came looking for me at the old Queen's Hotel and found me at the bar. We had a long chat, and following that evening, actually became friends.

As for warm-up, that was the start. The process evolved every year, and by 1979, players could throw stones in the pre-game warm-up but not on the sheet they were playing. The final step came at the 1980 Brier in Calgary when, for the first time, each team was allowed a ten-minute warm-up on the sheet of ice it was about to play and delivering of stones was actually allowed. Within the year, the same approach was adopted by the ICF.

CHAPTER 10
The Association of Competitive Curlers

WHEN RAY KINGSMITH and I had our historic discussion in Paris in March 1974, one of the things that was agreed was the need for an increased involvement of Canada's top curlers in the sport's administration. That task was thrown to me, and it wasn't long after I returned from Europe in March that I made contact with a number of the top players in Edmonton and across western Canada to discuss the idea of starting a group that I referred to as the Association of Competitive Curlers (ACC). We were clear from the start that it was not an attempt by the players to take over the CCA but to be more involved in a positive manner to influence matters that primarily impacted curling's top players.

By the fall of 1974, we were able to get ACC groups organized in Vancouver, Edmonton, and Winnipeg, with at least 300 members from the three areas. In addition, Regina, Saskatoon, Calgary, Ottawa, and Toronto were in the embryonic stage and getting things off the ground.

The next two years saw the program get up and flying, but there were many challenges. The media weren't exactly on our side and veteran reporters such as Jack Matheson of the *Winnipeg Tribune* and Doug Maxwell, who was at that time part of the CBC on-air team for curling and the executive director of the Air Canada Silver Broom, were anything but supportive. Larry Wood of the *Calgary Herald* wrote an article that was quite supportive of the whole ACC idea, and below is a transcript of the comments Maxwell sent to Wood in response to his column.

Mr. Larry Wood,
Sports Department,
Calgary Herald,
206 – 7th Ave. S.W.,
Calgary, Alberta

Dear Larry:

Thanks for sending down your May 29th column on the Association of Competitive Curlers, together with Ray Turchansky's story in the Edmonton Journal.

As I mentioned to you on the phone, Mattie also picked up your story and ran it in the column in the Tribune, and I am extending the same answers to him as I am to you.

I don't want to quarrel with some of Warren's philosophical ideas although I do not think they will stand close scrutiny. Basically he is applying an ethic of professional competitors in a professional sport to a game that still involves non-professionals in a non-professional sport.

Rather, I would like to point out a few of his errors of fact, give you the details and leave it to you to do with them what you will.

Let me quote from your story using Hansen's words and then I'll give a comment.

> *"The sponsors of the championship events are getting fantastic attention, their money's worth. The people staging Briers and Brooms have been filling their pockets. You place either of these events in the right city and it's like printing money."*
>
> *Comment: It's true that sponsors of championship events (Macdonald Tobacco and Air Canada) are getting fantastic attention, their money's worth. That is, they are now but that was not*

always the case. There are quite a bit of investment spending by both sponsors, before this present state of affairs came into being but surely that is one of the reasons that a sponsor does not get involved in the sport—to provide assistance to that sport and in so doing gain the goodwill of the people who are concerned about it. Surely they are entitled to this. I can't speak for the Brier and Macdonald Tobacco, although (like you) I have long been appreciative of their efforts. I think I can speak on behalf of Air Canada and the Silver Broom. While Air Canada is now obtaining significant attention to the event, you know as well I do that it wasn't always so and until quite recently, there were executives in the airline who believed that the attention obtained was not worth the money spent.

It's not true that Air Canada and Macdonald Tobacco have been filling their pockets from the staging of the Brier or the Silver Broom. It is true that organizing committees in some Brier and Silver Broom cities have made a profit, sometimes substantial, sometimes not, and on some occasions they have lost money. But surely it is obvious the only way they can make a profit is to utilize the volunteer support of large committees of committed curlers in each host city.

Take Regina as example. It's true that the profit that the Regina committee realized on the Silver Broom was approximately $41,000.

But remember that Laurie Artiss and his committee (of close to 200) worked like demons for almost an entire year in order to achieve such success. Air Canada did not gain one cent of that profit, nor did they wish to. They are in the business of transporting people, not making a profit from sporting events. If you divide that profit by the number of people involved it works out to about $200 per person, and that's very little money for an entire year's work. And don't forget that the entire profit has been ploughed back into curling in the Regina area.

As far as choosing the "right" championship location, while we try and select the best city for the event, the profit potential is of little importance in such a choice. In fact, there a number of cities where the profit is not necessarily taken for granted. If Megeve had not obtained government support, if Garmisch-Partenkirchen had not obtained a form of subsidy, if Berne had not assessed every curler in Switzerland financial support, then it is doubtful if any of these would have realized a profit on their operations. Yet they thought it was important to host the Silver Broom to help in the promotion of the world curling. We agreed with their assessment and we were happy to put the event into those places. Profit (or loss) was not a factor.

"Hansen says the curlers who put on the show, meanwhile, get as little as $75 for a week expense allowance."

Comment: Warren is right as far as he goes, but that's not really far enough. Just to set the record straight, here's what we provide to each national champion who comes to the Silver Broom. First of all, he receives first-class airfare from his home city to the site of the Silver Broom. In addition, a car and a driver is put at his disposal throughout the competition. Thus, he has no transportation costs from the time he departs till the time he returns home (compare that to professional golfers who must pay their own transportation to the competition and return).

We pay for his hotel room, completely, which is usually double accommodation. In the case of Berne, that hotel also provided breakfast each morning. What's left for him to pay? There are the various meals remaining, namely lunches, dinners, snacks, laundry, telephone calls and a few other incidentals. Early in the preparation of each Silver Broom we investigate the cost of meals, laundry, etc. and work out an allowance that will cover them for the full period. Don't forget too, that will cover them for the full period. Don't forget too, that on International Day, at the Get Acquainted Reception and the Swiss Party, there is no meal cost

> *to the curlers. In effect, we pay for all meals and eight lunches. We realized as well that many of the teams are provided with free meals by their hosts, but since this cannot always be taken for granted, we provide money to cover all meals.*
>
> *Thus we feel the allowance provided should be sufficient to cover their basic needs, although there is no argument that it will cover all of their needs. It will not cover entertainment, nor will it cover some of the costs involved if they wish to have a party with some of the other curlers. Some of the European Associations provide their national champions with an entertainment allowance to cover the cost of treating their opponents. We do not feel it is necessary for us to do so.*

In my opinion, both Air Canada and Macdonald Tobacco have been more than aware of the demands placed upon curlers at such championship events, and have shown themselves quite willing to work to the advantage of the curlers. In point of fact, nobody has ever complained before this (to us anyway) about the per diem allowance being too low. Incidentally, we're now working on the budget preparation for Perth, and I'm sure that Air Canada will be quite fair in their approval of a daily allowance sufficient to meet normal expenses.

I don't think I need to get too deeply into some of the other beefs that Warren seems to have, since most of them fall into the category of concern about various curling associations, provincial or national. My own opinion is he is somewhat naïve in his concerns. He says that curlers should be running the associations, that curlers should have a greater voice in the administration of the game, playoff systems, co-ordination of prizes, dates, etc. My own experience is that associations have done an excellent job involving competitive curlers in their deliberations. I agree that it was not always so, but in recent years, I think there have been very significant changes. In your own area, Ray Kingsmith surely must qualify as a concerned and experienced curling executive, sympathetic to the requirement of present day competition.

In Manitoba, such outstanding curlers as Bruce Hudson, Bob Picken and Don Duguid have been deeply involved with the MCA. If Warren thinks that only present day competitive curlers are fit to administer the affairs of an association, then obviously he has never watched Bill Lumdsen of the MCA at work?

In Ontario, we have such outstanding competitive curlers as Alf Phillips Sr., Earle Hushagen and Mac Bell working in key positions within the OCA.

As far as co-ordinating prizes and dates of bonspiels, that's a very easy statement to make and almost impossible to achieve. We have been trying to do this in a modest way in the Toronto area through the curling calander of the Toronto Curling Association, where we only have to worry about twenty-four clubs in the Metro area. We have found that it is almost impossible to get many clubs to work together to co-ordinate their major bonspiel dates. As soon as you move into a provincial or national situation, it becomes that much more difficult, and in my opinion, impossible to achieve.

However, my purpose is not to argue in these latter categories with Warren as he is entitled to his opinion even though it may differ from mine. I do want to set the record straight, however, regarding the finances that Warren mentions.

If you want to get any further details, or if I have neglected any area that you would like to explore, please don't hesitate to give me a call or call Peter Jerome or Don MacLeod at Air Canada in Montreal.

Doug Maxwell – His comments were typical of the old guard of the day who wanted nothing changed and desired to have everything left the way it was. *Photo credit – Michael Burns Photography.*

Yours very truly,

Douglas D. Maxwell
Executive Director
Air Canada Silver Broom

I might also add that Maxwell copied four senior executives of Air Canada with the aforementioned letter, including two who dealt with the Silver Broom Curling School contract. His comments were typical of the old guard of the day who wanted nothing changed and wanted everything left the way it was. Maxwell had power and control in his position with Air Canada and CBC, and the last thing he wanted was for the curlers to gain any influence over anything. He failed to understand that companies such as Macdonald

Tobacco and Air Canada were gaining huge benefits from their involvement with the Brier and the world men's championship, yet the curlers who were putting on the show were receiving the bare minimum to participate, without a chance of earning a cent. To play in the events, most had to take time away from work and families, which required time off without pay or use of vacation time. There was no desire by anyone to advance the sport down the road in any way.

I did not let Maxwell's attack go without a response, and below is a copy of the letter I sent to him and copied all the Air Canada people involved. Yes, I gave Larry Wood a copy as well.

Doug Maxwell
Toronto, Ontario

Dear Doug:

I appreciate your concern and comments regarding the newspaper articles mentioned, but I wish my exact opinion had been considered before the above mentioned letter was sent. Unfortunately, the sensationalism used in both articles does not exactly define the views, or express the exact purpose of the proposed Association of Canadian Curlers.

My name has been directly associated with one article mentioned, but my position with the operations is 'coordinator'. The points I am going to mention for the most part are those of a united front which involves people from coast to coast that are involved in curling at a competitive level.

I agree to a certain extent with your first comment regarding professionalism in a game that isn't professional, or completely professional yet. There are many large events presently being staged, with bigger and better ones with larger sponsors lurking around the corner. A degree of professionalism already exists, and the potential of it happening to a large degree is certainly present.

Your second point regarding the sponsors of championships is not a direct quote. The point is not directed at the sponsor at all, nor do I really think anyone intended it to be. No one is filling their pockets from national or international championships, although the potential is most definitely there. This would be of considerable benefit to sponsors if it were completely utilized. Also, for the most part, the Silver Broom would not as yet enter into any discussions of this nature since international curling is relatively new and has a long way to go.

However, the Brier is quite a different story. I do not wish to mention names since other people might receive unwarranted criticism as well; but recently a high ranking CCA official agreed completely with the following: Holding the Brier in a place like Fredericton doesn't any longer make any sense. The game has grown to the extent that national championships should only be held in areas where every possible financial benefit can be utilized. The Grey Cup is not held in a 6,000 seat stadium, with a gate admission of $1.50 and without the sale of TV rights being considered. Everyone involved in curling at a competitive level is aware of the sponsor having nothing to do with gate receipts for national or international competition. Local host committees do a fantastic amount of work, however, they also, as mentioned, gain whatever profit that might be derived. Is this really the best, most feasible way of doing things for sponsors, curlers, and everyone involved?

The matter involving expense allowances, etc. for someone like myself is not a factor at all. I'm completely involved with the curling business, and most definitely would be at all the mentioned events at company expense. Unfortunately, curling's national and international championships, as things exist is getting to the point where it is only available to those with time and money. We say it is not professional, yet it does have a professional image. Just ask average John Doe public. Consider curlers that are married with families, regular jobs and in many cases tight budgets. How do these people make up lost wages and time from their regular jobs and in many cases very tight budgets. In many cases differences are made up by donations from local curlers and firms. Is this right?

If you make a comparison with golf, practically every pro golfer has some sort of sponsorship. Sponsors in curling for individual teams is becoming more and more feasible. As a matter of intertest, last season the team I played on had a sponsor for the entire season until local Brier playdown time. We then had to sign a document indicating that if we were successful at the local level we would, from that point forward, wear only the sweaters and crests of the province/country we were representing. It's rather interesting to note that the sweaters chosen clashed with our slacks, but once again the curlers, who are not allowed a sponsor of their own, had to make up the difference. Also, pro-golfers are playing for large purses as well, which is quite a different situation.

It most definitely would not be the concern of the Association of Competitive Curlers to attempt to govern in any way the various curling associations. But a number of the decisions made by the associations only impacts one group of people, the competitive curler. It is the competitive curler's feeling that he should have an opportunity to express his opinion in matters that affect him. Most definitely there are a number of people involved in associations who might be competitively minded but no one has any way of knowing if their opinions are universal. The various curling associations are very essential for the administration of the entire game of curling. Associations are slowly changing and the people involved are becoming more progressive by the day. I for one am extremely delighted with the proposed "Curl Canada" program and feel honoured that I am involved and have been able to pass on some of my ideas for the promotion of the games. It is the feeling of the proposed group that the top curlers, as a body, could be very beneficial in promoting curling and would most definitely strive to work in co-operation with the various bodies.

There are many areas yet unexplored to a degree which are of great interest to competitive curlers but of little concern to curling associations. The main areas I refer to are: sponsorship of large events, negotiating TV rights, etc. Our current investigation into the areas mentioned indicates these commodities are definitely available. The intent of the proposed Association of Competitive Curlers is not to create problems or splits between the top players and the CCA.

For the most part, items picked up by the various media people were premature and emphasis was placed on points that possibly were relatively minor.

It is our feeling that such a body coming into existence would require many years of hard work to reach its potential. However, everything must start somewhere and with initiative the group should be a great asset to the progress and advancement of the game of curling.

Sincerely yours,

Warren Hansen
cc: P. Jerome
D. McLeod
H. Cameron
J.P. Turkel

I had made it clear from day one that the ACC did not wish to create a separate organization for the purpose of bucking the provincial associations or the CCA but to work with them to make things better for the sport's elite. The ACC's objectives were to assist in maintaining and improving the game of curling and promoting, fostering, encouraging, and hopefully operating better events for the competitive athletes of the day.

Warren Hansen originally planned to be at the helm of the players group but he had to step back because of the work he was doing for the CCA was deemed to be in conflict. Terry Braunstein of Winnipeg stepped into the president's chair. *Photo credit – Michael Burns Photography.*

Despite the problems and controversy, the organization was fully up and running by 1976, with most of the cities in western Canada harbouring a local chapter of the ACC. While I was originally planning on being the man at the helm, I had to step back because the work I was doing for the CCA was deemed to be in conflict, so Terry Braunstein of Winnipeg stepped up into the president's chair. The main thing accomplished in the first year was the establishment of a Super League in each of the cities involved that was exclusive for the curlers who were members of the ACC.

The Super Leagues all played with two very new and interesting rules as part of the constitution. The first rule that everyone agreed on was a big one: if a team blanked an end, it would lose the hammer. The second change was if you had a rock touching the button, it counted two points rather than one. If I look at some of the problems facing top curling today, I think adding both of these rules might be more appropriate rather than adding the probably soon to be considered six-rock rule. In addition to the Super League and the rule changes mentioned, discussions were taking place to possibly hold a western Canada championship in 1977 that would incorporate the new rules and involve the winners of each Super League.

A number of contacts were made in an attempt to find a sponsor, and in the summer of 1976, Carling O'Keefe Breweries agreed to be the sponsor of the newly formed western Canada Super League Championship, with the first event to take place in the spring of 1977. The event was very different in that it had three teams a piece from BC, Alberta, Saskatchewan, and Manitoba playing as a unit of three, and it also used the rules of no blank ends, and a shot touching the button was worth two points. In total, twelve teams participated in the event known as the Super Showdown in Saskatoon, February 24–28, 1977. Actually, the official name was the Carling O'Keefe Shield. The playoff system used had a mini round robin, with each of the four-team units playing a minimum of eighteen games. Then the top two provinces advanced to a final showdown—that is, three teams from BC, for instance, versus three from Manitoba, with the winner being the province who wins two of the three games. While there were few fans in attendance at the old Saskatoon Arena, everything else, including the curling, was first class. The preliminary aspect of the event went right down to the final draw before settling the two provincial squads for the Shield's final series.

Manitoba sent teams skipped by Rod Hunter, Barry Fry, and John Usackis, Saskatchewan's entries were led by Rick Folk, Larry McGrath, and Les Rogers, British Columbia skips were Glenn Pierce, Ken Neuman, and Brent Giles. Alberta was represented by Gil Svensen, Doug Johnston, and Tom Kroeger, and when the dust settled, those three teams carted the Shield back to Edmonton at the end of the event.

The Shield was held for a second time at Regina in April 1978, but following that event, Carling O'Keefe gave notice it would not continue as the title sponsor. After the 1979 season, Terry Braunstein stepped down as the president and the activities of the group more or less ground to a halt. Attempted meetings between the ACC and the CCA never really happened, and what could have been the start of a strong players group working hand in hand with the CCA never really got off the ground.

In its short life, the ACC was pretty organized. It actually developed a set of objects and bylaws while becoming a legal entity. The official objectives of the ACC were as follows:

1. To promote, foster, encourage, sponsor, develop, operate, and maintain the game of curling.

2. To promote, arrange, undertake, and assist in the operation and administration of competitive curling events, and in that regard, to solicit prizes, awards, and distinctions.

3. To fully cooperate and establish liaison with other organizations, whether incorporated or not, which have objects similar, in whole or in part, to the objects of the Society.

4. To provide instruction and programs, for the purpose of teaching and training persons in the game of curling, upgrading the calibre of same.

5. To acquire and hold, buy, lease, purchase, or otherwise dispose of all lands, buildings and appliances necessary for the equipment and maintenance of the game of curling.

The idea was attempted again in the nineties, and this time, the women's side of the equation joined with the men to attempt for the second time the formation of a players group. Under the leadership of Jim Armstrong and Anne Merklinger, progress was made, but leadership of the players group changed in 2000 and in 2001, as a result of growing frustrations amongst the curlers, a number of the sport's elite male curlers, led by Kevin Martin, started a boycott of the Brier in favour of the newly formed Grand Slam of Curling.

It is an entire story in its own right that I will not elaborate on at this point except to make a simple statement. Today, it is 2021, and a players group or association is badly needed in the sport of curling but still does not exist.

CHAPTER 11
The National Team Program Gets Underway

CERTAINLY, ONE OF my disappointments of playing in the 1974 Silver Broom was the lack of direction or involvement of the CCA when it came to preparing our team for the event and support during the event. We didn't even have a Canadian uniform. We simply wore the Alberta uniform used in the Brier with the Alberta rose logo on the back removed and replaced by a green CCA logo that said "Canada" across the bottom. One of the objectives I had in life going into 1976 was to begin to make all of this change.

It had to start somewhere, so going into the fall of 1976, I had two objectives regarding national teams. Foremost was to develop a Team Canada uniform that would be provided by the CCA, and the second was to provide some support and guidance for the junior teams playing in the relatively new world juniors. Remember, at this time, there were two world events: the men and the junior men. In 1976, the summer Olympics were held in Montreal, and for those who can remember, the Canadian team wore a uniform that had three vertical stripes of varying width running down its right side. I liked the look, and I thought because of the Olympics, the Canadian public would quickly identify the mark as that of a national team, and it would also plant a seed in many people's minds of curling and the Olympics.

So, for the first time, the Bill Jenkins team playing in the 1977 world junior and the Jim Ursel team playing in the world men's in Karlstad, Sweden, wore a Canadian uniform that was a white sweater (remember the curling sweater was still the stable dress in the sport at this time) with the three red stripes running down the right side of the garment. The other change that took place was the back crest. The old green maple leaf created from the old CCA logo that had been tooled into a back crest was replaced by a new, stylized red crest that was produced in the shape of the newly developed CCA logo. The sweater continued to be the garment of choice for most top curlers until 1991, so from 1977 to 1991, every Canadian team participating in a world championship wore the white sweaters with the three red stripes. The fashion world finally caught up to curling in 1991, when we changed the traditional sweater for a nylon jacket, and this was also the end of the white garment with the three red stripes look due to the difficulties in doing the stripes with the nylon garment.

The Canadian team at the 1977 world junior curling championships was the first Canadian team ever to have the support of a CCA appointed team leader. Canadian skip, Bill Jenkins hoists the trophy after winning the championship.

We took the three-stripe look into all the national development programs in the seventies. All the certified national instructors wore a navy-blue garment with the three stripes in white down the right-hand side, and when national officiating came into existence in 1981, for ten years, all the officials wore a white sweater with three navy-blue stripes down the right-hand side of the garment.

The year 1977 was the start of attempting to help the junior men's champions at the world level of play. The team representing Canada was skipped by Bill Jenkins from Prince Edward Island. Prior to 1977, the team was simply sent with its coach, who could be whomever they chose, and a representative of some sort from the CCA, who again could be anyone and in all likelihood had never attended a world event before in his life. The coach for the Jenkins team was well-known PEI curler Doug Cameron. Doug had played in about six Briers during the sixties, and I had actually played against him in the 1973 Canadian Mixed Championship, so we knew each other. The CCA rep assigned to accompany the junior men's team to the Uniroyal Worlds in 1977 was Bob Picken from Winnipeg. Picken himself had been a fair country curler and was a sportscaster for CBC Winnipeg. I approached Bob with the idea of providing some assistance for the Jenkins boys, and he thought it was a good idea.

The 1977 world juniors were in Quebec City, and this was in the days when the Canadian junior champion went to the world juniors a year after being named the Canadian champion. Not a good arrangement for many reasons, but that is the way it was, which was a situation created by timing because the world juniors were held in late February and the Canadian juniors were played near the end of March. Because of the arrangement, we had a good amount of time, so it was decided to take the team and the coach into Quebec City for a weekend to get them familiar with the area, facilities, use them to promote the event a bit and spend a few hours on briefing them on what to expect. Then when the event was happening, Picken and I were both with the team and gave them as much advice and support as possible throughout the event. The team won the world juniors. The experiment seemed to have worked, so it was decided to continue the same approach in 1978.

The 1977 Canadian juniors were won by Calgarian Paul Gowsell, who had also taken the title in 1975 and the world juniors in 1976. Gowsell had Kelly Stearne back at lead and two new players in John Ferguson and Doug MacFarlane, playing in the middle. Gowsell was a rebel and had created a fair amount of stir in the establishment of Canadian curling. In typical Gowsell fashion, he played the Canadian junior without a real coach; he had taken his second player from 1975,

Glenn Jackson, along as his coach, but everyone knew he was a coach in name only. The CCA executive of the day knew this was a potential problem with the team going into Switzerland for the world juniors without at least a person in the coaching position who the CCA knew would be cooperative. The CCA executive decided there was a need to send a coach with the team who could ensure everything happened within the boundaries of acceptability to the international curling community.

The Canadian team that won the world junior in 1978 at Grindelwald, Switzerland from the left, Paul Gowsell, John Ferguson, Doug MacFarland and Kelly Stearne. Gowsell and Stearne also won the event in 1976 with Neil Houston at third and Glen Jackson at second.

After deliberation, the executive decided I would fill the coach's role with the team for its trip to Switzerland. I was not totally comfortable with the situation but also understood how important it was for the CCA to start having coaches in place that looked like coaches if we were to make curling look like other sports that had a strong international and Olympic presence. Amongst other concerns was the fact that the world juniors was in Grindelwald, Switzerland, and it was starting before the Brier ended. This would mean I would have to leave Canada in the middle of the Brier, which would impact many things, including the six or so radio updates I would do each day for CKWX in Vancouver. This was made even more difficult because the Brier was, in fact, in Vancouver. Anyway, it was a chance to advance the coaching program, so I agreed to do it.

Bob Picken and I chatted about a development camp for the team similar to what we had done in 1977. We knew we did not have the budget to spend a weekend in Grindelwald, but we also wanted to get the team out of Calgary for a couple of days, so the camp was set for Edmonton in November. Gowsell and I knew each other but not well, so we decided before the camp got started the first item on the agenda would be a one-on-one meeting between Gowsell and me. We stayed at the Chateau Lacombe Hotel in Edmonton, and I remember Paul coming to my room, a small suite. I think the meeting started by Paul suggesting that it was rather a nice room, and I cut right to the chase from there.

Paul had a history of partaking in the consumption of cannabis long before anyone thought of it being legal. We were very aware of the situation, and it was one of the things I was told to take care of. I explained to Paul that I was there to be a technical resource for him if there was anything he wanted, but my main purpose was to ensure that all their needs were taken care of. If there were any issues with anything, he was to bring them to my attention. And then I said, "One more thing. We are going to Switzerland, and you are representing Canada. If there is any nation in the Western world with no sense of humour when it comes to drug use, it is Switzerland. So do not even slightly think of taking anything into Switzerland with you that in any way might be associated with pot."

I remember getting this sort of shrug from Paul and the Gowsell response, "Well, jeez, you didn't think I would do anything like that?"

I just smiled and said in response, "Of course not." Wink... wink... nudge... nudge...

The week in Grindelwald went fairly well, except for a couple of small issues. One I remember well, and it was about the second day we were there. There is a local brew in Grindelwald called Rugenbrau, known by the locals as "Ruggie," coming from a local brewery down the road in Interlaken. Grindelwald is a small alpine town. In the middle of ski season, it is a ski resort, so anyone walking down the main street who is not skiing is pretty obvious. I was walking down the main drag, and all of a sudden, I saw this very recognizable bearded person coming toward me, which had to be Gowsell. Firmly placed on his shoulder was a twenty-four pack of Rugenbrau. We passed, and I said nothing except to smile, but we had a little discussion later when I suggested that I was not denying him the opportunity to have a cool Ruggie on occasion but could he make it a little less obvious. He smiled and said sure.

While it wasn't a cakewalk for Gowsell, he won the championship and, by so doing, became the first team in the short history of world junior curling to win the title twice. But while the championship was over, the excitement wasn't. John Hudson, who was the head of CBC Television Sports, was on site and decided with Gowsell's record and previous curling success, he would invite Gowsell to the annual CBC Curling Classic, which was taped annually during early April in Winnipeg. He approached Gowsell on site with the offer, and Paul's reaction was, "Great, but I want my real team."

To Paul, his real team was the 1976 world junior champions with Neil Houston at third, Glenn Jackson at second and Kelly Stearne at lead. Hudson shrugged and said, "Okay."

Gowsell replied with one other request. Paul had planned on staying in Europe until the end of April, so he asked if CBC would fly him over to Winnipeg to play in the Classic and then back to Europe. Hudson thought for a moment and said, "Okay."

But Gowsell came back and said, "Just one more thing. My girlfriend is here with me, so could you fly her over and back as well?"

Hudson said no, so Paul gave up his one and only opportunity to play in the CBC Curling Classic. But it wasn't over yet. The closing banquet was being held around seven p.m. that evening at the headquarters hotel. Somehow, MacFarlane and Ferguson got wind of what Gowsell had done, and they were furious. The closing dinner was more than entertaining and not because of what was said or done at the dinner. I sat with Ferguson and MacFarlane on one side of me and Gowsell and Stearne on the other, with the Ferguson/MacFarlane side of the table wanting to kill the Gowsell/Stearne side.

Following that week, Paul and I became friends and remain so until this day. We had a couple of encounters along the way that will be referred to later in this book.

Things did not get any easier in 1979. Another Alberta team won the Canadian junior in Charlottetown, but this time from Edmonton with Darren Fish as the skip. I knew who Darren was, and I knew the father of the Barker brothers (Lorne and Barry), who were playing lead and third on his team. Jim Barker had been the ice maker at the

Greisbach Curling Club, which was the army base just outside the north city limits of Edmonton. Murray Ursuliak was the second player, and while I did not know him personally, I could remember him as a little boy at the Ottewell Curling Club in Edmonton riding a rock down the ice like a cowboy on a bronco. There was an added dynamic on this team because the coach was Ray Osborne, who was in his own right a pretty good curler but, along with his brother Bud, was a professional wrestler.

Paul Gowsell became a curling phenomena in the late '70's. He won the world juniors in 1976 and again in '78 while being the number one overall winner on the men's bonspiel circuit during the same period.

In all fairness, I remember Ray as a gentle soul, but he liked to party, and after a few cocktails, he could become a little crazy. I'm not sure of all the details from Charlottetown, except there were a couple of incidents and Osborne was part of them. The result was the CCA decided it would not be a good idea to send Osborne to the world junior in Moose Jaw, Saskatchewan. Thus, for the second year in a row, I was selected to not just be an adviser to the coach but to be the actual coach of the team. For the third consecutive year, it was decided to take the team for a weekend training camp in the fall of the year prior, which would serve, amongst other things, as a briefing session for the team from the CCA. Since the world juniors in March was being held in Moose Jaw, CCA International Chair Bob Picken decided Moose Jaw would be the site of the camp.

On the November weekend chosen, we travelled to Moose Jaw and were hosted for the weekend of the camp by the host committee for the world juniors. Things went pretty well, with the camp concluding on Saturday evening, and plans were in place for us all to travel home on Sunday. However, Bob Picken and I awoke Sunday morning to find that Darren Fish was missing in action, and no one else on the team was saying much about anything. While I do not remember the details, Fish was located later in the morning, and we found there was a fair story unfolding. Apparently, sometime in the night, a disagreement erupted between Fish and the lead Barry Barker. The result of the disagreement was Fish leaving the area where the argument took place, heading back to his room and locking the door. Barker was not pleased with the situation and apparently went to Fish's room and pounded down the door. Fish somehow escaped into the night and hence was missing in action the following morning. The CCA board became involved, and as a result, Barry Barker was suspended from playing in the world junior and was replaced by Murray Ursuliak's brother.

So, in February 1979, I headed to Moose Jaw with Team Fish and a new lead to play in the world juniors. Things went reasonably well, but it was not a smooth ride. One incident that was pretty humorous deserves some attention. Paul Gowsell showed up at the event in the middle of the week, and all of a sudden, on Wednesday evening, Fish disappeared when we left the arena. I asked the other team members where he was, and someone offered that Darren had gone back to the billet, where the team was staying, with Paul Gowsell. My antennae went up immediately, and I asked the team driver to take us back to the billet as quick as he could.

When we arrived, sure enough, there was Gowsell's van, with I assumed Fish inside. My fear was that Paul would be offering Darren some of his best cannabis, which would not be cool. I approached the van, and Paul rolled down the window. I suggested to Paul that maybe he could step out so the two of his could have a chat. I remember offering some pleasantries before saying, "Paul... leave this guy alone. He can get into enough trouble without your help." I do not remember his exact response, except I think it was along the line of how he was just trying to help. I think my comeback was, "If you really want to help, go back to Calgary." Team Canada did not emerge the winner, but the whole thing was respectable, and after three years, the team leader program for the junior men was up and flying.

In the spring of 1979, some major discussions took place at the board level of the CCA. It had become almost a nightmare, but Canada had lost the men's world championship for seven years in a row. The last Canadian team to stand on the champions podium was Orest Meleschuk, way back in 1972, and because American Bob LaBonte thought Meleschuk stole the 1972 Silver Broom from him, he had put a curse on Canada to not win the world curling championship for seven years. His curse had unbelievably come true. Whether anyone believed in the curse, it was, in fact, a reality. While we had started to deal more with the arrangements for the Canadian team prior to heading for the worlds, there still was not a representative of the CCA with the team at the world site to be constantly available to assist the team in any way possible. Some suggested a team manager, while others thought a person who could act in the capacity of a manager or coach, if required. By the fall of 1979, agreement had been reached that starting with the 1980 world men's championship in Moncton, a team leader appointed by the CCA would accompany the Canadian men's champions to the world championship. I was appointed to the task, and Garry DeBlonde, who had become the newly appointed technical director of Curl Canada, would move into the team leader role with the junior men.

While I certainly won't take the credit for the change, in 1980, the Canadian team skipped by Rick Folk turned the tide, and for the first time since 1972, Canada became the world men's champions. I served in the team leader role with the Canadian men's teams until 1989, a total of ten years, and Canada during that period did not win every year but turned the tide to claim seven world titles. The program was up and running and continues today for every Canadian team travelling to a world championship.

CHAPTER 12

The Macdonald Tobacco Bomb!

WALTER STEWART OF Montreal and George Cameron of Winnipeg were behind the start of the Brier in 1927. Stewart was the owner of Macdonald Tobacco, and Cameron, the president of W.L. Mackenzie and company, a subsidiary of Macdonald Tobacco, based in Winnipeg. With urging from Cameron in 1924, Stewart launched the start of the Brier in 1927. He felt the company needed to give something back to Canada for the huge support Macdonald Tobacco had received from Canadians over the years. With the help of Cameron, the two concluded that the one thing Canadians had in common from coast to coast was the sport of curling, and a fitting tribute to the sport would be to initiate an annual event where a men's team from every province was brought together to play in a national championship. In those days, curling was very much a male-driven sport, and while women played, their participation was very limited.

At the time, Canadian curling was divided between the use of iron stones and granites, with the latter being used in Quebec and Eastern Ontario and the former used in the balance of the nation. The granite camp held the advantage as Howard Stewart, brother of company president, Walter, supported the use of granites. He was thus able to influence the use of granite stones for the first Brier held at the Toronto Granite Curling Club in March 1927. Eight teams from across the country participated, representing western Canada, Quebec, New Brunswick, Nova Scotia, Northern Ontario, and Montreal. Games lasted fourteen ends, and each team played each other in a seven-game round robin with no playoff unless there was a tie for first.

The tobacco giant grew the Brier over the years and developed some interesting traditions for the event that still exist today. Many people think the term Brier is some unique ancient Scottish reference, but it isn't. Brier was the name of a pipe tobacco that Macdonald marketed back in the twenties. The symbol of being a provincial champion and a person who had played in the Brier was the purple heart, which still exists today with the same significance. I'm not sure why the purple heart was the symbol chosen, except history tells us that Brier tobacco had a small plug in each bag that was shaped like a silver heart and inside the silver heart plug was a small plastic purple heart. The Brier Tankard trophy that is still presented today is a sterling silver cup on a wooden base, where the name of each winning team is engraved on a silver heart.

The Brier was operated by Macdonald Tobacco for fifty years, ending in 1979. (Two years were missed because of World War II.) The Dominion Curling Association (later the CCA and now Curling Canada) did not come into existence until 1935 and never really had any role in the operation of Brier during the Macdonald years, except to standardize the rules of play.

In 1928, the Brier game was reduced to twelve ends from fourteen, and there were very few changes over the years until 1949, when Newfoundland received a direct entry to make the total number of teams eleven. A further change happened in 1975, when a twelfth team became a reality with the addition of a joint entry for Yukon and the Northwest Territories, known as the Territories. Until 1974, every stone had to be thrown in every Brier game played, but a change took place that year that allowed a team to concede before completing a full twelve ends. A further change was made in 1977, when the length of the game was reduced from twelve to ten ends.

Things changed for Macdonald Tobacco in the early seventies. By this time, Walter Stewart had been replaced by his son David, who was a bit of an eccentric who cherished the sanctity of the Brier over the years. David was also a historian and saw the Brier as a unifying event for Canada that brought all provinces and territories together annually in one arena to compete for the Tankard. He held an annual dinner on Tuesday evening at every Brier, where he hung a flag on the wall that he considered to be the true Canadian flag that had the entire nation connected by a chain of curling stones.

Government and industry pressures on Macdonald Tobacco forced David to sell the company to the American giant R. J. Reynolds in 1972, and things changed for the Brier as early as 1973. Under the Stewart family, the Brier was not used in any way as an advertising vehicle, and the commercial aspect was kept very low key. However, all of a sudden, at the 1973 Brier, there was signage everywhere, and it was obvious to everyone that things had changed. It was one of the issues that was creating ongoing conflict between David Stewart and RJR, along with increasing pressure from the Canadian government to eliminate tobacco companies from having anything to do with sport.

The actual people with the Brier who called most of the shots, including who would host the next event at least two years hence, were the three people who were known as the trustees, along with David Stewart, who was the chair. For all intents and purposes, the presence of the trustees went back to day one of the Brier, and it seems Macdonald Tobacco appointed them. The last three trustees were an interesting group and all were quite elderly. The group included Thane Campbell (a Charlottetown judge who was former premier of the Island), Collie Campbell (a former MP from Toronto, a brigadier general in World War II, a past president of the CCA, and the president of the ICF from 1967 until his death in 1979), and Ted Culliton (chief justice of Saskatchewan). Along with David Stewart, as the chair, nothing happened with the Macdonald Brier of any significance that the trustees did not approve. The other thing that ended with the 1979

Macdonald Brier was the trustees, as the direction and operation of the event were turned over to the CCA.

The 1977 Brier was held in Montreal for the first time since Macdonald Tobacco became the sponsor in 1927. Strange as it may seem, the event was held at the velodrome used for the cycling event at the 1976 Olympics in Montreal. There was an actual bicycle racetrack between the competitors and the fans, which was less than ideal.

In those days, the Brier started on Monday afternoon and ended on Saturday afternoon. I was part of the media contingent at the 1977 Brier, so I received notice of a special media conference called by David Stewart for the media room shortly after the start of draw one. Let me suggest this was unusual, and David Stewart was not in the habit of calling media conferences at the Brier. I walked into the media room to see Stewart sitting on a table with his legs crossed and looking very casual. Once everyone was in the room, he reached in his pocket, pulled out a package of cigarettes, took one out, lit it up, inhaled, and blew the smoke in the air. He then looked at the cigarette and addressed the media crowd with the following message. "You know, there is still nothing wrong with this product as long as it is used in moderation." I found the statement to be unbelievable. Following that acclamation, he then started talking about how new ownership at Macdonald and pressure from the Canadian government had changed a lot of things.

President of Macdonald Tobacco, David Stewart, called a media conference the opening day of the 1977 Brier. To the surprise of everyone Stewart announced that following the 1979 Brier in Ottawa the sponsorship of Macdonald's would be withdrawn.

The result was that following the 1979 Brier in Ottawa, Macdonald Tobacco would be withdrawing as the title sponsor of the Brier. The room went silent, and all the old boys in the room took a big gasp because they were all in love with Macdonald, David Stewart, and the Brier. However, I was positioned near the back of the room, and it was a good thing because I could hardly restrain myself. The majority of the people who worked on the Brier for Macdonald were in their sixties, and as long as they were in place, there was little to no chance of anything changing. It would now just be a matter of time before many things associated with the Brier and men's curling would be brought into the realm of today and out of the past. It opened the door for the push to make curling a recognized part of the Canadian sport mosaic and maybe ... just maybe, Olympic medal status.

CHAPTER 13

The Start of the Playoff System

IN 1973, MACDONALD Tobacco, in addition to being the title sponsor of the Brier, assumed the title sponsorship position of the Canadian Ladies Curling Championship, which became known as the Macdonald Lassie. When Macdonald announced in March 1977 that the sponsorship of the Brier would end in March 1979, the Macdonald Lassie met the same fate; Macdonald's sponsorship of that event would end in February 1979.

The 1978 Lassie was held in Sault Ste. Marie, Ontario, and was scheduled to be played at the Sault Ste. Marie Memorial Gardens, which was also the home of the Ontario Hockey League Greyhounds. I mention this because in 1978, Wayne Gretzky was a member of the Greyhounds. On the Wednesday morning of the Lassie, the ice crew arrived at the arena to find a lot of unexplained damage done to the ice and the hacks. Upon investigation, it seems the Greyhounds were in the arena very early in the morning to pick up their equipment as they headed out of town on a road trip. A few of them thought it would be a cool idea to give curling a try. While the Hounds ended up confessing to the deed, it was never really known whether Gretzky was part of the early morning curling experience or not.

Macdonald Tobacco held an annual dinner on Tuesday of the Brier and similarly a luncheon at the Scotties. In 1978, there wasn't any television coverage of the Lassie, but CBC did a thirty-minute nightly report from the Brier and live coverage of the final draw on Saturday. Remember, however, both events at this time determined the champion through round-robin play only, and it was never known if there would, in fact, be anything of consequence to televise. John Hudson, who was then head of CBC Television Sports, contacted the Canadian Ladies Curling Association (CLCA) and asked if he could come to address the CLCA and all the curlers at the annual luncheon. No one knew for sure what Hudson's message would be, but the CLCA quickly agreed for him to come as a speaker.

Hudson's message was very clear: if the CLCA and Macdonald agreed to go to a three-team playoff to determine the 1979 Lassie champion, following the round robin, CBC would televise both the semifinal and final live. The CLCA took the suggestion under advisement, but it did not take long for them to agree because everyone knew the Brier under the sponsorship of Labatt in 1980 would also be going to a three-team playoff. This move, however, would put the CLCA into the new system one year ahead of the men.

Interesting how things sometimes go. The 1978 Lassie in the Soo was the last time the champion was declared by round-robin play only. The Pidzarko twins from Manitoba had the last-round bye, but by the time they had finished all their games, they were the winners, so the last round of the Lassie had the winners sitting in the stands while the games on the ice meant nothing toward determining the winner. One year later, when the last round-robin-only champion was declared at the Brier in Ottawa, the same thing happened when Barry Fry, the champion, had the last-round bye and also sat in the stands during the final draw. This hammered the point home that in the new age of television and spectator demands, it was time for things to change.

CHAPTER 14

The Start of a New Era for the Brier

BY THE SPRING of 1977, a search committee was put in place to find a new sponsor for the Brier. The committee comprised of CCA First Vice President Clif Thompson, former Brier champion Harvey Mazinke, and curling entrepreneur Doug Maxwell. The search was completed by the fall of 1977, and at the 1978 Brier in Vancouver, it was announced that starting with the 1980 Brier, Labatt Breweries of Canada would be the new title sponsor.

I mentioned previously that during the Macdonald years, the CCA really had little to do with the Brier—it was all done by Macdonald Tobacco people, but the new agreement with Labatt saw the start of the CCA taking on the responsibility for everything that happened between the boards, which was all the competitive elements. Initially, the CCA board wasn't sure how this would all be handled, so I more or less became the liaison with Labatt on the coordination of the various activities that required CCA input or action. The man at the brewery who was charged with the implementation of the 1980 Brier in Calgary was Grant Waterman. I first met Grant in the fall of 1978, and it was the start of an interesting relationship that lasted until 1981, when Grant left the brewery to take a job with the Toronto Blizzard of the North American Soccer League.

Grant had a lot of ideas and seemingly a bottomless pit of money. There were things Grant decided he wanted to do, which we agreed on some and others not so much so. The Macdonald Brier Tankard was a symbol of the event that was synonymous with the Brier, but Grant decided it was going to be replaced and replace it he did with a new $50,000 gold-plated, double-handled beer tankard. A beautiful trophy, but to me... not the Brier. Labatt was the sponsor for twenty-one Briers through to Saskatoon in 2000. The following year, Nokia became the sponsor, and I quickly convinced the president of Nokia, Al Gilchrist, to bring back the old trophy. It is still being presented to the Brier champion each year just like it was in 1927.

The gold-plated Labatt Brier Tankard was presented to the winners of the Brier from 1980 until 2000.

Some other interesting things happened under Grant's direction, including the construction of ten new scoreboards made of stainless steel that pretty much required a forklift to move each one. They were beautiful, but not that practical. Plus, the cost was $30,000, and remember, this was 1979. Looking at today's costs, the boards would have been around $130,000. The promotion, player awards, and everything to do with the event was cranked up a notch, and a professional approach was attached to every aspect of the event. One other interesting change that happened, against my advice, was a change to the purple heart crest that every provincial/territorial champion playing in the Brier since 1927 wore with pride (although those hearts were red until 1935, but no one is really sure why). Grant thought it would be novel to have a new design where the actual crest would be in an oval shape with the purple heart design inside the oval. I did not think it was a good idea, but Grant did, and he was in control of all the items associated with the Brier. So, Grant changed the design of the purple heart for the first time in fifty years.

Before I tell the rest of this story, remember there would be players participating in the 1980 Labatt Brier who would have won numerous purple hearts prior to 1980. One example would be Peter Hope of Nova Scotia, who was playing in his fifth and final Brier; he would have four Macdonald hearts and now one Labatt. The players would receive their purple hearts when they became provincial champions so they could have them attached to their jackets/sweaters when they arrived at the Brier. No one said anything prior to arriving at the Brier, but once on site, the rumbling between the curlers was loud—no one liked the hearts. The complaint went out to all Labatt people on site, including Grant, but it seemed no one was listening. Labatt President Sid Oland arrived on the final Friday of the Brier to attend the closing dinner on Saturday evening and the Brier final on Sunday. He was approached by a few curlers who were pretty verbal regarding the change of structure to the purple heart. I guess Oland got the picture because, without notice to Grant Waterman, he stood at the closing dinner on Saturday night and announced he had heard from the curlers, and as a result, the purple heart would be changed back to the old version and immediately following the Brier an entire new set of purple hearts would be produced for the 1980 Brier participants. Grant Waterman was sitting next to me, and he was pissed... so much so that he immediately left the room mumbling something about "Damn Sid the Squid," which was the nickname a lot of senior staff gave Oland because he was from Halifax and had originally been the president of the Halifax-based Oland Brewery. So, for the first and only time in the history of the Brier, each participant of the 1980 Brier received two purple hearts.

Labatt President, Sid Oland, presents the Labatt Brier Tankard for the first time to 1980 Brier champion, Rick Folk.

The player benefits were also increased significantly. In the Macdonald days, each team received two rooms, airfare, and a small daily per diem of about $25/day. Labatt turned that around completely, giving every player his own room and a $75/day per diem. Toward the end of the Labatt sponsorship, that was turned into six rooms, as alternate players and coaches became the norm. In addition, Labatt did things for wives and families whom Macdonald did not acknowledge at all. Everything improved, yet there wasn't a dime paid in prize money, and the athletes were still not allowed to wear any advertising on their uniform other than those of the title sponsor.

For the first time in the history of the Brier, the CCA was in control of the ice area, which meant ice, rocks, ice technicians, umpires, and more. It had always been more than a sore point, in my opinion, that smoking was allowed to take place at the Brier and all curling events on the playing surface. It was one of the things that was a major issue with the sport advancing forward in the eyes of the critics and certainly wiped out any possibility of the sport ever gaining Olympic medal status. I knew it would be a difficult sell, but after giving it a lot of thought, I brought the idea to a CCA board meeting in Calgary in July 1979. I knew for sure I had two solid supporters on the idea with Ray Kingsmith and Herb Millham. The two were at opposite ends of the spectrum; Millham was the past president and Kingsmith the newly elected fourth vice president. People such as President Clif Thompson and First Vice Present Frank Stent were opposed, while Tom Fisher and Cec Watt weren't sure, but after about a one-hour discussion, the board finally gave me the green light to initiate a ban on smoking in the ice area at the 1980 Brier.

The official announcement on the ban was a week or so before the Brier started, and as expected, the old boys in the media jumped all over it with both feet about how disrespectful it was to announce this change in procedure just one year after the departure of Macdonald Tobacco. Interestingly enough, there was also a lot of grumbling from the curlers who smoked, but so be it—the decision was made and the decision held.

A New Job and the Start of the Publications

Grant Waterman also received a major pitch from Doug Maxwell, in 1979, to play a major role in the operation of the new Labatt Brier. Maxwell had been able to insert himself into the sponsor selection in 1978, thanks to the support of Clif Thompson, and everyone knew from day one that Maxwell's aim was to assume a role with the Brier similar to his executive director position with the Air Canada Silver Broom. However, Labatt was not like Air Canada and because of how the brewery business of the day operated, many of its staff had experience with events. In the end, Doug did not get the upper management position with the Labatt Brier that he had hoped, but Waterman did hire him on a two-year contract to manage the media aspect of the Brier. However, by the winter of 1981, Doug had some other challenges to face because John Hudson, now the director of marketing for Labatt, decided that following the 1981 Brier, he was going to hire another agency out of Toronto, the Houston Group, to direct the operations for the media at the Brier.

In the meantime, things were changing for me. In 1979, Sport Canada brought to Curl Canada's attention that I was the only technical director not housed at the National Sport and Recreation Centre in Vanier (Ottawa). They wanted that changed within the year. Faced with the situation, I advised the Curl Canada board I would not be continuing with Curl Canada beyond July 1981 if that was the case. The job was posted in the summer of 1980, and in the fall, Garry DeBlonde of Winnipeg was hired as the Curl Canada technical director; the plan was for me to continue in the role with DeBlonde until the spring of 1981. However, two members of the CCA board, President Cec Watt and President-Elect Tom Fisher, started discussions with me aimed at creating a new position that would involve media, marketing, and public relations. Doug Maxwell had some ears on the CCA board because Clif Thompson was now the president of the ICF, and of course, following the Brier sponsorship search in 1978, Clif had become good friends with Maxwell. Maxwell found out about the new position and attempted to get Clif to influence the CCA board in his favour. Clif tried, but it didn't work, and at the 1981 Brier in Halifax, the CCA announced that starting in May 1981, I would assume a new director of marketing and public relations position. The position involved liaison with curling sponsors and television, media relations, coordination of national championships, and overall marketing and promotion of the sport. Maxwell wasn't happy, and he managed to rally all of his old buddies in the media to grumble and bitch about the situation to anyone who would listen during the final days of the event in Halifax.

Garry DeBlonde became Technical Director of Curl Canada in the spring of 1981 replacing Warren Hansen.

When I had agreed to assume the new position, I had complained that I had not been making much money as Curl Canada technical director, and to take on the new position, the pay would need to increase substantially. While it was an increase, it still wasn't what I wanted, but I agreed to accept it as long as I could pursue other means of making money in addition to working for the CCA as director of marketing and public relations.

In the early eighties, a company in Toronto called Controlled Media had created *Score Magazine* for the Canadian golf world. *Score* was a guaranteed circulation magazine, which meant every golf club in Canada received a copy for each of its members, free of charge and delivered to the door. Controlled Media made the whole thing work by guaranteeing its advertisers that a copy of the magazine would be in the hands of every registered golfer in Canada. With the huge circulation, Controlled Media was able to charge enough for its ads to pay for the production and circulation of the magazine and still retain a profit. It was an arrangement where everyone was pretty much a winner, and I liked the idea. So, I asked the CCA board for a green light to go ahead and negotiate a similar deal for the CCA/CLCA and Curl Canada, if I could find a taker. I also made it clear that the magazine would require an editor, and I would be attempting to sell myself into that position. I did some research and found that besides Controlled Media, there was one other Toronto company, International Sports Properties, that was in the sports publication business. International Sports properties, amongst other things, published the programs for the Canadian Football League.

I held meetings with both companies and pitched my idea of a national magazine for curling that would resemble *Score*. I found both companies had an interest, but neither was prepared to offer the CCA any sort of royalty, but both were prepared to pay me to be the editor. I was talking with Grant Waterman about the idea, and he asked if I had considered speaking to Harry Littler. I said no, and I really wasn't familiar with Harry Littler or his company. Grant explained that Harry operated a number of companies under the banner of National All Sports Promotions, and he had a substantial contract with the Canadian Amateur Hockey Association (CAHA). Upon investigation, I also discovered that Harry's company was producing a guaranteed circulation publication called *Hockey Today*. I arranged for a meeting with Harry in his Toronto office, and within two weeks, we had reached an arrangement to start the production of an annual publication that would be known as *Curling Canada Magazine*, with the first issue set to be published in the fall of 1982. During the same year, initially at CCA expense, we started the publication of the first *Media Fact Book*.

We continued to produce both publications into the early nineties when Harry sold the company, now known as the St. Clair Group, to Tom Murray and John Barrington. About the same time, the contract with the CCA was extended to include the programs for the Brier and Scotties. In 1995, the St. Clair Group became the CCA agent for the Season of Champions and part of the arrangement saw St. Clair become the publisher of the programs for all the Season of Champions events, along with the annual *Media Fact Book*. The name of the books was changed, and every program, as well as the annual, became known as *Extra End Magazine*. St. Clair also took over the publication of the *Fact Book* as part of the deal. Laurie Payne became the editor of all the publications, and I assumed the role of managing editor, which I held until June 2015.

Labatt Instructional Series

Shortly after Labatt became the title sponsor of the Brier, Grant Waterman asked me if I thought there was anything special Labatt could do for curling in Canada. I thought for a minute, and sort of jokingly said, "How about doing a series of films on how to instruct curling with the methods and techniques of the newly developed Curl Canada program?" To my surprise, Waterman responded and suggested that was a great idea and he would look into it. A couple of weeks later, I got a call from Grant asking what I thought the cost would be to produce the series of six instructional films I had talked to him about. I wasn't sure, so off the top of my head, I suggested maybe $150,000. His response was, "Okay, do you think we could do that over two years rather than one?" I said sure, and he again suggested that I leave it with him for a few days. In less than ten days, my phone rang again. It was Grant. Everything was set, and he had arranged for $75,000 for the films in the 1980 budget and another $75,000 in the 1981 budget. He then asked if I could do some investigation with Chetwynd Films in Toronto to get some more details.

In the fall of 1979, I met with Robin Chetwynd and we worked out the details of producing the six films. Jim McKinley was assigned as the producer/director, and between the two of us, we produced the script for the first three films by late summer. In May 1980, we did the first shoot at the Chinguacousy Curling Club in Brampton, Ontario. CBC sports radio broadcaster Bob Picken was brought in to work with me on live commentary, and CBC television personality Don Chevrier did the voice-over. In the late fall of 1980, the first three films were officially released to the public through the Labatt Breweries across Canada.

The shoot for the final three films took place in May 1981, and again, Chinguacousy was the site. The final three films were released in the fall of 1981. The films were used for over twenty years, providing a teaching aid all over North America for anyone instructing people, from novice to advanced curlers. By the late nineties, the films, now on VHS format, were getting old and dated, and there was a need to replace them. While the desire might have existed to attempt to develop a replacement, there wasn't a financial source, and so the films disappeared into the perils of time. Below is an outline of what the series was all about, as it was outlined in a promotional brochure.

Labatt Instructional Series.....

LABATT CURLING CLINC INSTRUCTIONAL SERIES

This outstanding series of six films was created by Curl Canada and produced by Chetwynd Films in conjunction with the sponsor, Labatt Brewing Co. Ltd. The films feature a number of outstanding curlers whose expertise and style for specific demonstrations are recognized as ideal. The list includes Denis Marchand, Briar Boake, Carol Thompson, Alex Mowat, Bryan Wood, Kerry Burtnyk, Rick Folk, Ron Anton, Dawn Knowles, Garry DeBlonde, Bob Widdis and Paul Carriere.

Narration is provided by veteran curling commentator Don Chevrier. On camera monologue and dialogue are by CBC radio curing broadcaster Bob Picken and Curl Canada's Warren Hansen.

The series parallels the first three teaching levels of the Curl Canada certification program. Films 1, 2 and 3 match the teaching of Level I Technical; films 4 and 5 apply to Level II Technical, while the detailed teachings of Level III Technical are highlighted in film 6. The series is an excellent teaching aid for an instructor operating Novice, Intermediate or Advanced Clinics. In addition, groups of individuals interested in learning the sport or improving their present skills will enjoy the professional instruction provided by the films.

CHAPTER 15
Things That Needed to Change

FOR A SPORT to have a hope of being accepted as a full medal sport in the Olympics, there are many common-sense things that need to exist. First and foremost, the sport must have a solid set of rules and guidelines of operation, and if those rules/guidelines are violated, there must be a manner of dealing with the violation.

Through its history, curling did not have any team statistics, or for that matter, individual statistics other than game scores. Individual player statistics were being kept by a few journalists in the sixties and early seventies, but nothing was consistently being done at either national or international events prior to the late seventies. Prior to the introduction of the coaching certification program in the late seventies, training of coaches in curling simply did not happen. While coaches had existed junior curling for a while, there were no recognized coaches in either men's or women's curling before the eighties. Since the beginning of time, a curling team comprised of four people, and for the most part, if one of those regular players could not play for whatever reason, the team continued with three players, and the first player delivered four stones. To become an Olympic sport, curling would require a proper means of substitution, and a championship team would be required to be more than four players.

Officiating, Rules, and Umpires

Curling has always been a different sport, and because of some of its quirky style, there were those who have always referred to curling as a game and not a real sport. One of the quirky aspects was always the rules and enforcement of rules, and prior to 1979, there was never even any suggestion of any sort of rule enforcement being applied to curling even at the championship level. Curling is an old and historic sport, with origins as a friendly, social activity that was often referred to as a "gentlemen's sport." The sport always had few rules, and the rules that existed were often thought of more as courtesies than actual rules. If a curler breached a rule, they were expected to police themselves, and you were never to accuse your opposition of any violation of the rules. In the sixties, the sport took on more of a competitive atmosphere, and a few major cash and carspiels sprang on the scene. There were becoming more and more curling events, in addition to the annual competition for the Brier, where there was cash and major merchandise on the line. This resulted in more violations of the rules at all these events, in particular the hog-line rule, yet the older astute gentlemen who comprised the rules committee of the CCA did not want to acknowledge or even discuss the situation.

The annual national showcase of curling, the Brier, really did not have any game control people. There were always people present who were referred to as umpires, but they were usually older gentlemen from the local area that supposedly had a long history with the game and a lot of understanding. The umpires did not have any power, and if they were ever called upon to resolve any matter in dispute, it had the potential of ending in total disaster. A good example of such a disaster took place during the tenth end of the 1972 Silver Broom in Garmisch-Partenkirchen, Germany, which I spoke about earlier in the book.

I brought the rules committee's attention to the issue in 1976, but no one really listened until Calgarian Len Pasychny became the vice-chair of the rules committee in 1979. Pasychny and I knew each other pretty well because we had both served on the Curl Canada

Certification Committee since 1976. The rules committee still did not agree with the suggestion that a number of rules were being ignored by the game's best players. To finally prove the point one way or the other, it was agreed that a complete officiating system could be put in place for the 1980 Brier in Calgary, but all that would be allowed was for all rule violations to be recorded in the event final report. Since Calgary was Pasychny's home, he agreed to work with me on introducing an officiating system to the Brier in 1980.

In October 1979, Len arranged a meeting in Calgary with three local curlers who had shown an interest in being involved in the new steps we were attempting to take forward for curling and rule enforcement. The three gentlemen were Dave Petursson, Gary Pepper, and Rod Duncan. We talked about how the new officiating plan might take place at the 1980 Labatt Brier. Following that meeting, I worked with Dave, Gary, and Rod to put together the system that would be used in Calgary to observe and record all rule infractions. Below is what it looked like. Remember, prior to this, the Brier had a couple of older curlers from the area wandering around the ice area who were the supposed umpires of the Brier. There were no official lineup cards and no official stats kept. Only an official score recorded at the scorer's table (located at the side of ice level) at the end of the game.

Officials Guide for the 1980 Labatt Brier

Sheet Officials

1. *Two per sheet (one at each end). Primary task is CHARTING.*
2. *Make sure SCORERS properly indicate score, IMMEDIATELY.*
3. *If asked by players for a ruling, provide an answer if there is no doubt. Should there be any question call in a supervisor IMMEDIATELY.*
4. *If measurements are required the supervisor at the end will be summoned for the task.*
5. *Bring any immediate problems to the supervisor's attention.*

On-Ice Director (Home End)

1. *Assign all the officials for each draw.*
2. *Make sure scores at the home end are posted quickly and correctly.*
3. *Complete all measurements at the home end when necessary.*
4. *Make any decision necessary at the home end and if necessary, summon the head official.*
5. *Accept official lineup at the start of the game and submit to supervisor of stats.*
6. *Flips coin at the start of the game and team throwing red stones calls.*
7. *Responsible to make sure the official score card is signed and presented to the head official (umpire).*

On Ice Supervisor (Away End)

1. *Total supervision of officials and play at the away end.*
2. *Make sure scores at the away end are posted quickly and correctly.*
3. *Complete all measurements at the away end when necessary.*
4. *Make any decision at the away end and if necessary summon the On Ice Director or Head Official.*
5. *Responsible to make sure the on ice official at the home end completes the summary sheet at the conclusion of each draw. Also, complete the master summary chart.*

Eye In The Sky—Official

1. *In an arena with a gondola one official will be assigned per sheet of ice to the media gondola equipped with binoculars and a stop watch.*
2. *Gondola officials are directly responsible for timing each shot and observing hog line violations.*

Head Official

1. *Responsible for the complete direction of on ice operation during the time the competition is being played.*

2. *Head official answers directly to the curling body governing the competition.*

ALL UMPIRES MUST CLEARLY UNDERSTAND they may not intervene in any game unless requested to do so by one of the teams participating. When requested the official must provide an opinion and from that point the responsibility still lies with the skips involved to decide the course of action. The only exception will be when the curling body governing the competition gives the official authority to enforce certain rules or provide penalties.

It was obvious to many that a lot of rule violations took place at the 1980 Brier, but no one said much until the official report was released sometime later. Without question, the report provided some alarming results: total violations were 3,295, which included 59 sweeping, 253 hog line, 1,240 positioning, and 1,743 movement violations. Some were quick to argue that most violations involved positioning and movement, which many considered to be unimportant because these should have really be considered more courtesies than rules. Others suggested if that were the case, might it be safe to assume that intimidation could be considered part of top-level curling? Further, if a rule is thought to be unimportant, should it not be removed from the rules? If none of the current rules warrant concern at the top level of the sport, should they not be simply thrown out?

The most alarming violation was the 253 hog-line fouls, and the most shocking aspect was that over 120 of the violations recorded were not by inches but between a foot and a yard! This was interesting because the competitive curling world had lobbied hard to get the rule adjusted to be what most thought to be more manageable back in 1974. The rule adjustment was huge because it went from a curler having to bring their body movement to a full stop prior to crossing the line to being able to continue to slide as long as desired after the release of the stone. If there was any rule violation that got everyone's attention, it was this one. The efforts made to enforce it created a lot of discussion in the years that followed until an electronic device was invented with a sensor embedded in the handle some twenty years later.

Reluctantly, after studying the report, the management committee of the CCA agreed there was need for concern, but handling the matter going forward would require a delicate touch. Obviously, pressure would have to be applied, but to get majority buy-in would require a gradual approach. It was also clear and essential to start by applying pressure at the elite level of the sport because the various Canadian championships were without question the showpiece of the sport. If the game's rules were not totally adhered to at the top level of competition, those below could never be expected to follow the rules because they look up to the best players for the sport's image.

In 1981, the pressure started at all the Canadian championships, under the direction of the CCA/CLCA. The logging of all violations continued, but this time, the violation sheet was presented to each team at the conclusion of each game. The response was positive, as the total violations at the Brier dropped from 3,295 in 1980 to 591 in 1981.

This resulted in more pressure being exerted every year so that by 1984 the Brier only recorded 176 violations. The most important thing to note was the hog-line fouls had been reduced to five, all five stones were removed from play, and any stones that might have been displaced by the fouled stones were replaced. This all led to the procedures being tightened more annually until, by 1985, all the procedures and penalties were written into the rules.

The system has continued to be refined as the rule violations that existed in the seventies slowly disappeared. The world body, then the ICF, slowly adopted the same approach to officiating/umpiring that originated in Canada. Today, the world and Canadian systems pretty much parallel each other. The result was getting the sport of curling one step further toward what would be deemed acceptable at the Olympic level.

Statistics

Prior to 1976, keeping shots-made statistics (percentages) at curling events was done by many different individuals for their own use or interest. Sportswriters often kept them and published them to augment their newspaper stories, and some keen observers kept their own performance records for events of particular interest to themselves. These individuals often developed their own "scoring system." Consequently, various systems were used at different times, and these systems differed widely. Some used an eight-point maximum for successful execution of a shot; others used six, five and four-point maximums, and some had a "degree-of-difficulty" factor included in the evaluation.

At the Brier in Regina in 1976, the committee member (Al Heron) in charge of arrangements for the media attending the event decided to have "scorers" keep shots-made percentages for all games and distribute them. A four-point maximum was used, evaluations were manually recorded, and computation of the individual and team results was done at the completion of each draw, photocopied, and distributed.

In 1977, the ICF, working with Air Canada, decided to introduce statistics at the Air Canada Silver Broom in Karlstad, Sweden. Silver Broom Director Doug Maxwell contacted Ray Turnbull from the TU Curling Schools and myself from the Silver Broom School and asked if we would direct a statistics operation at the world men's championship. Each school provided three people, and for the first time, a four-point scoring system was used at the event. The idea was continued in 1978 at the Winnipeg Silver Broom and remained in place from that point forward. A team of scorers was trained and brought to it and subsequent events where official statistics were being compiled. Using the same team each year enabled enhancement of the system to include a degree-of-difficulty factor for each shot, determined in part by the scorers relying on their experience and knowledge of the game.

After a hiatus of two years, Al Heron was brought to Ottawa for the 1979 Brier, and Committee Chair Terry Begin recruited a group of experienced "competitive" curlers to act as scorers to provide "official" percentages for the event. Again, as in Regina, evaluations of each shot were recorded manually, and results for each player and the teams were prepared using hand calculators after the games were completed. It took at least an hour for the results to be compiled, checked, photocopied, and distributed to the media.

Since the statistics evaluated players' and teams' performances by turn thrown and shot type, the teams expressed great interest in having access to that information about themselves but, more importantly, about upcoming opponents. Consequently, the reports also were distributed to the teams for their own analysis.

In the fall of 1979, Ed Lavalley (vice-chairman of the CCA's public relations committee) approached Terry Begin and asked if he would undertake a review of several known shots-made percentages evaluation systems and make a recommendation as to the most appropriate system for the CCA to use at its championships. It was emphasized that the scorers for the events would be recruited from the local host committee at each site.

For consistency, it was decided to use a four-point system very similar to that being used at the world championships, but simplified by not having a degree-of-difficulty factor modifying each shot's numerical evaluation. This made it easier to train new statisticians at each site, as they only needed to record the turn thrown, categorize the shot in one of the same nine categories being used at world championships, and provide a numerical success evaluation of zero to four. Because some shots attempted (usually by skips or thirds) clearly were more difficult and/or critical to a game's outcome, the use of bonus values of five or six (still based on a maximum of four) was introduced. This partially compensated for a degree-of-difficulty evaluation being done for every shot and the resultant fractional values, which very much complicated computation of results.

Ed Lavalley then asked Terry Begin if he would volunteer to undertake implementing the system at its several major national championships, beginning with the Canadian Junior Men's Championship in Sault Ste. Marie, Ontario, in 1980.

He agreed and prepared documentation describing the system and its use: "Shot-making Percentage Statistics for Curling" and "Guidelines for Shot Evaluation." These documents were the basis for training the scorers at each site and are still in use today largely unchanged from the originals.

For each event, he contacted the host committee and asked the chairperson to recruit about a dozen of the most experienced current competitive curlers to act as statisticians. He travelled to each site prior to the event (usually two or three days in advance of its start) and conducted training sessions for the scorers. Then he stayed on throughout the competition to supervise the statistics function and the preparation of the various reports for distribution to the media and the teams after each draw.

The shots-made percentages continued to be compiled manually for the next several years. In 1982, Terry Begin also became chairman of the public relations committee of the CCA, as well as continuing in his role of head statistician, travelling each year to most sites of the major championships for about ten days to conduct training sessions and supervise the preparation of the statistics for the event. At the 1984 Annual General Meeting of the CCA, he was recognized with a unanimous vote of thanks for his efforts in developing and implementing the statistics system.

With the development of computer technology in the eighties, it became apparent that the computation of results was an ideal application, which could mitigate the onerous manual compilation function and speed the reports' preparation. In 1984/85, programs were written for the mainframe hardware installed at Sport Canada headquarters in Ottawa, the shots-made evaluations were entered, and reports were prepared, utilizing remote connections to it.

The rapid development of desktop computers and laptops, and continuing technical difficulties and costs associated with establishing remote connections to the mainframe hardware in Ottawa, pointed to their use as an obvious improvement to the system.

In 1985, Brian Cassidy, a member of the Systems Support Group in the Computing Centre of the University of New Brunswick in Fredericton, agreed to write programs for desktop/laptop computers that could be used for data entry and production of statistical reports without the need for remote data transmission. Brian observed the functions being performed, prepared preliminary software, and via correspondence, telephone, and visits by Terry Begin to Fredericton, he developed the application.

Fortuitously, the 1986 Tournament of Hearts and Brier were being held in London and Kitchener, close to one another, and they provided the first real test of his work. Brian accompanied Terry to these two events, and the system was debugged and implemented.

To save travel and accommodation costs, the CCA decided to send only Brian to the major championships in 1987, and he took over the role of head statistician from Terry Begin, who had developed and implemented the system and fulfilled that function for the previous seven years. Brian continued to refine the system and its reports as he attended all of the major championships and supervised the statistics function for each of them over the next two decades. Today, computerized statistics are part of every official Canadian and world championship, and this put the sport another step closer to possible full acceptance by the IOC.

Coaching

Certainly prior to the late seventies, coaching was anything but an accepted part of curling. The only age group that even suggested a coach was a worthwhile addition to the team was the junior men's, which was known until 1976 as the Canadian School Boys Championship. Yes, each team travelling to the Canadian School Boys had a coach, but for the most part, that person was really a chaperone and often a teacher from the school the team attended. That is because all four members of the team had to attend the same school to be eligible to enter. So, for those reasons, the coach was often a teacher, and if that coach knew anything about curling, it was often by accident rather than design. Outside of the School Boys event, coaching really did not exist in the sport except in a few instances where a well-known curler, nearly 100% of the time a male, became attached to a team as a coach but was never a recognized part of the team.

When the Coaching Association of Canada became involved with Curl Canada in 1974, they supported an instructor training program in year one but only under the condition that a coaching course or accreditation had to be started in year two. So, as promised, the Level I coaching program was rolled out in the summer of 1976, and the first courses were held that fall. Coaching certification requirements were suggested to the National Junior committee going back as far as 1978, but it was a few years later before it became a mandatory requirement for a coach to have at least Level I credentials. One of the problems was that the coaching course had three legs: technical, theory, and practical. A big hassle was the fact that post-secondary institutions in each province provided the theory course, and because these courses applied to all sports, not just curling, it was sometimes difficult to get enrolled when desired. Nevertheless, by 1983, it was required that all coaches at the Canadian Junior Men's and Women's Championships hold at least Level I credentials.

Shortly after the official coaching program was underway, I wrote a position paper for the CCA, CLCA, and Curl Canada. Below is that document.

Coaches in Curling—Long Overdue

The sport of curling has thrived for centuries despite a persistent non-progressive attitude that has hung around like a persistent like a coastal fog. The absence of coaches in curling has been part of the age old tradition that still exists despite the recent introduction of a coach certification system. Certainly, this is fine at the non-competitive level, but we have reached a point where competitive players need the continued assistance and guidance of a properly trained coach. Curling is the only team sport that I can think of that doesn't consider a coach to be part of a top caliber team. Furthermore, most individual sports also utilize coaches when the sport simply has the highly skilled, trained athlete pitting himself against time, distance of a single opponent.

If I had to pin-point an area where a coach could benefit a curling team the most it would be in psychological development and strategy. Curling strategy and different approaches to the game are currently learned through experience which is why many players never really learn the proper approaches, even at the top competitive level. Would it be fair in football to have a budding young quarterback develop his technical and strategical skills without the benefit of a coach? No, it wouldn't be dreamed of in football, but it is in curling. From the same point of view, you wouldn't expect the quarterback to fully understand and deal with the emotional and arousal level differences of each and every player. Yet, in curling we expect the skip to carry that burden and much more, when the task requires a person with specialized training and understanding of the details.

Consider this, in curling the skip is responsible for calling the shots, analyzing the ice conditions, analyzing the skills of the opponent, policing their own team, being the psychological leader and making all of the most important shots in every game for their team. Under our present system there is little doubt that it requires the strongest of personalities to be able to cope with that sort of pressure and responsibility. Little wonder a lot of skips crack under the strain in critical situations. In sports such as hockey and football, the coach constantly works on building the confidence of their key players, the goalie and the quarterback. In curling there isn't any coach to assure this constant ego boosting of the skip so it falls back to the hands of the other team members. If a player becomes disenchanted with a situation of any sort they can completely shatter the skip's confidence. Then there has always been the challenge of determining who is going to play the different positions which again falls upon the shoulders of the skip. Many things need to be considered including emotional makeup, leadership ability, experience, throwing ability, sweeping ability, sweeping judging skill, etc. The largest single problem facing most teams in competitive curling today is the fact that about half the curlers on the ice are playing out of position. Again, it may be difficult for a skip to make necessary changes in a line-up but a coach would have little problem.

Practicing and team conditioning has also become a necessary part of the competitive game but again there is no one around to direct these very essential sessions. Again, someone with a good deal of knowledge in this area must establish and set-up such a program making sure all necessary areas are covered.

Who is going to be the enforcer if three players follow a strong training and practice schedule and one does not.

It is obvious that curling has come of age and we need trained coaches for competitive teams at all levels. We don't, however, want to fall into the grips of the incompetent coach who has cast his shadow on so many sports. Professional hockey and football players are prime examples of gross coaching incompetence (with some exceptions). For the most part, these people have a great deal of experience, playing the particular sport and have had it pass them by because of age. Experience alone does not a coach make. The coach must possess a large amount of leadership ability and be schooled in the most current approaches for physiological development and psychological approach. In addition, he must be prepared to attend additional courses when available to keep himself abreast of new developments in both the coaching and technical areas.

Curling to some degree is lucky because we will not have to overcome existing problems with incompetent coaches. A new part of the Curl Canada Level II Instructor program will offer the first detailed sessions on coaching in the very near future. The course curriculum will include: Coaching Principles in Curling, The Coaches Scope of Influence, Psychology for the Curling Coach, Team Selection and Position Responsibility, Training Principles and Diet and Practice Schedule and Evaluation of Players.

In curling I foresee the coaches role as being multi-fold with the following providing some idea of responsibility.

1. *Make sure each curler on the team is playing the best position to give the team an opportunity for success.*
2. *Develop the best possible training program for each team member along with proper advice on diet.*
3. *Coordinate and direct regular, objective practice sessions.*
4. *Determine seasonal goals for the team that are within their reach.*
5. *Offer detailed advice on curling strategy.*
6. *Provide the necessary guidance for proper mental preparation taking into consideration such things as the different arousal levels of the athletes involved.*

7. *Organize beyond the benefit of a doubt all travel arrangements, etc., for the team. The players should have one responsibility curling.*
8. *Provide an analysis or scouting reports on opponents to be encountered in the future.*

There are certainly other areas of involvement for the coach as well but the key ones have been mentioned. Ultimately, the coach will probably be allowed to confer with his team a certain number of times during the game which could be the answer for elimination of the current game delays by indecision. Coaching in curling! Just around the corner.

Things changed with the Brier in 1980, and for the first time, coaches were recognized, but none of their expenses were paid and they were not permitted any consultation with their teams during the game. In 1981, the function of coaches travelled a little farther down the road as they were permitted one consultation with their team after the fifth end and provided a seat at the media bench. The number of coaches present at the Brier increased to nine in 1984, and by 1985, ten of the twelve teams had coaches. Similarly, the advisory committee for the 1981 Air Canada Silver Broom in London, Ontario, allowed coaches for the first time and provided them seating at the media table. However, the coaches were not provided the opportunity to confer with their team at any time during the game.

By 1986, things had moved one step further toward coaches being an accepted part of the Brier and all Canadian championships, as well as adding credence to the curling coaching certification program. To be a coach at the 1986 Labatt Brier, a person had to be at least a certified Level II coach, and if possible, have completed Level III Technical. Coaching was now becoming an accepted part of the game, and with curling's demonstration appearance at the Calgary Olympics less than two years away, it was just in time.

Alternate Players

The substitution rules for curling for many, many years were very strange. There was usually room for some sort of a substitution at most levels of the sport, but for the Brier until 1980, the substation allowed was simple... it wasn't. The way it worked was like this: If a player was lost for whatever reason, you would continue to play with three players, and there was really no substitution. From the time a team started the playoffs to the Brier, up to and including the world championship, should a player be lost for one game, two games, or the balance of the competition, the only substitution allowed was from the same club that the team played out of. There was one stipulation, however: the player coming in as a substitute could not have played in the playoffs for the Brier, even at the club level. The Brier had another provision in place. If a player was lost to a team during the competition, a curler from the local area could be brought in as a sweeper but could not throw stones, just sweep eight stones each and every end while the lead player threw four rocks. I always found it strange that a sweeper from the local area was fine, but a thrower was only allowed from the home club of the team. It was sort of like the sweeper wasn't really part of the team—just some sort of an add on.

Ron Anton played third for Hec Gervais when they won the Brier in 1961. Anton did not attend the world championship in Scotland because of university exams but the process for his replacement was complicated.

The strangest application of this rule ever was in 1961, when Hec Gervais won the Brier and his third, Ron Anton, could not attend the world championship in Scotland because it interfered with his university exams. It was only the third year of the world event that was pretty much a curling tour of Scotland and the foregone conclusion that Canada would win, so Anton did not feel he was missing anything too special. Anyway, because the team had to get someone from its home club, and it had to be someone who had not even entered the playdowns at the club level, the person selected was a man by the name of Vic Raymer, who was well into his fifties and considered a senior curler. Fact is, however, he had not entered the playdowns at even the club level, so he was eligible.

Things changed at the first Labatt Brier in 1980, when a pool of local curlers was put together, and if a team required a substitute for whatever reason, they could choose one of the local curlers to fill in at the lead position. For the next couple of years, the substitution pool continued to be provided by host committees, but teams actually brought an alternate player at their own expense in some cases. Finally, in the spring of 1984, the title sponsor, Labatt, agreed that starting with the 1985 Brier in Moncton, funds would be provided to pay for the alternate player or fifth as they are often called.

It was again just in time as curling prepared for its presence in the 1988 Olympics in Calgary as a demonstration sport. By this time, it was an accepted position at both the men's and women's worlds and carried forward into the 1988 Games. I always thought that once it was agreed that an alternate player would be funded for both the Scotties and Brier, teams would use the alternate player to their advantage. But for some reason, this never seemed to happen. Rather than have the alternate accept a regular rotation into the team lineup, they were sparsely used, except in the event of an accident or illness. Unfortunately, as well many teams selected a friend or buddy to join them at a national championship, and because of this, some non-believers referred to the alternate player as "the pizza man" (suggesting his main job was to get the team its late-night pizza delivery). Nevertheless, despite some negative comments, the alternate player position continued and is still in place today.

CHAPTER 16

Women's Curling Finds a New Sponsor

WHEN MACDONALD LEFT as the sponsor of the Lassie in 1979, the Canadian Ladies Curling Association (CLCA) was not as fortunate as the CCA in coming up with a sponsor to step into place for 1980. The result was that in 1980 and 1981, the CLCA sponsored the event itself. However, during that time, Robin Wilson, who had herself won the Macdonald Lassie twice, became involved in finding a new sponsor. I met Robin in 1975 when I travelled to Vancouver in April to play in a mixed bonspiel with Jim Armstrong, Robin, and her sister Dawn Knowles. I moved to Vancouver in the summer of 1975 to curl with Jim Armstrong for the following season. I started dating Robin's sister Dawn and, as a result, became involved as the coach of their curling team, skipped by Lindsay Sparkes, with Dawn playing third and Robin at second. I coached the team for both of their Lassie wins in 1976 and '79, and as a result, Robin and I also became very good friends. Following are the words of Robin Wilson, telling us how the sponsorship of Scott Paper fell into place:

I started working in Marketing at Scott Paper in New Westminster on graduation with a Bachelor of Commerce from UBC in 1968. The Dean of Commerce had asked that I apply for all positions in Marketing when recruiters visited campus as some companies specified that only men could apply for interviews. Like many other companies, Scott Paper Limited at the time did not hire women in sales or their corporate head office. My friend Lee and I (both with names that could be assumed to be male) applied for everything. We were pretty cocky but somewhat to our surprise received several second interviews.

Robin Wilson, a two-time Macdonald Lassie champion, convinced Bob Stewart, President of Scott Paper Ltd., to consider having the company become the title sponsor of the Canadian women's curling championship.

My final interview was with the Vice President of Marketing at Scott Paper Limited in New Westminster. Bob Stewart was a tall and imposing personality and as I would learn over the years one of the smartest and kindest men I would every have the pleasure of knowing. I was truly shocked when offered a job in sales working with an entire male workforce. I was even more surprised when I was later offered the position of Marketing Brand Manager at head office. I was the first woman to be hired into management. My early relationship with Bob had some ups and downs as he called me out on numerous occasions but always behind closed doors. He provided guidance, motivation, emotional support, and role modeling.

Getting together with two great wonderful friends, Lindsay Sparkes and Lorraine Ambrosio, and my sister Dawn, we formed what would become a formidable curling team.

We won our provincial championship in 1976 and earned the opportunity to represent BC at the Macdonald Lassie in Winnipeg. I was thrilled with the support that our team received from Scott Paper employees across Canada, including Bob, who sent us a personal note of congratulations. We beat Alberta in a playoff to win the championship.

In 1979, I left Scott Paper when I became pregnant with the first of our three children (this was widely considered the norm at the time). Our team was still together when we went on to win the Lassie for a second time in Mount Royal, Quebec. This was the last Lassie sponsored by Macdonald Tobacco.

In the summer of 1979, I met up with John Leonard, President of Walker Leonard Advertising, and asked if he would team up with me and make a presentation to Bob Stewart proposing that Scott Paper become the title sponsor of the Canadian Women's Curling Championship. We were thrilled when he agreed, and the CLCA blessed the change after two years without an official sponsor.

Bob had me promise we would work together to make the Scott Tournament of Hearts into the premier women's sporting event in Canada. And he reminded me that he intended to be actively and personally involved in all aspects of the event. True to his word, Bob or "Mr. Stewart" as so many referred to him in deference to his imposing profile, would personally phone the skip of every team after they won their provincial and territorial championships. Imagine their shock when the now-President of Scott Paper called to personally congratulate them. If necessary, he would call repeatedly until he could speak with every single skip.

Bob would become my "mentor" and the driving force behind Scott Paper's long-running sponsorship of the Canadian Women's Curling Championship.

Once moving forward with the event we needed a new name and logo for the event. My sister Dawn and I grabbed a bottle of red wine after dinner at Mom and Dad's one night and retreated to the living room where we started to brainstorm. The idea of the 4 hearts logo representing the four players that make up a team seemed obvious, and it was synonymous with the friendships developed through curling. Also obvious was that "Scott" had to be included in the name that replaced the Macdonald Lassie. After tossing out idea after idea, we agreed on The Scott Tournament of Hearts.

Betty Summerville (an independent graphic designer) was contracted to create the artwork for the logo. This design was incorporated into the creation of the perpetual trophy which was created by Clarkes Recognition Products. The four heart columns were to be different heights to differentiate the four positions on the team—Skip, Third, Second, and Lead.

The media had some fun with the new name likening it to football's Tournament of Roses, celebrated annually in California on New Year's Day. However, we forged ahead, and they eventually cooperated with us to cement the name in the history books. Because the newspapers had a policy of not mentioning corporate sponsors, the press buried the STOH name in their copy hoping it would be missed by editors. Radio reporters had no such constraints and called the championship by its designated name from the beginning. In gratitude to the media and their support, Bob would host a media lunch at every Scott Tournament of Hearts no matter where it was being played and he personally thanked every reporter and journalist for their continued support.

Now it was time to share the news about Scott Paper becoming the new sponsor of women's curling in Canada. Bob, the senior executive team and I set off for Newfoundland, where the 1981 national Championship was being played at the Memorial Centre in St. John's. We took the new Scott Tournament of Hearts trophy with us, paying for an extra seat so it could ride alongside us on the plane. And we shipped 1000 yellow daffodils to St. John's to be distributed to the spectators at the arena. The new trophy was escorted by the RCMP onto the ice and the crowd roared. The stands were packed to overflowing as Sue Anne Bartlett's hometown team took on Susan Seitz' Alberta team. The crowd was shouting "atta boy girl" throughout the match to their dismay, the Seitz team won.

The first Scott Tournament of Hearts was hosted in Regina, Saskatchewan, in February of 1982. Again, the entire Scott executive team was there in their new uniforms; grey slacks and burgundy jackets with the Scott Tournament of Hearts crest proudly displayed. Colleen Jones' team from Halifax, Nova Scotia, won the Scott Tournament of Hearts, earning the right to represent Canada at the Women's World championships in Geneva, finishing a disappointing fifth.

Bob Stewart as President of Scott Paper became the driving force behind the company's sponsorship of the Scott Tournament of Hearts.

Working with Bob and Don Pettit, who was Vice President of Marketing, we agreed on a strategy to build the coverage and profile of women's curling on television and in newspapers. I made numerous trips with Don to Toronto to visit both television and newspaper outlets, promoting the Scott Tournament of Hearts and the merits of increased exposure of women's curling. At the time, coverage of women's curling was minimal. CBC was covering the semi-finals and the finals but that changed in 1985 when TSN came on the scene and introduced round robin coverage.

From day one of the sponsorship, the curlers and their families were treated as extended family. The foremost highlight of the annual event was the closing banquet on the last day of the championship. I was given pretty much carte blanche in organizing the banquets, working closely with the hotel staff to create a unique and unforgettable experience. Each banquet was themed, and the decorations were elaborate. The food included multiple courses. Every venue was different, and I had a generous budget to hire some amazing entertainment. The banquets wound up with a retrospective set to music which included photos of every curler.

Traditionally, engraved silver trays had been presented to the top three teams at the Lassie and a trophy in the image of the "Lassie" on a package of Macdonald cigarettes. While the trophies were unique and treasured, the silver trays not so much. This was a practice followed by many other sporting organizations at the time. We replaced the trays as prizes with custom engraved miniature copies of the official four heart trophy on a teak base for each member of the winning team.

Bob was adamant that we find other ways to recognize the first, second and third place teams and we agreed that jewelry would be an innovative and universally desirable replacement. Plus, there was no comparable prize in women sports. Our new team prize structure focused on gold rings in the four-heart design with 1/4 carat diamonds (1st place), emeralds (2nd place) and rubies (3rd place). These were in addition to the four heart pendants which the provincial/territorial team winners were presented with. These were created in the same theme with a diamond or emerald or ruby stone at the center of each one of the four hearts as winners repeated.

Looking back, I can see that we really did not think this whole prize package through at the time. It was not long before we had multiple winners at the provincial/territorial and national levels. What to do now? Ultimately, we agreed that with every repeat win at the provincial/territorial level the curler would receive a four-heart necklace and pendant. If she was a repeat winner a diamond would be added to one of the pendant's hearts. This was a short-term fix as winners continued to repeat and the pendants were soon full. So, we created gold bracelets with adjoining hearts. Each heart had a diamond inserted as soon as a curler had filled their necklaces.

Colleen Jones team from Nova Scotia won the Scott Tournament of Hearts six times. We needed to get creative once again and, in the end, they had their choice of snowmobiles or trips anywhere in the world (with a ceiling of $10,000). However, as Colleen and team continued to dominate, we knew we needed to think to the future and create a lasting theme and prize structure. We stuck with jewelry and to this day curlers wear their necklaces and rings with great pride. Repeat wins at the national level are recognized by increasing the size of the diamonds in the rings. There are several curlers who proudly wear rings featuring full one-carat diamonds.

The 1985 Scott Tournament of Hearts was played in Winnipeg and Linda Moore's team from BC won with a 11–0 record, the first time any women's team had gone undefeated. With the win, the team earned the right to return to the national championship in 1986 as Team Canada without needing to qualify by winning their provincial championship. This was an initiative of Bob's and mine. We recognized we needed to have a repeat championship team that would bye into the Scott Tournament of Hearts. This would allow us to promote, advertise and further build the championship nationally and help grow women's curling in Canada. Scott Paper invested millions of dollars in advertising support of women's curling in Canada. However, there was considerable controversy in curling circles at the time.

The 1986 Scott Tournament of Hearts was held in London, Ontario, and for the first time Linda Moore's team as defending champions received an automatic berth in the competition. It was 19 years later, in 2015, that Team Canada became part of the Brier. The resulting final was testament to the validity of Team Canada. Moore's team and Marilyn Darte's Ontario team finished the competition with one loss each. In the final game, the Darte team won the final 7–3.

In 1997, Kruger Products acquired a long-term licence for the Scott brands and is now the owner of Scott Paper products in Canada. The Scott Tournament of Hearts was officially re-named the Scotties Tournament of Hearts now recognized as the longest national corporate sponsor of amateur sport, in Canada.

CHAPTER 17

Hexagon . . . Grief the Curling World Didn't Need

I HAVE MENTIONED Doug Maxwell on a couple of occasions, and I think it is quite obvious that Doug and I had conflicts, to say the least. I can still remember walking into a meeting in Montreal in the summer of 1972 that I thought was going to be the final step in completing a long-term arrangement with Air Canada, only to find Maxwell sitting across the table from me. Although it was not totally obvious at the first meeting, it soon became evident that Maxwell did not want me or anyone else near what he thought was his self-created toy—world curling, and certainly at that time, the sponsor of the world men's championship, the Silver Broom. Doug was sort of a double-edged sword. With one forward swing, he had created a lot of good things in curling, while he had created an equal amount of destruction with the backswing. The problem with Doug was he had one foot in taking curling in a lot of bold new directions, but the other was stuck in ideas and ways of doing things from the past.

In and around 1967, Doug made a pitch to someone at Air Canada about the airline becoming the next sponsor of the world men's curling championship. The idea sold, and Air Canada became the sponsor of the first-ever Air Canada Silver Broom, held at Pointe Claire, Quebec, in the spring of 1968. Maxwell established himself very well with the event and was named as the executive director. At this point in time, the then-ICF was a very small organization that could not manage a world curling championship any more than the CCA could operate the Brier. Maxwell pretty much took the model Macdonald Tobacco created for the Brier and applied it to the men's world curling championship, which was now known as the Silver Broom.

From 1968 until 1978, things went like clockwork for the Air Canada Silver Broom and Maxwell. The 1978 Silver Broom was held in Winnipeg, and it was a huge success—it was hard to believe how much better the event could become. However, something happened about one month after the Winnipeg Silver Broom that I'm sure shocked Maxwell to the bone. Don MacLeod was the vice president of marketing for Air Canada, and he was the man Doug had to directly report to regarding the Silver Broom sponsorship. Unannounced, MacLeod retired, and a new vice president of marketing and man responsible from Air Canada would have to be appointed. MacLeod loved Maxwell, and in his eyes, Doug could do no wrong. Many of us thought that Pierre Jerome, who worked under MacLeod as the director of public relations, could possibly be the replacement, which would allow everything to stay unchanged. But that was not the case. A young French-Canadian executive by the name of Michel Fournier was named as MacLeod's replacement. In addition, the two people directly under Fournier who would be the ones really responsible for the Silver Broom would be Lillian Rayson and Ken Meek, both new to the Silver Broom and to curling.

It immediately seemed it would be business as usual, and the 1979 Silver Broom was returning to Berne, Switzerland, for the second time in five years. The event in 1974 had been well attended by Canadians, as was the 1979 event. In addition, Peter Attinger was again the team representing Switzerland, as he was in 1974, and the Swiss again had high hopes of the home nation performing well. So, in addition to the 3,000-plus Canadians in the seats when the Swiss team was on the ice, at least 4,000 Swiss were usually present.

Another item that I have not talked about yet is Max Holling Travel. Doug Maxwell was the executive director of the Air Canada

Silver Broom, but with it came a few other little tidbits that were never talked about much. One of them was the travel packages primarily sold to Canadians going to the Silver Broom. No one ever knew the exact relationship between Holling Travel and Maxwell, but with what was about to happen in March 1980, there is one thing for sure: Holling Travel was not connected to Air Canada. Michel Fournier travelled to the 1979 Silver Broom in the middle of the event, and upon arrival, investigated a few things. Whether by accident or design, Fournier discovered Holling Travel had transported a large number of the Canadians at the Silver Broom in Berne on Swissair... not Air Canada. Upon his return, Fournier apparently called a meeting of the troops and started a review and investigation of what exactly was taking place with the Silver Broom.

Nothing much reached the rumour mill until the 1980 Silver Broom in Moncton, New Brunswick. Fournier flew in early in the week and called a meeting with Maxwell. In a very short period, Doug's world changed. Fournier informed Maxwell that going forward, the airline would have a much more hands-on involvement with the Silver Broom, starting with the travel packages being established and sold to spectators attending the Broom. Maxwell was told that Air Canada's in-house agency, Touram, would be handling all the tour packaging, and Holling Travel was out. A number of Maxwell's other responsibilities were reduced, including the fee he was being paid and the number of Air Canada flight passes he could access. Doug's immediate response was, "I quit!"

He then went to all of his media buddies. The group, led by people such as Laurie Artiss and Bob Picken, approached Fournier and asked for a meeting. The meeting was granted, and the old boys' group convinced Maxwell and Fournier that they needed to kiss and make up. That they did, sort of. Maxwell was told that he would be dealing directly, on an ongoing basis, with Ken Meek, who would be reporting back to Lillian Rayson and Fournier. Maxwell agreed to it but was obviously unhappy. He was caught between two eras. He came from the era of the Macdonald Tobacco, Dominion Stores, and Seagram's type of sponsorships, where the corporation used the sponsorship as a public relations venture aimed at being good corporate citizens. The sponsor owned the event from top to bottom and did the whole thing as a public service. In 1980, when Labatt became the sponsor of the Brier, it was made clear they had no interest in being responsible for the technical aspects and day-to-day operations of the event. Labatt had the new vision for sponsorship, which was marketing-driven, and its investment and efforts to increase sales and loyalty. Under Michel Fournier's direction, Air Canada wanted the Silver Broom sponsorship to go in that direction, but Doug didn't see it that way.

Another thing happened in 1982 that gave Doug another step up on the Air Canada conflict: the election of Clif Thompson to the presidency of the ICF. Remember, Doug and Clif had become close back in 1978, when they both served on the committee appointed to find a new sponsor for the Brier. It was Clif whom Doug turned to for help in 1981 when he felt the new job I was hired to perform for the CCA in marketing and public relations should have belonged to him. The day Clif became the ICF president, Doug had another ear that would listen to his complaints about Air Canada being a "bad sponsor."

Remember, I had an agreement with Air Canada for almost ten years for the operation of the Silver Broom School and as such developed relationships with a number of people inside the company. Ken Meek often called me to ask questions and seek opinions. Usually, those questions were about how Labatt handled different aspects of the Brier and the desire for Air Canada to direct its sponsorship of the Silver Broom more toward a marketing approach and less of a public relations vehicle. In May 1983, Meek called a meeting at the Toronto York Hotel of an interesting group of people, which included Clif Thompson, Ray Kingsmith, who was then-first vice president of the CCA, and me. No one was totally sure what Meek had called the meeting to discuss. Upon arrival, we quickly found out that he was looking for advice. Air Canada was in the airline business and not the curling business, and while they wanted to continue as the title sponsor of the Silver Broom, they wanted the relationship with the ICF to be more like the Labatt relationship was with the CCA, as it pertained to the Brier. In a nutshell, Air Canada wanted to be the sponsor but void itself from the operation of the event.

Clif Thompson suggested the ICF was not really in a position financially to take on the responsibility of event operation of the Broom. Ken Meek suggested that Air Canada could possibly provide some help. Both Ray and I were shocked at Meek's candid comments about Maxwell with Thompson in the room, but maybe that was the plan? He suggested that Air Canada was anything but happy with Doug Maxwell, and if Meek had his way, Maxwell would be gone tomorrow, even though there were two years left on his contract with Air Canada.

Within a couple of months, Air Canada announced that Doug Maxwell was no longer under contract to the airline. For the two years he had left on his contract, he would be working for the ICF but paid by Air Canada (the minutes of the ICF meeting from March 1984 suggest Maxwell was being paid $60,000 per year).

The next phase of the saga was at the 1984 Silver Broom in Duluth, Minnesota, at the annual meeting of the ICF. Doug's number one cheerleader through most of his adventures was Laurie Artiss of Regina. Laurie was an old newspaper writer turned curling entrepreneur and the owner of a growing curling supply and pin business in Regina. Artiss had also chaired the 1973 and 1983 Silver Brooms in Regina. In 1982, he was appointed by the CCA as the chair of its international committee, which made him the number one representative from Canada to the world body.

Laurie was a likeable guy and had done some great things for curling and the merchandise business. I actually worked closely with Artiss for a few years, when we were both in the equipment business, and we actually did some joint purchasing of product from White Ram for a few years. Truth is, when our company, Curlers Corner, got in some financial trouble Artiss supported us through the storm. Laurie, like Clif Thompson and a few other well-meaning people, got pulled into Doug's web, which we will talk more about as this story unfolds.

Another thing needs to be remembered about this whole thing... Doug was desperate. For sure Air Canada would not renew his contract when it expired in spring 1985, and in those days, the ICF did not have the means to pay Doug $60,000 per year plus expenses. If Doug did not find a way to get rid of Air Canada by the summer of 1985, he was finished with world curling.

In Duluth, it became obvious that certain ICF members were determined to pressure Air Canada and possibly even submit an ultimatum for the airline to continue as the sponsor. Ray Kingsmith, who was the CCA president, shared with me that Laurie Artiss had been advised in writing not to support any discussion of this nature or the proposed ultimatum. All indications coming out of the ICF meeting in Duluth were that relations between the ICF and Air Canada were improving, and some positive discussions took place.

However, at a special executive committee meeting held on the morning of April 7, it seems the tone changed. Some unfavourable comments were levied at the airline's travel arm, Touram, but the brunt of the objection seemed to be led by Doug Maxwell and Laurie Artiss. Maxwell felt the airline was receiving value far in excess of its investment, and he suggested that cutbacks to things such as computerized stats shouldn't happen. He also stated that the airline had turned the event into a marketing operation and that it should be totally public-relations orientated (old thinking for the eighties).

The meeting resulted in a notice of termination to Air Canada if it didn't meet certain demands by August. The two main demands were for the airline to get rid of Touram and Maxwell's main adversary, Ken Meek. It is also interesting to note the main supporters of the demands, besides Maxwell, were Clif Thompson and Laurie Artiss, despite the fact that Artiss had been told by the CCA to not support any ultimatum proposed to Air Canada.

The executive committee agreed to set up a meeting with Air Canada at which time the sponsor would be informed that (a) the ICF wished the sponsorship to continue but with changes in personnel with specific reference to Ken Meek, (b) the ICF wished to invite tenders from other travel agencies to replace Touram, (c) the ICF wished to discuss a new cost structure that would realistically express the value of the Silver Broom, and (d) the ICF, dependent on agreement regarding the first three points, wished to give Air Canada notice of termination of the sponsorship contract. Let me also tell you loud and clear the contract in place was through to and included the 1986 Silver Broom in Toronto.

From there, we go to Maxwell's book, *Tales of a Curling Hack*, and in his own words:

> *In June of 1984 the Canadian Curling News sponsored a promotional seminar in Brandon, Manitoba. As publisher and editor, I was there with the invited presenters, one of whom was Laurie Artiss, a key member of the ICF's executive committee, and one whose Silver Broom roots stretched back as far as mine. He had twice served as chair of an organizing committee (1973 and 1983) and in 1976 had chaired a Regina Brier. He had helped rewrite the ICF rulebook, he had been a major player in the television negotiations involving the federation and TSN and was one of the most astute international curling people around. No one doubted his great love of the game.*
>
> *Also present were a pair of Dons—Lewis and Turner. Don Lewis, whose ice-making expertise had been a boon in the early days of the Silver Broom, had been more than an ice maker as he made himself invaluable in a variety of ways. In later years he would go on to chair the 1992 Regina Brier and in 2001 to become president of the CCA. Don Turner, a retired farmer from Weyburn, Saskatchewan, was probably one of the most intense curling devotees I have ever met. He'd been one of Regina's key organizers in both 1973 and '83 and when he wasn't collecting memorabilia, he was an enthusiastic spectator.*
>
> *After the seminar, Laurie, the two Dons and I were sitting around with our feet up when the conversation turned to the fragile world sponsorship situation. While the ICF's opting out notice had been given, in Duluth, basically as a defensive move, what would happen, we wondered, if Michel Fournier decided to call their hand? Did the federation have any other option but to*

fold? Before we left Brandon, we were on the phone to Scotland and New York to acquaint Chuck Hay and Kay Sugahara about our concerns and thoughts. What if we offered a plan to the ICF that would serve to stiffen their resolve?

Chuck Hay is, of course, one of the giants of world curling. Some of his accomplishments have already been covered, but to remind you... not only was he (at the time) Scotland's only world champion, it was his example that had revolutionized competitive curling in Scotland in the sixties. He had been a player in the final Scotch Cup, 1967, and in the first Silver Broom in 1968. He had been president of the Royal Caledonian Curling Club, a valued Scottish representative to the ICF, and the first Scots curler to be honoured by the Queen with an MBE (Member of the Order of the British Empire). Like Laurie Artiss he had been chair of a Silver Broom organizing committee, in 1975. He had also been a chief umpire for the event. Blunt-spoken he may be, but when he speaks, his words had a ring of truth to them. Sincerity, intensity, wisdom and conviction are other words that come to mind.

I hadn't met Kay Sugahara until the 1981 Silver Broom in London, Ontario, but had quickly recognized his enthusiasm for curling. I also discovered he was one of the smartest men I have ever met—and certainly with the means to indulge his passion.

Before I continue this part of the story, let me say this: I did then and do now have the utmost regard for Artiss, Hay, Sugahara, Turner, and Lewis. Lewis has, in fact, been a good friend for over forty years, but unfortunately, they were all pulled into a web by Doug and became convinced that Air Canada was bad for curling. However, none of them had a background that would provide them with the understanding or knowledge of the world of sponsorship, how it was changing, and that Air Canada did not want to leave world curling but simply wanted to change the relationship.

The scene now moves to Montreal on August 9, 1984, and a series of meetings involving the executive committee of the ICF. For the sake of clarification, the executive committee consisted of representatives from Canada, the USA, the United Kingdom, Scandinavia, Central Europe, and the president, vice president, and director of competitions (Maxwell). Interesting to note that Laurie Artiss was representing Canada and Doug Maxwell was a member of the ICF staff as the competition director.

The first item on the meeting agenda on the morning of August 9 was a proposal circulated by a Toronto law firm on behalf of a client who did not wish to disclose its identity. The client had indicated an interest in becoming the sponsor of the world men's curling championship and wished to purchase all the rights, including the travel package, for a fee of $100,000 annually plus a percentage of the annual aggregate revenue (the travel package alone was estimated to be worth between $1 and $2 million, dependent on the site). The client had also indicated that if it were possible for the rights to be acquired for the 1986 Silver Broom in Toronto, it would be prepared to pay an additional $50,000 rights fee. Keep in mind, the Air Canada contract went through and included the year 1986.

During a discussion on the proposal, Laurie Artiss told the meeting he was a member of the group the Toronto law firm was representing, and as a result, he would refrain from any comments because of a possible assumed conflict of interest. When Artiss made that declaration, Canada was left without a voice in whatever the final decision would be, which should have set off an alarm bell in someone's head. The largest curling nation in the world was left without a say in what was one of the ICF's biggest decisions. It might be compared to NATO holding a meeting and declaring a nuclear war without anyone from the USA in the room. Later, some in the room argued that President Clif Thompson was a Canadian and could have represented Canada's interest, but he wasn't even present at the annual meeting of the CCA in 1984 where the issue of the future of Air Canada and the CCA position was discussed.

The second meeting was held the afternoon of August 9, and this time, three members of Air Canada, led by the vice president of public affairs, Michel Fournier, joined the meeting. Accompanying Fournier was director of community affairs, Lillian Rayson, and manager of community affairs and Silver Broom chairman, Ken Meek.

Clif Thompson, was President of the International Curling Federation (ICF) in 1984 when Air Canada was terminated as sponsor of the world men's championship in favor of six curling enthusiasts that formed a management group known as Hexagon International.

The sponsor's response to the Duluth notice of termination was circulated. Air Canada had been requested to reduce its overall costs by 25%, but the airline wished to continue its sponsorship.

Fournier indicated that most of the items in the proposal might be negotiated. But he said the airline was adamant that the ICF could not retain Doug Maxwell in any capacity that involved the Silver Broom. He said that the interest of Air Canada was being badly serviced, that the sponsorship was not working to Air Canada's advantage, and if Maxwell were retained, the problems could continue.

One of the proposed items was contracting a national public relations firm to handle the Silver Broom that was familiar with managing a large sports property. The Houston Group was doing the job for Labatt with the Brier, and Fournier thought the same company might be contracted for the Silver Broom.

Following the departure of the airline representatives, President Thompson noted that the ICF's Duluth proposal had been totally reversed and that the situation boiled down to a personality clash between Ken Meek and Doug Maxwell.

Further discussion with Lillian Rayson indicated that Air Canada would be prepared to withdraw its sponsorship after 1985 if the ICF found another sponsor. On the morning of August 10, the ICF committee, excluding Maxwell and Artiss, met with the members of the Hexagon group who was the mystery client that had declined to be named and its legal representative. Upon considering Hexagon's thirteen-page proposal, the committee agreed to recommend its acceptance to the ICF. Whereupon Laurie Artiss, according to the minutes, suggested the ICF executive committee should inform Air Canada that its proposals were not acceptable and that it sponsor the 1985 Silver Broom but withdraw from the 1986 Silver Broom in Toronto.

On the afternoon of August 10, the ICF committee, which included neither Artiss nor Maxwell, met with the Hexagon group and a press release announcing the "withdrawal" of Air Canada and the surfacing of Hexagon was discussed. Joining the meeting were the members of Hexagon, Chuck Hay, Don Lewis, Kay Sugahara, Doug Maxwell, and Laurie Artiss. It was now obvious why Maxwell and Artiss were not on the ICF side of the table.

Hexagon made its presentation, and before its representatives left the meeting, the following was noted:

1. A contract should be established with the group for a minimum of five years. The group would retain income from television for the Silver Broom (interesting that at this time, there wasn't any television revenue and the only network providing any coverage was CBC).

2. Vice President Freddy Collioud of Switzerland asked about the rights of future sponsorship and who decides sponsor arrangements. Maxwell said it was clear that Hexagon would retain all sponsorship rights. He suggested the group intended to negotiate major sponsorships with the approval of the ICF. It was noted that the ICF would have no involvement in negotiations between Hexagon and potential sponsors. If, in the unlikely event that no sponsors were interested, then Hexagon would pay the costs of running the Silver Broom.

3. Don McKay of the USA raised the position of some form of guarantee of the amounts payable to the ICF. Kay Sugahara

stated that a guarantee for five years would be difficult, but a bank letter on a year-to-year basis or a revolving line of credit would be possible. Doug Maxwell stated he appreciated that some form of guarantee would be granted, but some form of agreement would be provided once the contract was signed.

4. If the new contract received approval, then it would be left to Clif Thompson and Doug Maxwell to liaise with the 1986 Silver Broom committee in Toronto. The Hexagon group left the meeting.

The president then stated that in his opinion, the presentation offered a completely new concept as far as the ICF was concerned. It would considerably minimize the duties of the president of the ICF's involvement of the negotiations with sponsors and television. The president concluded his opening remarks by stating that he was sure that a good working relationship would exist in the future for all concerned and further stated that Doug Maxwell had remained loyal to the ICF.

When the group returned to the meeting, the chairman announced that the executive committee was prepared to recommend the acceptance of the Hexagon proposals to the ICF. Laurie Artiss suggested that the ICF executive committee should inform Air Canada that the airline's proposal was not acceptable, and he further suggested that after the 1985 Silver Broom in Glasgow, the Air Canada contract would be terminated.

At two p.m. on the same day, August 10, a meeting was held with Air Canada and the executive committee where Air Canada was told that following the Glasgow Silver Broom, its contract as sponsor of the Silver Broom would come to an end.

In a final meeting on the morning of August 11, it was agreed that a press release would be issued by the president and Doug Maxwell between August 24 and 29, announcing the termination of Air Canada and the new agreement with Hexagon.

One month later, CCA officials let it be known that they did not like the way the ICF had handled the situation. President Clyde

Opaleychuk cited the earlier CCA directive regarding the ultimatum to Air Canada and asked for the resignation of Artiss at the association's semi-annual meeting in September.

The scene then moved to Mozine, France, and the semi-annual meeting of the ICF, where the Hexagon proposal would be put forth to the entire membership for approval. There were actually two other sponsorship groups that submitted proposals to the meeting in Mozine, but in the end, the Hexagon proposal was accepted despite Canada's objections.

It was rumoured that all six Hexagon partners had put $50,000 into the organization to get things rolling, which meant there was $300,000 in the Hexagon bank account. However, before any thoughts were put into what would be required to run the 1986 championship in Toronto, the ICF would need to be cut a cheque for $150,000 and, for the 1987 event in Vancouver, another $150,000. Certainly, two things were assumed by the principals: first, that a travel agent appointed by Hexagon would be able to sell a large number of packages to the new world men's championship, and second, that at least one sponsor would purchase the title. A Regina travel agent was given the travel rights, and with the 1986 Silver Broom being in Toronto, packages that were expected to be sold were not and a title sponsor was not acquired.

While the event in Toronto was okay, it was very evident that the "touch" Air Canada had put on the Silver Broom was missing, and so were the fans. The Silver Broom had been held in Moncton in 1980, London in 1981, and Regina in 1983 all before sold-out crowds. That was anything but the case at the new world men's championship held in Toronto in 1986 in the old Toronto Coliseum, which had about 6,000 seats. At no time was it even close to being full. Before the Toronto championship was over, it was already apparent that things were not good in Vancouver, where the 1987 world men's was scheduled to be held. Without a major sponsor associated with the event, money was becoming a problem. The only member of the Hexagon group who probably had the resources to continue to play in this game without a major sponsor was Kay Sugahara. By the time things got to Vancouver, he seemed to be more and more the only member of Hexagon prepared to continue to play the game.

The 1987 event in Vancouver happened, still without a title sponsor, and attendance was not much better than in Toronto a year earlier. Things seemed to be getting tougher. By now, Sugahara had become the main face of Hexagon, and it was obvious he was paying most of the bills. During a meeting with Sugahara and the ICF in Vancouver during the '87 event, he noted Hexagon would not be honouring its contractual commitment to pay the ICF the $100,000 rights fee owing for the '87 championship, and unless they could obtain a sponsor, the same situation would occur in the 1988 Lausanne, Switzerland, event. He did, however, make a commitment to provide transportation and accommodation for the teams for 1988. The other thing made clear by Sugahara was that if no sponsors were obtained by December 1, 1987, Hexagon would not be continuing with the contract or any financial support after Lausanne. Hexagon had some favourable discussions with some potential sponsors over the summer of 1987, but nothing materialized, so on December 1, 1987, Sugahara advised the ICF in a letter that Hexagon could not provide any further funds beyond Lausanne and that the federation was free to pursue other sponsorship arrangements.

The CCA had been very vocal about its disappointment in the ICF's decision to terminate Air Canada, a seventeen-year sponsor, for what seemed at best to be questionable grounds. It was obvious to the CCA that the whole thing had been pretty much created by Doug Maxwell and his displeasure with the airline when it decided to move its sponsorship into current times. Maxwell came from the old school and the days of Macdonald Tobacco, when sponsorship was considered a public relations venture and the way a corporation could expand its goodwill to the community, expecting nothing in return. That whole concept changed for curling in 1980 when Labatt Breweries became the sponsor of the Brier, being clear the main objective of their sponsorship was to sell more of its beer to Canadians involved with the sport of curling. Air Canada wanted to do the same thing with its sponsorship of world curling, but Maxwell did not like it and was not prepared to accept it.

Maxwell claimed that numerous sponsors had been close to signing an agreement with Hexagon, but something always happened to sideline the final signing. He indirectly blamed the CCA because of its failure to ever accept Hexagon, but what Doug forgot about was Air Canada. The airline was extremely disappointed with what had taken place and was not quiet about it. Think for a moment. If you were a major corporation about to sign a multi-year deal to sponsor the world men's championship, might you not check out what happened with the previous sponsor before making any sort of a commitment?

I had a good relationship with Air Canada, going back to my ten-year association through the Silver Broom Curling School. So, on two occasions, I met with Ken Meek and Lillian Rayson between 1986 and 1992 in an attempt to get Air Canada involved with the CCA as a sponsor. Both times the meeting was very amicable, and both times I was told by Rayson and Meek that they were interested; however, it would never pass muster from those above. It was clear Air Canada was well aware Doug Maxwell was still involved with curling through the Ontario Curling Federation and the Canadian Curling News (monthly curling newspaper), and as long as Doug had any official association with curling, Air Canada held no interest in the sport.

In the end, the entire venture set world curling back on its heels, and for a period between 1989 and 1991, things were pretty touch and go. The Air Canada public relations director for western Canada was Hal Cameron in Vancouver. I was in Hal's office for a chat in 1986 before Vancouver was hosting the new Hexagon world men's championship. I will always remember Hal's parting comment: "I will never understand Doug Maxwell. We would have been in world curling forever, and Doug would have had the job forever. All he had to do was be quiet and do what he was told by the sponsor who was paying the bills." Doug was an interesting study; despite all the negative things that happened, in the end, he did a lot to advance curling around the world. It is unfortunate that he could not find a way to work with

Air Canada through a new type of sponsorship that differed from his vision of a title sponsor.

I guess you ask: What did all of this have to do with curling not becoming a medal sport out of the 1988 Olympics in Calgary? In a word… lots. It would be very incorrect for anyone to assume that the entire scenario with Air Canada went unnoticed by the sporting world and the IOC. The ICF sponsorship dustup with Air Canada, along with a lot of other unfavourable things that happened, which will be elaborated on later, all combined to paint a picture that the IOC would not be impressed with.

CHAPTER 18
The Start of the Olympic Trail

ON SEPTEMBER 30, 1981, from Baden-Baden, Germany, the IOC announced that Calgary, would host the first Olympic Winter Games in Canada from February 13–28, 1988. In the initial announcement, nothing was said about demonstration sports, but once we were well into 1982, the topic began to be tossed around with the media. During this time, a host committee could request the inclusion of demonstration sports to the IOC. The request usually came from a host city because of the strength of the sport involved in the host country and the desire of the host city to assist the sport in possibly becoming an Olympic medal sport at some point in the future. It was interesting to muse as to curling being a demo in the 1988 Games if Italy or Sweden, the other two bidding nations in 1988, had won the bid. In the early eighties, curling was nowhere in Italy, and while Sweden had won a couple of world championships, it still was not a household conversation in Sweden. Would there have been a curling voice strong enough to make it happen? To be clear, the request for a sport to be demonstration had to come from the host committee, *not* the national or international body. In the end, the host committee required the support of the National Sporting Association (NSO) and eventually the International Sporting Organization (ISO), but the request had to originate with the host.

In September 1982, I put in a phone call to my friend Ray Kingsmith in Calgary and asked if he had heard anything about the process a sport would need to go through to gain demonstration status for '88 Games. Ray did not know, but he would find out. About two weeks later, he got back to me and indicated a meeting had been established in Calgary to discuss the topic with the organizing committee he wanted me to attend.

It was a cold, frosty morning on December 7, 1982, and the winter wind penetrated my skin as I walked toward the Westin Calgary from the Delta Bow Valley, where I was staying. An eight a.m. breakfast meeting had been set a few weeks prior by Ray with Brian Murphy, vice president of sports from the Olympiques Calgary Olympics (OCO), organizing committee.

Murphy was friendly and informative, and the points that Ray and I needed to know were on the table. Murphy indicated that in addition to curling, ski orienteering, freestyle skiing, short track speed skating, dog sledding, and ballroom dancing were being considered for demonstration status. Only three would be selected, and Murphy agreed he would advise us as soon as he was aware of the procedure to be followed for acceptance. He did, however, indicate that the facility for curling could be difficult, and the acceptance of the proposal might have to be based on the event being held at the Calgary Curling Club. It was strongly recommended that the approach should include men's and women's curling as part of the demonstration.

Nothing happened for a while, but on June 6, 1983, Ray finally received a letter from Murphy asking for a detailed questionnaire on curling to be answered. Following that, on August 22, we would be called upon to make a presentation to the executive board of the OCO. We were advised that the presentation would be verbal and should outline why curling should be a demonstration sport, what it would do for the Games locally and internationally, and would the financial returns from curling in the Olympics be significant? I contacted Bob Moir, CBC Television Sports executive producer, and he put together a presentation video that, along with my written documentation, answered the three questions and a lot more. About a week before the presentation was to happen, Ray was advised by his employer, Cominco, that he would have to travel to Trail, BC, for an executive meeting on the day of the OCO presentation. I would have to do the presentation to the OCO without him. August 22 was an anxious moment as I sat like a school kid waiting to do my "stuff."

In early September, Ray was informed by Murphy that OCO had officially accepted curling, along with short track and freestyle skiing. IOC President Juan Antonio Samaranch had endorsed curling and freestyle while IOC Director of Sports Marc Hodler recommended curling and ski orienteering. Ray was "unofficially" assured that curling was in. The only question still to be answered: Which of the other sports would be chosen? OCO advised at the same time that the IOC had recently recognized curling at an executive committee meeting. In late October 1983, the IOC officially announced that curling, short track, and freestyle skiing would be the three demonstration sports in the 1988 Winter Games.

On March 29, 1984, Murphy wrote Kingsmith a letter that suggested the ICF would have to provide the event with its blessing while OCO would operate the demonstration in conjunction with the CCA.

In November 1984, Ray Kingsmith sent ICF President Clif Thompson a letter outlining the position and plan for curling in the 1988 Winter Olympics. This was the first official communication with the ICF after the acceptance of curling as a demonstration sport in the '88 Olympics. You will notice the plans outlined in the letter changed significantly in the months that followed before a final agreement between the ICF, CCA, and OCO was reached for curling's demonstration appearance in Calgary.

Dear Clif,

The following is an update on the plans to date covering curling in the 1988 Olympic Winter Games. I'm sure the member nations of the ICF are anxious to hear of our plans as it is now just a little over three years until the Games begin.

Curling as a Demonstration Sport falls under the control of the ICF to the extent of insuring that international guidelines, rules and protocol are properly followed.

The CCA, as the national governing body, must and did, make application to the ICF for sanction to hold the tournament in Canada. The operation of the tournament, whatever it is called, then falls under the auspices of the CCA.

The actual operation of the tournament is the responsibility of the Calgary Olympic Committee and I have accepted the job of chairing the curling committee. The volunteers required will be drawn from the Southern Alberta area so the legacy of the training will be to the benefit of the area where the Games are staged.

It is our intention to run the tournament as two open 16 team events. That is sixteen men's teams and 16 ladies' teams. The ICF should extend invitations to their member countries to declare by January 1, 1987 whether or not they will send or not likely to send a men's and/or ladies' team. Assuming we get sixteen teams of each, they would be split into an A and B competition and two seven game round robin series would be played. The first and second place finishers of each round robin series would then enter a sudden death semi-final and final round.

I would suggest that the A and B groups would be seeded to some degree to insure that the games are interesting and as even as possible. That does not mean that all the top teams would be in A, but rather based on the 1987 world championship final standings. The first-place finishers in A, second in B, third in A, fourth in B and so on. Not unlike what is now done in hockey.

The round robin games would be played in a curling club with viewing facilities beginning on the Tuesday before the Olympic Games and finishing on the Friday. Saturday, February 13th is left for the opening ceremonies and the semi-final and final games would move into the Corral on either Sunday and Monday and Tuesday after the official games begin.

As is the case all Olympic Sports, a country sending a team or individual is responsible for the expense of transportation to the hosting city and accommodation and living expense while at the Games. The hosting committee will arrange for the accommodation etc. and transportation within the city while the team or individual is participating.

As you can appreciate Clif, all plans at this time are in the formative stage and much work is still to be done. If you or any member of the ICF have any ideas or suggestions they would be most welcome. As mentioned earlier, at this time we have not even selected a name for the competition.

As plans progress, I will keep you informed by way of periodic updates. Good luck with your deliberations at the semi-annual meeting in Morzine, I trust all things will work out for the betterment of our game.

Yours sincerely,

Ray Kingsmith

In March 1986, at the ICF annual meeting in Toronto, an Olympic Committee was finally established within the ICF that consisted of President Phillip Dawson of Scotland, Harvey Mazinke of Regina, representing North America, Pierre Thuring of Switzerland, representing Europe, and Ina Light of Winnipeg representing women's curling. The first major decision indicated the selection of countries for the '88 Olympics would include Canada, plus the top seven finishing countries (men and women) in the 1987 world championships. This was contrary to the original proposal from Ray Kingsmith that had suggested a total of sixteen men's and sixteen women's teams should be involved. But remember, at this time, the total membership of the International Curling Federation (ICF) was less than twenty nations, so the manner of even how you would determine what the sixteen nations would even be was far too complicated to consider. Other decisions that came out of the Toronto meeting were:

1. The on-ice officials (umpires) would be from Canada and appointed by the OCO committee, working with Curl Canada.

2. The Curl Canada statistics program that was in place would be used for curling in the Olympics.

3. The draw was submitted by the Calgary Committee and approved.

4. The teams would be limited to a maximum of five members.
5. The amateur standing situation would be dealt with between the ICF and the IOC.

A bit of a crisis took place in the fall of 1986, when an attempt was made to move curling from the Calgary Curling Club to the Max Bell Arena. The Calgary Curling Club was the initial venue selected by OCO, but Ray and I had never agreed with that decision and felt curling needed to be in an arena to be properly demonstrated. Our original thought had been the Calgary Corral, which hosted the 1980 Brier, but that was rubbed out early in the game when it was determined the Corral would be required for hockey and possibly some of figure skating. Max Bell was an arena that had about 2,500 seats, but OCO had decided it would be the host site for another demonstration sport, short track speed skating. In the end, it was agreed that the funds required to bring the arena in line to host not only short track but also curling would be approved in a venue where it could really put its best foot forward. The final decision was curling would be held the first week of the Olympics and short track the second week.

Things were now in place and what was left for Canada was to determine who would represent Canada at the Games in Calgary. That was about to open another huge can of worms.

CHAPTER 19

An Unexpected Distraction

IN 1976, JOHN MacLeod was hired as the executive director of Curl Canada, and with the help of Sport Canada, an office was set up at 333 River Road in Vanier, Ontario, in what was then the National Sport and Recreation Centre. Initially, John shared a part-time secretary, but by 1979, the office was a bustling place with a staff of three people, along with yours truly, who was working as the technical director of Curl Canada but from my home office in Vancouver.

In the meantime, the CCA operated its office from the home of its secretary-manager, Charles Scrymgeour, in Winnipeg, while the Canadian Ladies Association moved its books from the kitchen table of one president to the other. In 1979, the CCA decided it wanted to move its office from Charlie Scrymgeour's Winnipeg home to the Curl Canada office in Vanier (Ottawa). Charlie was into his early sixties, and the CCA was pretty sure that Charlie would retire rather than root up his home in Winnipeg and move to Ottawa. However, the CCA guessed wrong. Charlie decided he would move to Ottawa and took up an office at 333 River Road, adjacent to John MacLeod, in July 1979.

On a Friday afternoon in October, John drove Charlie to the airport as he was flying to Winnipeg for the weekend to complete the sale of his house. It was pre-arranged that John would go back to the airport on Monday morning and pick Charlie up on his return. John arrived at the airport on Monday morning as arranged, but Charlie did not appear. John checked with Charlie's wife, Val, who was in Ottawa, but she had not heard from him. A day went by, then a week, and finally three weeks when Charlie's brother Doug located him in San Diego. Needless to say, Charlie was done with the CCA, so in the fall of 1979, John MacLeod became the general manager of the CCA, as well as the executive director of Curl Canada. John MacLeod was a good honest worker and a sound administrator, but as time passed, toward the middle eighties, there was an element of the CCA board who felt most of the current staff were not of the calibre required. During a couple of late-night board gatherings, where a few had probably consumed more alcohol than they should, the suggestion was dropped that it was time to clean house and come up with a new staff. This would have probably included John MacLeod, Garry DeBlonde, technical director, and yes, me, who was now serving multiple roles, which included public relations, marketing, and competitions.

The feel of this movement was in the air, and it got stronger toward the summer of 1985. John, who was a retired military guy and into his late fifties, announced in June 1985 that in July 1986, he would retire. I had met with John privately and discussed the matter in detail. I tried to urge him to hang in there, and if they wanted to get rid of him, to not make it easy. But John made it clear he was considering retirement, and he did not want to get into a nasty fight with the CCA, even though he fully understood what I was saying and agreed he wasn't the only one in the crosshairs.

I enjoyed my involvement with curling and the CCA, and by now, I also had my sights set on the bigger prize, which was to get curling accepted as full medal sport in the Olympics. I had other business interests in addition to my work with the CCA/Curl Canada and really did not have an interest in either moving to Ottawa or becoming the general manager of the CCA, but I also felt the squeeze. If I did not go after the general manager's job, I was afraid my life within curling and the CCA/Curl Canada could end as soon as a new GM was in position. In my opinion, there were two CCA board members who saw things in a different way, and I also knew that once a new GM was in place, my reporting would be to the GM and not the board. The GM could potentially be influenced by a couple of board members to possibly go in... "a new direction." I thought about it long and hard and finally concluded that I had to apply for the job or potentially be finished with the CCA. My thought process was of possibly taking the job until curling was accepted as an Olympic medal sport and then hopefully move onto something new that would allow me to move back to the West Coast.

The 1986 Brier was being held in Kitchener–Waterloo, Ontario, the first week of March, and it was during that week that the deadline for application fell. I wrote the official letter before I left home for the Brier, but I didn't mail it. The day for the deadline got closer, and I thought more and more about what I really wanted to do—if I didn't mail it, my future with curling was probably done, but did I really want to do this? I remember it well. On the day of the deadline, I walked from the Valhalla Hotel to the street where the K–W post office was about two blocks away, where I registered the letter and sent it to the hired headhunter in Toronto. I knew for sure it would send a couple of CCA board members into a complete tailspin, and that actually brought a smile to my face.

By early April, I received a letter from the headhunter inviting me to an interview on April 22 at his office in Toronto. He informed me that I was one of three interviews that would be completed that day, and following the interviews, a vote by the five people involved would determine who the next GM for the CCA would be. I was advised who four of the five people interviewing would be Ralph Boyd, president of the CCA (meeting chair), CCA Joe Gurowka, CCA second vice president, and from the CLCA, President Elsie Crosby and President-Elect Aileen MacLean. The one that made little sense was Gurowka, who was way down the CCA, ladder as the third in line to the presidency. However, President-Elect Jerry Muzika from PEI worked for the Government of Canada and apparently could not take the added time off to be part of the hiring process, so it was passed to the first VP, Harvey Mazinke of Regina. Mazinke passed the responsibility to Joe Gurowka for reasons unknown because Mazinke owned his own farm implement business, so getting the time would not be a huge issue—however, there was probably more at play than met the eye. The fifth person and final key to the puzzle was Ray Allard, who was the consultant from Sport Canada. At that time, he had a definite concern and involvement with the operation of the CCA, CLCA, and Curl Canada. I did not know for sure who the other two people being interviewed were, but the rumour mill told me that one person was the executive director of Badminton Canada and the other a member of the host committee in Kitchener–Waterloo that had just hosted the Brier.

Ralph Boyd was President of the CCA in 1986 and was chair of the commmittee assigned the responsibility of hiring a new general manager for the CCA.

The interview went well, and I felt I answered all the questions in a very convincing, professional manner. I felt pretty confident that I would have the votes required to win the day. Ralph Boyd was from Campbell River, BC, and had been a friend, I thought, for some time. I got along well with both Aileen and Elsie, and I also knew Ray Allard pretty well. The wild card was Joe Gurowka, and although I had worked well with Gurowka for a number of years on the Curl Canada program, he was tightly aligned with Mazinke. I knew Mazinke was the driving force behind wanting the administration of curling at the senior level in Canada to change. Following the interview, the headhunter advised me that he would be in touch within twenty-four hours to provide me with the results. I left the interview and went back to the Delta Chelsea Hotel, where I was staying. I knew that Crosby, MacLean, and Boyd were also staying at the Chelsea. Gurowka lived in the Toronto area and would have driven in for the day.

I went out that evening for dinner and returned to the hotel around nine p.m. There, standing in the lobby, were Aileen MacLean and Elsie

Crosby. I went over to chat, and after a few moments, Elsie asked me if Ralph had spoken to me. I quickly said no and asked what should he be talking to me about? Elsie explained that when they left the meeting in the afternoon, I had won the vote, and Ralph was instructed to contact me to advise of the result and begin a discussion about a contract. Elsie no sooner got the words out of her mouth when the doors of the elevator opened. Out popped Gurowka and Boyd. Almost in unison, the two women said something like, "Those bastards... they've been talking to Mazinke." Gurowka and Boyd headed out the front door and did not come near us. After chatting for a few minutes, the women informed me that both Boyd and Gurowka had voted against me, but I had received the votes of the two women and the Sport Canada consultant, Ray Allard. The women were clear in suggesting the "boys" weren't happy. They went onto tell me further about being pretty sure Mazinke was behind it, and Gurowka supported him, while Boyd did not really agree with them but was afraid to go against Harvey's wishes.

Not only did I not hear from Boyd that evening, but I did not hear from him, period. I went back to Vancouver, and the following Monday, I talked to John MacLeod and explained to him what had happened. He reluctantly told me more. Apparently, Ralph Boyd contacted Elsie and Aileen following the meeting and told them clearly that the CCA could not accept the decision made on April 22, and there was going to be a need to discuss the matter further. The women dug in their heels and told Boyd the decision had been made and it would not be changed. John indicated to me that it was a standoff, and he did not know what was going to happen next.

In July of 1985 John MacLeod announced he would retire from the position of general manager of the CCA in July of 1986.

April ended, and May began, but still no movement by anyone. Ralph Boyd, before all this, talked to me quite often, but there was not a word from him. John MacLeod was well aware of what was going on and kept me pretty much informed. There was a Curl Canada meeting scheduled for Ottawa toward the end of May, and it was decided the committee would reconvene at that time to resolve the stalemate. I was part of the meetings that would take place on May 24 and 25, and I remember the tension in the room being pretty high, as Boyd, Gurowka, Crosby, and MacLean were all in the same room as me. The Curl Canada meetings ended Saturday morning, and John told me that the hiring committee would reconvene its meeting around one p.m. on Saturday afternoon.

From what I was told, the meeting started with some early fireworks, and the standoff continued. The women and Ray Allard were still firmly in my corner, while Gurowka and Boyd were pushing hard for the person who was the executive director of badminton.

After about an hour, Ray Allard from Sport Canada apparently left the meeting after telling the group he was not going to interfere with their decision and did not want any part of it. The arguing continued and the headhunter finally suggested that since the group could not agree on one of the people from the top three on the short list, they should look deeper into the pool and consider the person short listed in fourth, fifth, or sixth place. Upon review, it was discovered that Earle Morris was number five on the short list and lived in Ottawa. After discussion, all four agreed to call Earle and see if he might be available for a chat. Remember, it was now about four p.m. on Saturday afternoon. Boyd reached Earle and asked if he was still interested in the job and if he was could he come to downtown Ottawa for an interview. Morris suggested he was on his way to a function in Kingston but could be available for an interview on Sunday morning, if that would work.

The group reconvened the meeting at around ten a.m. Sunday, and the women gave in and agreed by noon to offer Earle a contract. The offer was accepted by Monday afternoon, as Boyd finally called me on Monday evening to advise that I had not been successful in my quest to become the general manager of the CCA. I guess he thought I might simply quit, so in the call, he offered an olive branch, suggesting that I didn't want to move to Ottawa anyway, and he wanted me to consider a new job title, which would be director of competitions and media relations. I'm not sure Boyd even consulted other members of the board or Earle Morris with his offer, but by the time Earle came on board, he was informed by Boyd that my job responsibilities had changed slightly and were more directed toward the major championships. However, my reporting responsibilities now turned toward the general manager and not the board, which was where Mazinke wanted things to go. I was okay with the move because it would allow me to continue with the organization of curling as a demonstration at the 1988 Olympics and my work within curling in Canada would continue. I doubt that Mazinke or Gurowka were happy with what Boyd had done, but there was nothing they could do about it for now, at least. I received a letter from the CCA president-elect, Jerry Muzika from Charlottetown, in June, suggesting that he would like a summary from me each month indicating what I was doing and where I was planning to travel. I felt this strange, since starting in July, I would be working directly under Earle Morris. I think I filed one report to Muzika, and the whole thing faded away. It was obvious that the directive did not come from Muzika.

Earle Morris had recently retired from the military and had skipped team Ontario at the 1985 Brier in Moncton, so Earle and I knew each other. In addition, I had toured to the Canadian Forces Base at Lahr, Germany, in 1983 to direct an instruction program along with Garry DeBlonde, and Earle had been the military officer from Canada assigned to accompanying us to Germany. From my experience with Earle, I found him to be a likeable guy and initially we did not have any issues. I did, however, wonder if he had any idea of the process that had taken place for him to get the job, and to this day, I still don't

Earle Morris became the third general manager of the Canadian Curling Association in July of 1986.

know the answer to that question. The fall of '86 went okay and so did spring 1987, but in July '87, I received an ultimatum that was the beginning of the end of things between Earle and me. By July 1, 1988, I would be required to live in Ottawa and work out of the CCA/Curl Canada office. I was shocked to some degree, after Ralph Boyd had told me there was never going to be a need for me to live in Ottawa. But Ralph was no longer on the board. I knew pretty much where the directive had come from, and it wasn't Earle.

In the early fall, friction developed between Earle and me. Things came to a head at a board meeting in Ottawa in November 1987. A faction of the CCA board and all the CLCA board were not happy with how Earle had acquired the position, and to a large degree saw him as an extension of Mazinke and Gurowka. Two members of the CCA board, Ed Steeves and Don MacLeod, were not in support of Earle, but they were probably more opposed to Mazinke and Gurowka. A couple of things happened at that meeting that painted Earle into a corner and, for the most part, made it difficult for him moving forward. In addition, I advised the CCA and CLCA boards that if I was going to be required to live in Ottawa to maintain my position with curling, I would be finished as of July 1, 1988. The majority of the CCA/CLCA board agreed with me, further undermining Earle. Again, this decision was not as much against Earle as it was opposing Mazinke and Gurowka.

The Olympics were held in Calgary in February, and I spent a month at the Games working for OCO as the director of technical operations for curling, under the direction of my friend and confidant, Ray Kingsmith. Earle was there, along with most of the CCA/CLCA board members, but I did not see much of them because I was at a different hotel and pretty busy. In addition to working for OCO, I was doubling up as the media attaché to the curling venue for the Canadian Olympic Association. I travelled directly from Calgary to Fredericton, New Brunswick, for the Scotties, and from there to Chicoutimi, Quebec, for the Brier. In both cases, Earle was there, and I chatted with him about various things. Everything seemed fine. However, at the Brier, tension grew, and it became obvious to me, after a couple of days of the CCA meetings at the Brier, that Earle was falling further to the back of the line. On Thursday, March 10, the CCA AGM was held, and things seemed somewhat normal. However, when I woke up Friday morning, there was a letter shoved under my door. As I later found out, the same letter went under the door of every staff and board member in the hotel. It was a letter from Earle, which clearly stated that effective immediately, he was resigning as the general manager of the CCA. I think most of us were shocked, yet we knew Earle had been backed into a corner where there was only one way out. I always felt bad for Earle because he entered into a situation from day one that was almost impossible to win as he became the man in the middle between feuding board members.

Things continued as normal for the next few months, with each of us continuing with our specific jobs and reporting directly to the board. Mazinke became the past president on the men's side, and Gurowka moved into the president's chair. On the women's side, Marilyn Barraclough became president. Barraclough and Gurowka headed up a hiring committee for a new general manager. I received a call from Marilyn, asking me if I was interested or might consider applying for the general manager's job. We had a lengthy discussion, and at the end, I suggested I might consider the job if it were offered to me, but that was not an option, so I passed. I had absolutely no interest in repeating the drama I had experienced in the spring of 1986.

The job was advertised, and through a comedy of errors, no one applied who anyone on either the CCA or CLCA felt was qualified. Somewhere along the line, an application from Dave Parkes had been misplaced, but it was found and he was offered the job. Parkes had worked for me as one of the Brier's head officials, so he was known to many of the board members. Later in the summer of 1988, he was offered the job, but he initially declined the offer. Within a few hours, Garry DeBlonde was offered the job through a phone call from Gurowka. DeBlonde told Gurowka he wanted a day to think about it. In the meantime, before DeBlonde got back to Gurowka, Parkes changed his mind and asked if the job were still available to him. Gurowka said yes, and Parkes moved from his position as the director of recreation at Morden, Manitoba, to Ottawa to fill the GM position. There is an entire story of the nineteen-year working relationship between Parkes and me, but that is for discussion at another time.

CHAPTER 20

The Olympic Plan Begins for Canada

IN THE FALL of 1984, the board of directors of the CCA/CLCA agreed to experiment with the selection of teams to represent Canada at the 1988 Olympics, subject to funding from Labatt and Sport Canada. Garry DeBlonde and I had both put forward the case that we needed to make the approach fair, and in addition to accepting actual teams into the trials, we also needed to provide individual curlers the opportunity to be part of the Games. An ad hoc committee was established, known as the National Team Program Committee (NTPC), which would be responsible for creating and implementing the Olympic selection process. The committee consisted of CCA Vice President Harvey Mazinke (chairman), CLCA Vice President Dot McRae (vice-chairman), National Coach Garry DeBlonde, Dr. Art Quinney (physiologist), Dr. Vera Pezer (former four-time

The National Team Program Committee (NTPC) held its first meeting in April of 1986 to discuss how curling teams for the 1988 Olympics would be selected. From the left, Ron Anton, Art Quinney, Garry DeBlonde, Vera Pezer and Warren Hansen.

Canadian champion and psychologist), Ron Anton (two-time Brier champion and national course conductor), and myself (the first technical director of curling, national course conductor, and member of the national coaching core).

The first official meeting of the NTPC happened in Calgary on the weekend of April 13, 1985. A lot of discussion initially took place regarding funding that would be required to operate the trials and train the teams for the '88 Games. It was agreed that the approach should be to develop A, B, and C plans regarding areas of potential funding. Sport Canada might only supply partial funds, and then it would be necessary to revert to a different plan. If sufficient funds could not be raised the plan would be revised. In addition, an application for official medal status needed to be made to the IOC prior to January 1986, which would be the ICF's responsibility.

By early 1986, the funding was given the green light from Labatt and Sport Canada. The final budget for the project $287,000, with $240,000 coming from outside funding.

It was also agreed in the meeting that team selection for the trials would involve an eight-team playoff for both men and women. The first Canadian Olympic Curling Trials would take place in the spring of 1987 at the Max Bell Arena. The eight trials teams for each gender would, however, be selected from a combination of the traditional selection methods, as well as a series of training and selection camps. The traditional process would involve the following teams.

Men's Division	Women's Division
87 Labatt Brier winner	87 Hearts winner
86 Labatt Brier winner	86 Hearts winner
87 Brier team	87 Hearts team
87 World Junior team	87 Junior women's champions

The '87 Labatt Brier and '87 Hearts teams would be a team chosen by the Olympic team head coach and a selection committee from the best competitors at that event, excluding the winning teams. If the '86 and '87 winners were the same teams, then the '87 runner-up team will be selected. By the summer of 1985, it was decided it wouldn't be feasible to have junior teams as part of the trials, so it was determined to take the runner-up teams from the 1987 Brier and Hearts. It was also decided that the third team from both the Hearts and the Brier would be a selection made by the national coaching committee.

Regional Training Camps

Three or four of the training camps were planned for the fall of 1986, with the possible locations being Moncton, Toronto, Winnipeg, and Kelowna. Numbers invited to each camp would be dependent on registered curlers in each province. If four regional camps were held, a total of 400 athletes from across Canada would be involved (200 male and 200 female). The following points were noted.

- Flexibility would be used as to which camps athletes attended. For example, an athlete from Kenora might attend a camp held in Manitoba rather than Ontario.
- Thirty-two male and thirty-two female athletes would be selected from the four camps.
- The athletes selected would attend a national training camp to be held in November 1986.
- The best sixty-four athletes in Canada would be selected for the national training camp. The same number of curlers would not necessarily be selected from each regional camp.
- The CCA and CLCA could invite a limited number of athletes to camps in addition to those chosen by associations.
- It would be advantageous if regional camps and national camps were to all occur in the fall of 1986. This would provide more time to plan the camps and afford the provincial associations more opportunity to select their athletes and access funding

sources. Media interest would also be enhanced. This would also allow the selected teams an opportunity to compete together.

National Training Camp

- The national training camp would be held in the late fall of 1986 (well before playdown season starts).
- Sixty-four players (thirty-two male and thirty-two female) would attend.
- A total of four male and four female teams will be chosen, with alternatives.

Training Camps and Assessment Procedures

The regional and national camps would be designed to emphasize the training aspect of the elite athletes. This would be of benefit to the curling athletes and an attractive aspect of the Olympic program. The idea was also to help develop a process and a body of knowledge to assist in training programs for elite curlers into the future.

The second aspect of the camps would be to provide an assessment procedure for the selection of Canada's Olympic athletes. Some criteria for the selection process were as follows:

- curling skills
- curling accomplishments
- knowledge of the game
- biographical information
- physical fitness characteristics
- demonstrated willingness to train for the Olympic team
- psychological assessment
- coachability

For all the athletes involved, it was determined the assessment would be of benefit going forward since they would become fully aware of their strengths and weaknesses. Teams already selected for the trials before the training camps would be invited to attend a separate training camp to have the opportunity to benefit from the assessment.

The committee, through discussion, felt there were a number of advantages to the process that was finally agreed to, which included:

- All Olympic-calibre athletes would have more than one chance to qualify for the trials: national championship success or training camps.
- The process would also ensure every high-performance athlete would have an opportunity to compete in the trials, even if they did not win the Brier or Scotties in the years leading up to the Olympics.
- With teams able to qualify through two different paths, it would be possible to compare both methods to determine the relative strengths of each.
- The current selection method will still be part of the process, considering it has produced a number of excellent champions over the years.
- Initiation of a new and innovative (for curling) method of selection, which could prove to be of great value for the future. It provides an opportunity to explore a new idea for curling.
- The CCA/CLCA would be assured of having sixteen world-class teams in the Olympic Trials.
    - This should provide a much better likelihood that two of the best teams would represent Canada at the Olympics.
- A new body of knowledge would emerge with the development of the training camps and skills assessment techniques.
- The training camp concept could be effectively directed toward junior training and development programs across Canada.

- The new system would stimulate interest amongst curlers, in general.

Athlete Application Process to Attend a Regional Camp

The committee developed a set of guidelines to determine the process that each team and athlete would need to go through to register for a regional camp. This was the process decided on:

- Individuals and or teams could apply to provincial/territorial associations.
- A set of guidelines would be developed and sent to each association with criteria for choosing athletes.
- Possibly 200 male and 200 female athletes would be chosen to attend three or four regional camps.
- Each province would set up a committee to choose athletes from that province. The committee might consist of one person recommended by the CCA/CLCA, two qualified coaches, and a person from the association.
- The associations would be encouraged to stress a youth element in their selection because. the camps would also be looking to the future, to a large degree.

Team Support Staff

The committee held a discussion about the staff requirements for each regional camp as well as the two teams finally selected to represent Canada at the Olympics. The committee recommended the following:

- For the regional camps, one head coach, six assistant coaches, a sport psychologist, and the required administrators should be named by the fall of 1985.

- The support staff for the Olympics that should be named by the spring of 1987 would include a head coach (act as manager), two assistant coaches, team psychologist, and possibly a physiotherapist.

During the summer and early fall of 1985, discussions took place between the committee members until the second meeting was held in November 1985 in Edmonton. The conclusions of the Edmonton meeting were as follows:

Procedures for Provincial/Territorial Selection of Athletes for the Camps

On December 5, 1985, a letter was sent to all provincial/territorial associations regarding their nominations of athletes to one of two Olympic selection camps scheduled for the fall of 1986.

- Athletes nominated must be of Olympic or world-championship calibre.
- Selection was to be based on the best and most promising athletes.
- Selection could be made of entire teams, or team units (i.e., lead, second, third and skip), or individual curlers.
- Nominations to the camps would be based on the following criteria, listed in order of importance.

    1. recent international competitive experience at world championship level
    2. top three place finishing in Canadian championships
    3. multiple recent provincial men's or women's champions
    4. outstanding individual performance at recent Canadian men's or women's championships
    5. recent outstanding performance at major bonspiels

6. multiple recent outstanding performances at final provincial-level play in men's or women's championships

- Applicants were to have a team position declared (some flexibility would be applied by a national selection committee; for example, a player designated as a second could be selected in the lead position as well).
- Of all nominations received by all provincial associations, sixty-four male and sixty-four female athletes would be invited to attend one of two national camps. Selection would be made by a national committee based on the six aforementioned criteria. Selection would be based on curling excellence.
- If selected, each athlete must be prepared to commit the time necessary to properly prepare in the areas defined by the national coaching staff, which would. include skill development, psychological preparation, and physical preparation.
- The committee also recommended that each association form a committee to select its athletes. The following groups would be included in the committee structure: coach, competitive curler, and provincial association representative.
- Provincial associations would submit all athletes' names to the national office by March 31, 1986, if they were selected to attend one of the national camps.
- Associations would submit detailed biographical information on each nominated athlete.
- All expenses incurred by the athlete, if invited to a national camp, would be borne by the association or the athlete.

Selection Procedures for Athletes to Attend Camps

The selection committee appointed. included Ron Anton, Vera Pezer, Art Quinney, Garry DeBlonde, Dot MacRae, Harvey Mazinke, and myself.

- Detailed selection parameters would be established by January 31, 1986.
- Selection parameters and names of all nominated athletes would be sent to the selection committee by April 15, 1986. The committee would then meet in early May 1986 to complete selection.
- An attempt would be made to select equal numbers for each position.
- All athletes attending the camps would be provided with the following information: camp's structure and procedures, resource material in areas of skill development, psychological preparation, physical preparation, diet, etc. Athletes would also be given access to resource material and resource person, if desired.
- All athletes attending camps would be required to sign an agreement similar to the ones signed at the Brier and Scott Tournament of Hearts. The agreement specified the willingness to commit the necessary time for training, willingness to be coached, respect for sponsor agreements, and replacement, if necessary.

Criteria were developed to determine the athletes that could be selected from each province/territory to attend the camps, based on a score. This was calculated as follows:

1. Competitive curling background—70% of the total
2. Program commitment—15% of total
3. Sport/fitness background—15% of total

1. Competitive Curling Background Since 1980

1.1. International	-	*Maximum 15 points*
Appearances	-	*Once = 5 points (2 pts for Juniors)*
	-	*Twice or more = 10 points (5 pts Juniors)*
Finish	-	*First = 5 points*
	-	*Second = 3 points*
	-	*Third = 1 point*

1.2 Canadians	-	*Maximum 20 points*
Appearances	-	*Once = 5 points (2 pts for Jr & Mixed)*
	-	*Twice or more = 10 points (5 pts for Jr & Mixed)*
Finish	-	*First = 10 points (5 for Jr & Mixed)*
		Second = 5 points (2 for Jr & Mixed)
		Third = 3 points (1 for Jr & Mixed)
		Points may be assigned for finishing positions and for appearance between given values, depending upon frequency of being in the competition (i.e., two second-place finishers may merit more than the 5 or 2 points assigned).

1.3. Provincial Playdowns	-	*Maximum 15 points*
Appearances	-	*Once = 3 points (1 if Jr & Mixed)*
	-	*Twice or more = 5 points (2 if Jr & Mixed)*
Finish	-	*First = 10 points (5 if Jr & Mixed)*
	-	*Second = 5 points (2 if Jr & Mixed)*
	-	*Third = 3 points (1 if Jr & Mixed)*
		Lower finish points may be assigned for frequent appearance teams.

1.4. Success in Bonspiels	-	*Maximum of 20 points*
		1985 – 86 season of major bonspiels – 0 to 5 points

1984 – 85 season of major bonspiels
– 0 to 5 points
1983 – 84 season of major bonspiels
– 0 to 5 points
Points to be based on performance, consistency, and bonspiel category (A, B, or C)
A maximum of 5 points may be assigned by considering factors as:
(These additional points are for A bonspiels only)
1) Number of major events entered,
2) Consistency of finish,
3) Success in "top 3" events.

2. Program Commitment

A maximum of 15 points awarded on the basis of coachability (5 max), willingness to commit time and energy to the program (5 max), and receptibility to a program of physical, psychological and skill preparation (5 max).

3. Sport and Fitness Background

A maximum of 15 points, of which 10 may be assigned to individuals with a strong, broad background in individual or team competitive sports other than curling. Up to 15 points may be assigned for personal fitness or recreational sport activity.

CHAPTER 21

Onto the Camps and Trials

Plan for National Camps

A final decision was made on the regional camps, and while it was initially felt there could be three or four, it was finally determined that two camps would be held, one in the east and one in the west, in the fall of 1986. It was also determined that a total of sixty-four athletes (thirty-two male and thirty-two female) would be invited to each camp.

Western Camp	October 31 to November 3	Edmonton
Eastern Camp	November 14 to November 17	Toronto

The clubs selected for the camps would be required to have at least six sheets of ice and complete club facilities for the four-day camps. In each case, the camps would have two groups. Group one would participate Friday, Saturday, and Sunday, while group two would participate Saturday, Sunday, and Monday.

The elements to be covered in the camps were discussed, and in the end, it was agreed the following would be involved in each camp:

- a delivery evaluation (using a checklist); drills such as hit, draw, peel drills, etc., would be used to test for flexibility and consistency
- a sweeping evaluation (judgment and technique)
- points curling as a method of evaluation
- a mini game where the coaches would structure the teams
- a video analysis could be an option but requires further investigation
- a discussion between a coach and a team to discuss their preparation process, which might be done in log-book form
- other areas that could be involved but would not form part of the selection criteria, such as a psychological and/or a fitness and nutrition assessment

A pilot camp would be necessary to test all the camp components. The pilot camp would involve twenty male and twenty female athletes, who would be run through a two-day trial camp in the summer of 1986. All the athletes involved would come from the local area and would probably be junior curlers.

From the final camps, a total of four teams (men's and women's) would be selected from the camps and invited to compete in the 1987 Olympic Trials. The final selection would not necessarily be two teams from each camp, and selection would be based on the best athletes. The selection could involve complete teams or individuals could be chosen to be part of a team put together by the selection committee. The final team selections would be completed shortly after the completion of the second camp.

To assist at the camps and to select athletes after the camp, a number of coaches were also named, including Dr. Vera Pezer, Dr. Art Quinney, Ron Anton, Garry DeBlonde, Gerry Peckham, Jim Ursel, Joyce Myers, Rhonda Wood, and Keith Reilly.

The national coaches for the 1987 training camps for the 1988 Olympics. Back row from the left, Keith Reilly, Ron Anton, Art Quinney, Jim Waite, Gerry Peckham and Warren Hansen. Front row from the left, Joyce Myers, Jim Ursel, Garry DeBlonde, Rhonda Wood and Vera Pezer.

National Coach

In February 1986, Sport Canada agreed it would fund a national coach for curling over a two-year period from July 1986 until July 1988. The national coach would oversee the entire Olympic program and report directly to the general manager and the CCA/CLCA. The national coach would assume the responsibility of training the Canadian Olympic curling teams, as well as serving a similar role with the Canadian teams at all world championships. While the position was initially for two years, it was assumed that if curling were to acquire official Olympic medal sport status following the 1988 Games, the national coach position would continue.

It seemed obvious that either Garry DeBlonde or I would assume the job, but the question was which one. Garry turned to me and suggested I should have the first option for the job, and after thinking it over carefully, I suggested things would probably work better if he took the position. We agreed, and in the summer of 1986, Garry officially became the national coach for Curl Canada and the CCA/CLCA.

Each Olympic team would be led by an assistant coach appointed by the national coach in conjunction with the NTCP. If one of the teams invited to the trials had a club coach, the national coach would work with the club coach until after the trials. After the trials, the national coach will assign an assistant coach to each of the Canadian teams.

A number of other important meetings took place after January 1, 1986. One of those meetings was between Jack Lynch, who was then the technical director of the Canadian Olympic Association (COA), and Greg Mathieu, who was then the director of operations for the COA.

A major part of that discussion was around the lobbying required for curling to have a chance of medal status following the Games. The key people from the Canadian Olympic community would be Frank King (chair of the OCO), Dick Pound, and Jim Worrall, the two Canadian delegates to the IOC. Lynch pointed out if Pound and Worrall were only lukewarm toward curling getting into the Olympics, it would be a problem. Lynch felt Pound would be onside because his father was a curler and had been a member of the Montreal Thistle Club. It was also stressed that the ICF needed to have all of its members lobby the Olympic Association in each of their countries. In addition, the ICF needed to begin direct communication with the IOC and request an in-person hearing.

Greg Mathieu indicated the ICF would also need to start communication with the IOC Program Commission ASAP. The program commission is the IOC committee responsible for recommending to the IOC executive whether a sport should be considered for medal status. The site for the 1992 Olympics was to be named in October 1986, and the 1992 committee would need to have some idea whether curling was in or out by that date. Mathieu also felt curling would have a difficult time getting into the Olympics because the sport was not well known by most IOC members. The conclusion was that the ICF had a lot of work to do... fast!

1987 Canadian Curling Olympic Trials

Dates—Monday, April 20, to Saturday, April 25, 1987

Playoff Format—Eight-team round robin with the top three teams in the playoff

Draw—Four draws each day, Monday to Thursday. Round robins will be completed by three p.m. Thursday. Tiebreakers scheduled for Thursday evening and Friday morning. Finals scheduled for Saturday morning and/or afternoon. Exact scheduling as governed by television and host committee requirements.

The process was now ready to get underway, and the overall rationale behind the final decision on the process could be summarized as follows:

- Give all the game's best players an opportunity to participate in the Olympics, individuals as well as teams.
- In anticipation of medal status in 1992, develop a system of selecting athletes and teams that would meet acceptance by the Canadian Olympic Committee.
- In anticipation of medal status, develop a system for carding athletes that would have to start immediately upon being granted medal status.

In the spring of 1986, every potential camp attendee, except teams skipped by Ed Lukowich and Marilyn Darte (Canadian champions in 1986), was sent a camp invitation for the fall of 1986.

Camp Invitation

On September 17, 1986, National Coach Garry DeBlonde sent out an invitation to the training camp attendees.

From Friday, October 31, to Monday, November 3, the first of two Olympic selection camps was slated for the Shamrock Curling Club in

Edmonton. The second camp, involving another thirty-two men and thirty-two women curlers, was scheduled for the Mississauga Golf and Country Club from Friday, November 14, to Monday, November 17.

In total 128 curlers will attend the two camps (64 men and 64 women) that are aimed at selecting eight teams (four men's and four women's) for the Labatt's National Curling Trials slated for Calgary, April 19th to 25th, 1987.

All athletes from B.C., Alberta and Saskatchewan will attend the Western Camp. All athletes from Ontario and from all provinces east of Ontario will attend the Eastern Camp. Manitoba athletes will be divided east and west so that numbers are the same at both camps.

The camps for all athletes will be three days long with the times each day being approximately 8:00 am until 10:00 pm. Each day will have three sessions and each athlete will have rest time between each session.

The following is an example of how the schedule will work. The eight leads will be designated numbers A1 to A8. Seconds will be labeled B1 to B8, thirds C1 to C8 and skips D1 to D8. Following is an example, the women's second designated as B4 would follow these activities:

Saturday	*8:30 – 9:00 am*	*Orientation to Program*
	9:30 – 10:15 am	*Interview and Practice*
	10:15 – 11:30 am	*Peel Drill*
	19:00 – 20:15 pm	*Takeout Drill*
	20:15 – 22:00 pm	*Mini Games*
Sunday	*12:00 – 13:15 pm*	*Fitness Test*
	13:15 – 14:30 pm	*Video Testing*
	18:15 – 19:30 pm	*Fitness Feedback*
	19:30 – 21:15 pm	*Mini Games*
Monday	*8:30 – 9:45 am*	*Points Curling*

It has been determined that the eight teams selected from the camps in some cases will be made up of individual players that have played together before as units or they may be made of individual athletes who have not played together before as a team. The camp coaches will make all the final decisions on the teams chosen.

Camp Coaches

Garry DeBlonde	*National Coach*
Warren Hansen	*BC (Curl Canada, Director, Marketing, P/R and Competitions)*
Art Quinney	*Alberta (National Team Program Committee—NTCP)*
Ron Anton	*Alberta (NTCP)*
Vera Pezer	*Saskatchewan (NTCP)*
Jim Ursel	*Manitoba*
Rhonda Wood	*Saskatchewan*
Joyce Myers	*Nova Scotia*
Jim Waite	*Ontario*
Keith Reilly	*Ontario*
Gerry Peckham	*BC*

Camp Attendees

Western Camp—Men

British Columbia

Brent Giles
Glen Jackson
Steve Skillings
Greg Monkman
Allan Carlson
Ron Thompson
Alan Roemer
Brad Giles

Alberta

Pat Ryan
Paul Gowsell
Randy Ferbey
Don Walchuk
Donald McKenzie

Saskatchewan

Eugene Hritzuk
Kirk Ziola

Manitoba

Mike Riley
Bob Ursel

Randy Woytowich
Lyle Muyres
Robert Miller
James Packet
Nick Paulsen
Craig Muyres
Art Paulsen
John Grundy
Garth Muyres

Mark Olson
Brent Mendella
Russ Wookey
Gerald Chick
Dan Hildebrand

Western Camp—Women

British Columbia
Linda Moore
Lindsay Sparkes
Pat Sanders
Christine Stevenson
Debbie Jones
Louise Herlinveaux

Alberta
Susan Seitz
Judy Lukowich
Judy Erickson
Sandra Rippel
Penny Ryan
Betty McCracken
Allison Earl
Jennifer Buchanan

Saskatchewan
Nancy Kerr
Lori McGeary
Kathy Fahlman
Gillian Thompson
Sandra Schmirler
Chris Gevais
Kimberley Armbruster
Jan Betker
Sheila Kavanagh

Manitoba
Karen Fallis
Darcy Kirkness
Patti Vande
Barbara Kirkness
Faye Irwin
Lynn Fallis
Barbara Fetch
Kathie Ellwood
Jackie Rintoul

Eastern Camp—Women

Ontario
Cathy Shaw
Carol Thompson
Alison Goring
Pam Leavitt
Kristin Holman
Susan Bell
Beverley Mainwaring
Cheryl McPherson

Nova Scotia
Colleen Jones
Virginia Jackson
Penny Larocque
Kay Smith
Monica Jones
Catherine Caudle
Joan Hutchinson
Susan Robinson
Barbara Jones Gordon
Margaret Cutcliffe
Mari-Anne Vautour
Stephanie Jones
Mary Mattatall

New Brunswick
Denise Lavigne
Sheri Smith

Newfoundland
Debbie Porter

Prince Edward Island
Kim Dolan
Kathy Gallant

Manitoba
Chris More
Laurie Allen
Connie Laliberte
Janet Harvey
Corinne Peters
Janet Arnott

Eastern Camp—Men

Ontario
Al Hackner

Newfoundland and Labrador
Jeff Thomas

Ed Werenich
Earle Morris
Russ Howard
John Base
Paul Savage
Rick Lang
Glenn Howard
Lovel Lord
William Adams
Ian Tetley
John Kawaja
Tom Wilson
Dave Merklinger
James Adams
William Fletcher
Pat Perroud
Neil Harrison
Geoffrey Cunningham
John Allan
Neil Young

Quebec
Dennis Marchand
Kevin Adams
Malcolm Turner

Nova Scotia
Steve Ogden
Peter MacPhee
Andrew Dauphinee
David Wallace

Manitoba
John Bubbs
Dave Iverson
Clif Lenz

The male athletes that participated in the Eastern Olympic Trials Training Camp that was held in Mississauga, Ontario in November of 1987.

The second and final camp was completed on November 17 in Mississauga. The camps were felt to be successful, and it seemed the curlers enjoyed participating. However, it was a very new and foreign approach for curling, and not everyone was totally comfortable with the process. Every player invited was aware that two avenues were available to qualify for the trials. Finish on top of the 1987 Brier and Scotties, or be chosen to play through the camps. Every curler invited also knew the camps were going to involve testing and evaluating. Some players—such as Bernie Sparkes, Kerry Burtnyk, Rick Lang, and Al Hackner—didn't agree with the process and, as a result, didn't attend either of the camps. One team, however, skipped by Ed Werenich was not fully prepared to accept whatever verdict the NTPC handed down.

As previously mentioned, the assessment of each player at the camps was based on a figure of 100. The number was heavily weighted toward three-year curling performance, shot-making assessment from the camp, and program commitment (85%), with a small number for fitness and psychological testing (15%). The physiological and psychological aspects were more of a fact-finding exercise than anything else because there wasn't any history or known stats regarding how the top curlers might perform in either aspect.

On the morning of November 18, 1986, the NTPC met in Toronto to evaluate the records of the participants in the two camps and to launch the process of selecting the teams for the trials. A number of items were discussed prior to making the selections, and the following was agreed upon:

- *The first and second place teams at the Brier and Hearts will compete at the Trials and no player changes can be made on any of those teams. If a player or players have already qualified through the camps, they will have a choice of which team they will play. All camp selected players will be made aware of this decision.*
- *All curlers selected for the Trials from the camps will compete at the Trials. This is the case even if some of their selected teammates qualify through the Brier or Hearts.*

- *The NTPC will select a third team from the Hearts and Brier. The team will be chosen from all of the competitors at the Hearts and Brier excluding those who place first or second. This could be an intact team or four individual curlers. The third team picked from the Hearts and Brier could have athletes who have already qualified through the camps or the Darte and Lukowich teams (already qualified by winning the 1986 Hearts and Brier). In this case more athletes would be chosen from the camps.*
- *Alternates named from the camps will not be informed that they are on the first alternate team. The NTPC will make the alternate selections, if necessary, after the 1987 Hearts and Brier.*
- *A total of four teams from the men's and women's divisions will be selected to compete at the Trials. In addition, 16 men's and 16 women's alternates were selected in the event that more curlers are needed after the completion of the Hearts and Brier.*
- *If an alternate is required for the Trials the National Coach will work with the team involved to make a selection from the alternate list.*
- *Any change in the order of players on any selected team must be done in consultation with the National Coach.*
- *NTPC members cannot coach Trials teams prior to or during the Trials. NTPC members could be available to assist any of the Trials teams along the way.*
- *Six of the camp coaches are available to coach any of the Trials teams if they decide to.*
- *Each Trials team will be provided a list of available Level II coaches.*

During the selections, a problem came to the table. Everyone knew Ed Werenich had not taken the trials very seriously, and his results were dismal, while the other three members of his team had done quite well.

I first met Werenich when I played in the 1974 Brier in London, Ontario. He was second on the Ontario team skipped by Paul Savage. Ed, to me, was just another Brier player, and we did not pay much attention to each other. It was an interesting Brier finish for our Alberta team, which lost to Ontario in the round robin. I had previously written about the interesting finish we found ourselves in when we playing Jim Ursel of Quebec and Savage tangled with Larry McGrath of Saskatchewan. For us to win, we had to beat Ursel, and Savage needed to upset McGrath, and like clockwork, it happened and we became Brier champions.

The next time I saw Werenich was at the 1977 Brier in Montreal, where he was playing third for Savage, and the result for Ontario wasn't much better for the Ontario foursome than 1974. I was at the entire event, and if I had anything to say to Werenich, it was probably, "Hi"—maybe I got a reply and then again maybe I didn't... I don't really remember.

Camp coach Jim Waite (left) and camp participant Ed Werenich at the Eastern Camp in Mississauga, Ontario in November of 1987.

Labatt became the Brier sponsor in 1980, and in 1981, with the event in Halifax, Werenich was again representing Ontario, this time as skip. This was an innovative year for the Brier, as it was the first time any organized officiating was ever attempted. I was the head official for the CCA and in charge of orchestrating the entire on-ice operation. The Werenich team did not give us any problems. At the team meeting, I recall he made a gruff objection to the playoff system that had been put in place in 1980, but his objections did not go beyond the team meeting. However, Werenich (known by many as the Wrench) left his mark on the 1981 Brier, or maybe that should be the Ontario Curling Association (OCA). By the conclusion of the seventh draw on Tuesday afternoon, the Wrench had only picked up two wins in six tries. On Tuesday evening, the OCA took the Wrench and team to dinner prior to the annual Ontario/Northern Ontario party, which Ontario was called upon to host because of the 8–7 extra-end win by Al Hackner over Ontario. It became common knowledge that the dinner got well out of hand, with the Wrench attacking the OCA for spending more than $1,000 on a dinner while failing to provide his team with what he considered adequate financial support. Later in the evening, the Wrench arrived, heavily under the influence of the grape, at the annual Brier media party, to which the Brier participants are not normally invited. He climbed up onto a chair and further berated the OCA, in front of the media. No one was really amused, and finally some of the Wrench's friends from the *Ontario Curling Report* convinced him to get down from the chair and depart.

The balance of the Brier was uneventful for Werenich. He finished tied for third with a 7–4 record along with Saskatchewan and BC, and he lost the tie-breaker to Bob Ellert of Saskatchewan 6–5 in an extra end.

The 1983 Brier saw the emergence of Werenich again, but with a new team of third Paul Savage, second John Kawaja, and the only holdover from 1981, Neil Harrison, at lead. The curling world, especially those in Ontario, praised this team and referred to them as the super team, which had an enormous potential. Werenich had it all together on the ice this time, finishing the round robin in second place, easily disposing of BC's Bernie Sparkes in the semifinal and Alberta's Ed Lukowich in the final. Werenich was well behaved, and the championship was virtually uneventful.

From the Brier in Sudbury, Ontario, it was on to the world men's championship in Regina. The CCA designated me as the manager of the Werenich team. Most of the pre-event arrangements and the discussion during the championship were between Paul Savage and me. All in all, I probably didn't say two dozen words to the Wrench, and for the most part, we got along all right. I always liked Paul Savage, and over the years, we have got along well, and for that matter, I always liked John Kawaja and Neil Harrison.

On Friday, April 8, 1983, Werenich and his team were scheduled to arrive in Regina shortly after noon, and my flight did not touch down until around two p.m. I had made tentative arrangements with Savage to meet at the team hotel, the Sheraton, around three p.m. to review some of the procedures and CCA items of concern. I arrived at three p.m., but the "boys" did not, and by about four p.m., I managed to track down Larry McGrath, who was the Canadian team driver, and he gave me the good news. The boys were in the bar around the corner and really in no condition to discuss the finer points of world curling or the finer points of anything else, for that matter.

However, we finally had a meeting of sorts, and the Silver Broom got underway without any major incident. Things went well on ice and without incident until the fifth round on Tuesday afternoon—and the game against Steffan Hasselborg of Sweden. Werenich was struggling a bit and was in a four-way tie for second place at 3–1 with Hasselborg, Scotland and Norway. The game with Hasselborg is now part of curling folklore.

In the seventh end, Werenich walked over to Hasselborg and verbally threatened to place the working end of his broom firmly to a particular portion of Hasselborg's anatomy where the sun doesn't shine. Werenich had taken a reasonable delay to discuss a shot and clean broom corn debris from the ice left by the Swede's. Hasselborg, annoyed by the delay, gave the Wrench a little applause when he finally went to deliver his shot, and Werenich said his piece in response. The media jumped on it, and for the most part, Canadian fans and the Regina host committee were disgusted over the incident since Canada was the host country. The matter went one step further the following morning, when the Hasselborg team approached Werenich in the hotel restaurant to discuss the matter further. However, nothing developed, and the week continued with Werenich eventually defeating Keith Wendorf of West Germany in the final.

Werenich got it going again in 1984, and returned to the Brier in Victoria. However, before the Brier could even get underway, Werenich made his presence known to the CCA. In 1984, Joe Gurowka was the president of the OCA. It had been known for a while that Werenich did not like Gurowka. Who knows why? But for sure, there had to be a reason. Werenich sent his team driver to the CCA management meeting on the Friday afternoon before the start of the Brier with a message that was straightforward and simple: "If Joe Gurowka is sitting at the Ontario table at the CCA dinner this evening, my team will not attend." Rather than tell Werenich to take the next ferry out of town, the CCA bent to his demands and asked Gurowka to move to another table. Werenich was reasonably quiet for the balance of the Brier and struggled to a third-place tie with New Brunswick and Saskatchewan. He won tiebreakers with New Brunswick and Saskatchewan, and took out Ed Lukowich in the semi before falling victim to Mike Riley of Manitoba in the final.

After the 1984 Brier, no one in CCA circles really saw much of the Wrench prior to the Olympic camps in the fall of 1986.

By the end of the selection camps, the name Werenich certainly came to the table, and some interesting discussion followed. After a lot of differing opinions, everyone on the selection committee eventually agreed that Werenich had not made the cut. The whole thing had seemed to be a joke to him, and he did not take any aspect of it seriously. The physical and psychological aspects of the camps were never intended to be areas that determined whether an athlete would be invited to the trials. However, only one of the 128 curlers involved had a score of one out of ten in both categories... that would be Mr. Werenich. While his numbers on shot-making and three-year performance were okay, they certainly weren't great, and a number of other skips were definitely better. Meanwhile, all three members of his team—Paul Savage, John Kawaja, and Neil Harrison—had taken the process seriously and certainly did well enough to move forward. But the big problem was in the interviews conducted with all four team members. It was clear they were only interested in competing as a team.

A thought went through my mind. *Why did you guys even bother going through this process when you must have known Ed was not going to take it seriously?* From where I sat, we were painted into a corner... we were going to be damned if we did and damned if we didn't. I liked all three members of the team, but I had a hard time cutting Werenich any slack because he had certainly never cut me an inch of slack. The discussion within the committee went around and around. Although not a fan of Werenich's, the chairman insisted that we had to find a way to justify putting the whole team into the trials, while two of us on the committee argued otherwise. My comment was that Ed knew the rules coming in, and if he didn't make it by the rules we had developed, why in hell were we changing things to accommodate him? My thought was to give the other three players on the team a skip who earned the right for the position, and if the other three guys decided to not participate without Werenich, that would be their decision. Someone finally came up with a suggestion that made me choke. Werenich, along with two other curlers—Randy Ferbey and Paul Savage—had not attained a minimum fitness level of four. Maybe if we requested that all three of the curlers meet the minimum level of four by February 1, 1987, we could justify putting all three in the trials? Two of us spoke loudly against the idea, but slowly and surely, the other five committee members agreed to the idea. When the vote was taken, I voted against, and the final count was five in favour and two opposed. I can remember the comment that I made to this day. "We will all live to regret this decision."

So, it was final that Werenich, Savage, and Ferbey would be given until February 1, 1987, to meet the minimum fitness requirements. In each case, it meant, amongst other things, they would have to lose a few pounds. The difficulty for me was the fact that I was also the director of media relations, which meant I would become the face of this entire soon-to-be-nightmare. I knew a lot of people, including Werenich, would take direct aim at me and Garry DeBlonde because we were the two staff people on the selection committee.

I wrote the announcement that was set to be released on December 1, 1986, but the executive of the CCA had a management meeting scheduled for Winnipeg on the weekend prior, and because the three curlers involved were males, the men's association needed to approve the approach. Mazinke convinced the CCA board to exclude the fitness requirement from the media release on the trials, but the message did not get to me before the release was sent out. The following memo, issued by General Manager Earle Morris on December 4, 1986, explains what happened.

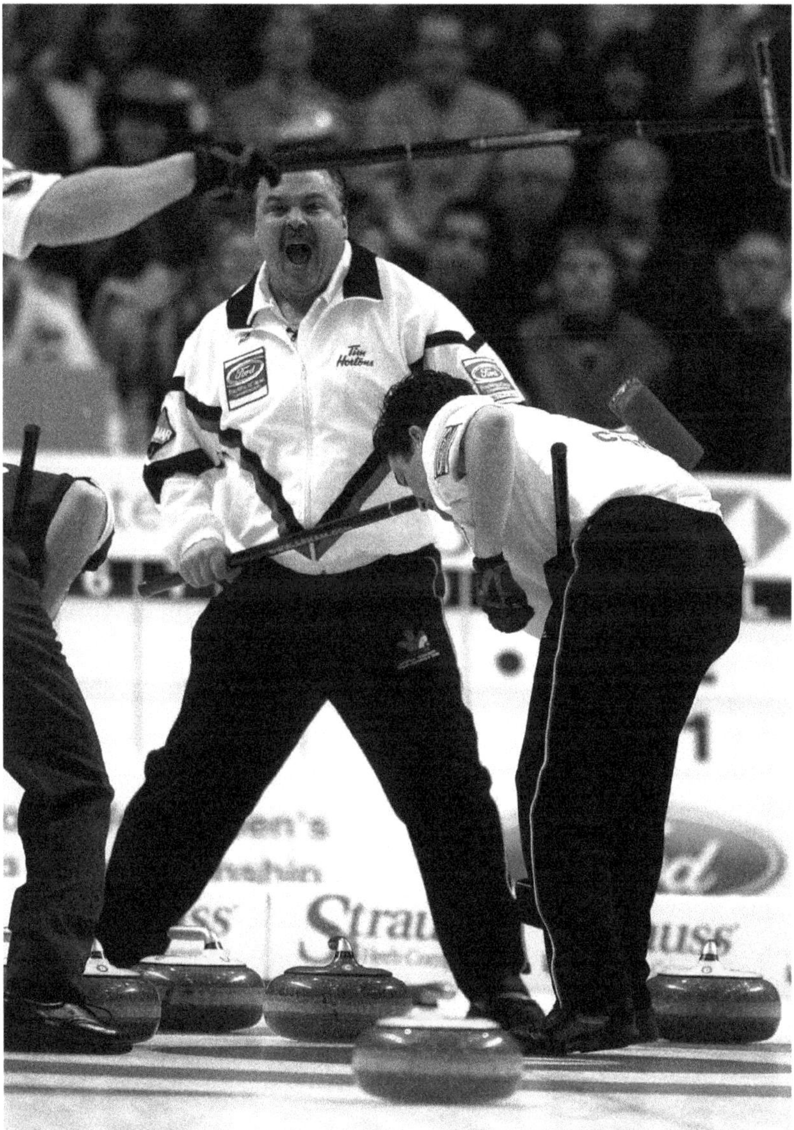

Randy Ferbey was put on a fitness program following the 1987 Camp in Mississauga. Ferbey went on to win six Briers and four world championships following the 1987 Trials. Ferbey celebrates during the 2005 world men's championship in Victoria, B.C.
Photo credit – Michael Burns Photography.

All CCA/CLCA Management

Press Release—Labatt's National Curling Trials

The attached press release which refers to the requirement for 10 of the male players to meet a minimum physical fitness standard by February 1, 1987, was released by our office to the media. The problem is it names those who are not fit; contrary to what had been agreed upon at our management meeting in Winnipeg, November 27–28, 1986, where it was agreed to deal with fitness in a more general sense.

The incident took place because the press release had been prepared prior to the management meeting so that it would be ready to go out on time when the Calgary announcement was made. Regrettably the staff were not advised to make changes as a result of the management meeting and consequently the original was released.

This oversight is regretted.

Yours sincerely,

Earle Morris
General Manager.

To say the least, all hell broke loose! The minute the story was out, the Toronto media were all over Savage and Werenich like a blanket. Savage showed a good deal of class about the matter, but Werenich showed little restraint, and his criticism was loud and long. To a large degree, I really couldn't blame him as the whole thing was a massive screw-up! National Coach Garry DeBlonde took the brunt of the attack from Werenich, but I received a fair share of the abuse. Other members of the selection committee were in the wilderness and escaped the storm. The worst media piece was telecast on the CTV documentary *W5*. Interviews with Werenich and DeBlonde were conducted in two separate locations. This allowed extensive editing to take place that painted the CCA in anything but a positive position. The controversy continued right up until February 6, 1987, the final dates for Werenich, Savage, and Ferbey to complete the physical assessment.

The interesting thing about this whole thing is a total of eleven curlers were fingered: the three who were named to the trials, and eight (seven men and one woman) who were named as alternates. This whole thing was aimed at justifying the naming of Werenich to the trials, and I guess, as the old saying goes, there is safety in numbers. The CCA management committee thought it could slip under the radar if they suggested eleven players had to meet a minimum fitness level rather than saying there was one concern, and that was Ed Werenich. Even if the media release that was sent out listing all eleven players had not named them, Werenich would still never have kept it secret because it was too much of an opportunity for him to pass up. Whacking at the CCA, who now had rendered themselves almost defenceless, was now easy for him. As this all unfolded, I thought back to the decision made by the selection committee and how much easier the whole thing would have been if Werenich had simply been denied an opportunity to participate because he did not meet the requirements. The other side of the coin was the curler who got cut out because the rules were bent to give Werenich access. The player who should have been named as the skip of the three Werenich players was Paul Gowsell of Calgary. The interesting thing about all of that was Gowsell knew it, and when I ran into him at the trials, he went up one side of me and down the other as to why he wasn't in the trials. All I could say was, "I know Paul, but I can't tell you why. Sorry."

The day of the announcement, February 6, I was attending the Canadian Juniors in Prince Albert, Saskatchewan, when Tom Slater of the Toronto Star called me on yet another matter to do with the Olympics. It seemed Pat Ryan and Ed Lukowich had numerous concerns about apparent rumours involving the contracts of athletes participating in the Olympic Games. They had heard that a) the CCA would completely control the Canadian Olympic curling teams, b) the CCA would take all the earnings of the Olympic teams in the fall of 1987, c) the Olympic teams would lose all endorsements to the CCA, and d) the Olympic teams would not be able to compete in the

1988 Scotties or the Labatt Brier. To calm the air, a few days later, Chairman Mazinke ensured all participants in the trials that a favourable contract would be negotiated with the winners.

Paul Savage, left and Ed Werenich were put on a fitness training program following the 1987 Olympic Trials selection camps. *Photo credit – Michael Burns Photography.*

However, before any of us could say much regarding any of these stories about the contract (most of which were idle rumours rather than fact), another story grabbed the limelight. On the same day, by coincidence, Werenich and Savage were given their final tests. We had the results in our hands by five p.m. ET, and it indicated that Werenich had lost nineteen pounds while Paul Savage was down seven, exactly half of what was required by the rules laid down. DeBlonde consulted Art Quinney (the selection committee physiologist) and Chairman Mazinke. Following that discussion, I reluctantly wrote the media release announcing that Savage, Werenich, and Ferbey were in the trials. Ferbey did very well, and later indicated, he was considering legal action against the CCA because he made the requirement while Savage and Werenich had not. Randy was more than justified in being pissed off!

The media release was as follows:

Werenich, Savage and Ferbey Meet Fitness Requirements

(Prince Albert) — It was announced today by Curl Canada National Coach, Garry DeBlonde that Ed Werenich and Paul Savage of Toronto along with Randy Ferbey of Edmonton achieved the fitness level requirement to be selected to the Labatt's National Curling Trials in Calgary, April 19–25, 1987.

"Ed lost 19 pounds and improved his flexibility, strength and aerobic capacity," said DeBlonde who is currently at the Canadian Juniors being held in Prince Albert, Saskatchewan. "Werenich did not attain the minimum requirement in two tests but his improvement was sufficient to be selected," he continued.

Paul Savage did not lose all the weight required but as with Werenich it was felt that Savage improved enough to continue as third for Werenich in the April Trials.

Randy Ferbey, third for Pat Ryan, achieved and surpassed all the fitness requirements.

All three curlers had been selected for the Labatt's National Curling Trials through the camps held last November but failed to pass the basic physical requirement. As a result all three were given until February 1, 1987, to meet an acceptable fitness level if they wished to participate in the Trials.

With the announcement, the final confirmation of the teams selected from the camps for the trials was confirmed, as follows:

Women

Linda Moore	Connie Laliberte	Colleen Jones	Chris More
Lindsay Sparkes	Janet Harvey	Kay Smith	Kathy Fahlman
Debbie Jones	Corinne Peters	Kim Dolan	Pat Sanders
Penny Ryan	Janet Arnott	Cathy Caudle	Louise Herlinveaux

Men

Pat Ryan	Ed Werenich	Eugene Hritzuk	Russ Howard
Randy Ferbey	Paul Savage	Ron Mills	Glenn Howard
Don Walchuk	John Kawaja	Ian Tetley	Denis Marchand
Don McKenzie	Neil Harrison	Bob Ursel	Bill Fletcher

Three teams would come from the Hearts/Brier. The first two would be easy because it simply involved the selection of the two finalist teams, but the third team was not as clear. It was left to the NTPC, and it could be a complete team or an all-star team selected by the committee.

The Hearts were held in Lethbridge, Alberta, and the decision on the three teams had some tension, but it was straightforward. Pat Sanders of BC and Kathie Ellwood of Manitoba met in the final, which put those two teams straight into the trials. Helen Tousignant of Quebec defeated Kathy Fahlman of Saskatchewan in a tie-breaker, so one might have thought that Quebec should have been the third team in from the Hearts; however, all three members of the Fahlman team—third Sandra Schmirler, second Jan Betker, and lead Sheila Schneider—were first-team all-stars, so the entire Saskatchewan team was selected as the third team from the Hearts. It all made sense.

The NTPC reconvened in Edmonton during the final weekend of the Brier. The main topic on the agenda was the selection of the third team from the Brier for the trials. After considerable deliberation, the final recommendations were made regarding the selection of the third team from the Brier. Newfoundland (Mark Noseworthy) was playing BC (Bernie Sparkes) in the Brier semifinal, and Russ Howard was in first place with a bye to the final. The other team in the mix was Quebec's Kevin Adams, who won six out of his first seven games before losing four in a row, including being defeated by Noseworthy. If Newfoundland won the semi, it was decided that a team would be created with Sparkes and BC third Armstrong, along with the Quebec front end of Don Reddick and Ian Journeaux. If BC won the semifinal, then the entire Quebec team of Kevin Adams and Malcolm Turner would join Reddick and Journeaux. The media was concerned about the all-star team selection process, but it seemed to be the opinion of the committee that the media usually voted the all-star teams from the player percentages, and Noseworthy was well down the list.

I was at the Canadian Curling Reporters meeting on Saturday morning where the all-star teams were announced, and I was shocked to find out that Noseworthy had been voted in as the second team all-star skip. I immediately got in touch with Mazinke and asked him to call a meeting of the committee for early Saturday afternoon. I brought to the committee's attention that because Noseworthy has been named as a second team all-star, we should consider changing the decision on the third team. I can remember suggesting that if Noseworthy did not win the semi, and we did not name him to the third team, there would be huge backlash. Others felt if we did that, it would clearly be a political decision. Others felt that not selecting Quebec could have the same political repercussions, so it was decided to stick with the original choices. I was told to prepare a media release on the decision and to release it just after the start of the final game on Sunday afternoon. I again suggested everyone should brace themselves because this was not going to go down well if Noseworthy lost the semifinal. Again, like clockwork, BC took out Newfoundland in the semi, and I knew Sunday was now going to be another interesting day.

Just before the start of the fifth end of the final, it was becoming obvious the word was out. From my position on the media bench, I could see that Noseworthy was holding his own little media conference. When the fifth-end break started, the media mob moved toward me, and I knew the game was on. Anton was working as an on-ice official at the home end, and I can remember leaning over the front row of the bench and suggesting to him that the fun was about to begin, and Chairman Mazinke was nowhere to be found.

Otto Jelinek, then Federal Minister of Sport was called by the Premier of Newfoundland and Labrador, Brian Peckford, days after the 1987 Brier demanding that Newfoundland and Labrador's team at the Brier skipped by Mark Norseworthy be named as one of the teams in the Olympic Trials.

Two days later, a telegram arrived in the CCA office from the premier of Newfoundland, Brian Peckford, demanding that Noseworthy be named as the third team from the Brier for the trials. And it did not stop there, as Peckford sent a letter to then-Minister of Sport Otto Jelinek asking for Sport Canada to intervene in the situation. Jelinek indicated to Peckford that he would ask the CCA to explain the process of how curlers were selected for the trials.

Mazinke settled the situation by suggesting Noseworthy and his third Randy Perry would be put onto the alternatives list, but when two positions opened, the committee filled the vacancies with Kirk Ziola of Kitchener, Ontario, and Mark Olson of Winnipeg. On March 23, at a media conference in Calgary, I finally named all the teams for the trials.

Final Teams Named for Labatt's National Curling Trials

(Calgary) — The final line-up of teams for the Labatt's National Curling Trials, being held at the Max Bell Arena in Calgary, April 19–25 were announced today by the National Team Program Committee (NTPC) Chairman, Harvey Mazinke. Five vacancies, on previously established teams, were created as a result of the success of Russ and Glenn Howard at the Labatt Brier and Pat Sanders, Louise Herlinveaux and Kathy Fahlman at the Scott Tournament of Hearts.

In the women's division three new players have been selected to the Chris More team which includes her twin sister Cathy Shaw at third, Chris Gervais at second and Sheila Kavanagh at lead. Shaw and More previously played together on the 1978 Canadian Ladies Championship team while Gervais and Kavanagh were the front end for Saskatchewan's Lori McGeary in the 1985 and '86 Scott.

Kirk Ziola of London, Ontario (formerly of Regina, Saskatchewan) has been named skip of the front end of Denis Marchand and Bill Fletcher while Mark Olson of Manitoba will take the third spot. Ziola finished strong in the 1987 Ontario Labatt Tankard while Olson had an outstanding year as third for Vic Peters of Winnipeg.

Following the 1987 Labatt Brier the management of the Canadian Curling Association (CCA) instructed the NTPC to include the names of Mark Noseworthy and Randy Perry (skip and third respectively for Newfoundland in the 1987 Labatt Brier) on the alternate list for the Trials. This was done and both were given due consideration along with the other sixteen alternates previously named. However, after taking all points into consideration the committee felt the most appropriate alternates in the skip and third positions were Ziola and Olson.

"The mission of the selection committee was to select the best individual curlers and teams to compete to represent Canada at the 1988 Winter Olympics in Calgary," said Mazinke. "Although the task was onerous and extremely difficult the committee did its best to fulfill its objectives," continued Mazinke.

One other change has been required as a result of Marilyn Darte's lead player Jan Augustyn withdrawing for personal reasons. The Darte team has selected Sandra Rippel of Edmonton as the replacement.

The two winners declared on April 25 will represent Canada in the 1988 Winter Olympic Games in Calgary.

The complete list of the teams who have qualified is attached.

TEAM MEMBERS LABATT'S NATIONAL CURLING TRIALS

WOMEN	*(S) Scott*	*(C) Camps*	
Marilyn Darte (Ontario)	*Kathy McEdwards (Ontario)*	*Chris Jurgenson*	*Sandra Rippel (S) (Ontario)*
Linda Moore (BC)	*Lindsay Sparkes (BC)*	*Debbie Jones (BC)*	*Penny Ryan (C) (Alberta)*
Connie Laliberte (Manitoba)	*Janet Harvey (Manitoba)*	*Corinne Peters (Manitoba)*	*Janet Arnott (C) (Manitoba)*
Colleen Jones (Nova Scotia)	*Kay Smith (Nova Scotia)*	*Kim Dolan (Nova Scotia)*	*Cathy Caudle (C) (Nova Scotia)*
Chris More (Manitoba)	*Cathy Shaw (Ontario)*	*Chris Gervais (Saskatchewan)*	*Sheila Kavanagh (C) (Saskatchewan)*
Pat Sanders (BC)	*Georgina Hawkes (BC)*	*Louise Herlinveaux (BC)*	*Deb Massulo (S) (BC)*

Kathie Ellwood (Manitoba)	*Cathy Treloar (Manitoba)*	*Laurie Ellwood (Manitoba)*	*Sandra Asham (S) (Manitoba)*
Kathy Fahlman (Saskatchewan)	*Sandra Schmirler (Saskatchewan)*	*Janice Betker (Saskatchewan)*	*Sheila Schneider (S) (Saskatchewan)*

<u>MEN</u>

Ed Lukowich (Alberta)	*John Ferguson (Alberta)*	*Neil Houston (Alberta)*	*Brent Syme (B) (Alberta)*
Pat Ryan (Alberta)	*Randy Ferbey (Alberta)*	*Don Walchuk (Alberta)*	*Don McKenzie (C) (Alberta)*
Ed Werenich (Ontario)	*Paul Savage (Ontario)*	*John Kawaja (Ontario)*	*Neil Harrison (C) (Ontario)*
Kirk Ziola (Ontario)	*Mark Olson (Manitoba)*	*Denis Marchand (Quebec)*	*Bill Fletcher (C) (Ontario)*
Eugene Hritzuk (Saskatchewan)	*Ron Mills (Saskatchewan)*	*Ian Tetley (Ontario)*	*Bob Ursel (C) (Manitoba)*
Russ Howard (Ontario)	*Glenn Howard (Ontario)*	*Tim Belcourt (Ontario)*	*Kent Carstairs (B) (Ontario)*
Bernie Sparkes (BC)	*Jim Armstrong (BC)*	*Monte Ziola (BC)*	*Jamie Sexton (B) (BC)*
Kevin Adams (Quebec)	*Malcolm Turner (Quebec)*	*Don Reddick (Quebec)*	*Ian Journeaux (B) (Quebec)*

So, things were finally all set to go for the trials... but there was still more fun to come. Werenich had kept a low profile in the weeks leading up to the trials, but the attention he had garnered through the whole weight loss issue continued with an endless stream of articles and editorials from coast to coast. He had still been making a number of statements that were covered by numerous media outlets, and he continued to condemn the CCA, Garry DeBlonde, and the entire trials process.

When the Wrench arrived in Calgary, Friday, April 17, he went straight to the room of Labatt employee Fred Storey to pick up team shirts and jackets. The Wrench had obviously partaken of the sponsor's product on the flight to Calgary because he was higher than the plane before it landed. With Storey in the Labatt room was National Coach Garry DeBlonde, and upon arrival, the Wrench set forth to berate both Storey and DeBlonde in front of a number of other trials curlers. After creating an uproar in the room for about thirty minutes, the Wrench departed.

The next morning at ten a.m., the NTPC convened for a meeting at the Delta Bow Valley Hotel. The first item on the agenda was the scene caused by Werenich in the Labatt room on Friday evening. After discussion, it was decided that a committee would be appointed to review the situation that would not have either Garry DeBlonde or myself as part of the committee. The review committee appointed involved the two national association presidents, Elsie Crosby and Jerry Muzika, Vera Pezer, Art Quinney, Dot McRae, and Ron Anton. The two Labatt people on site, Mike Buist and Fred Storey, had input to the committee. The committee met with the Werenich team, and the issue was discussed fully. While most of the committee felt Werenich should once and for all be suspended from the trials, Mazinke and Muzika felt he should be given yet another chance, so he was. Werenich was told if he wrote a letter of apology, he would be allowed to play in the trials. But before the letter could be written, the Sunday edition of the *Calgary Sun* hit the newsstand, and the sports section featured an article in which Werenich again spewed venom at the event and a number of the other participants. Nevertheless, everyone looked the other way one more time and the letter of apology was released just prior to the first draw.

Statement From Ed Werenich

It's obvious that I have had a number of differences with the National Team Program Committee regarding the entire selection process and the program to choose the Canadian teams for the 1988 Olympics.

However, my team and I had a meeting with the National Team Program Committee on Saturday and I believe the lines of communication were opened and have certainly improved between us. There is a clearer and better understanding of our differences.

While not misquoted in the story that appears in today's Calgary Sun, I regret the fact that many of the points I listed in the story, for which I had been interviewed several days ago, were also resolved satisfactorily in yesterday's meeting with the committee.

I hope that my comments have not detracted from the overall quality of the field at the Trials nor from the efforts of the organizing committee and the many volunteers. As a curler, I have great appreciation for the work that goes into putting on a competition of this caliber and magnitude.

So, I really have nothing more to say about the matter. I've said what I felt and as of today, I'm here and ready to curl.

Ed Werenich
April 1987

From that point, Werenich was pretty much muzzled, and the trials got underway. In the end, four teams on the men's side ended tied for second place with a record of 4–3, which included Werenich, Howard, Sparkes, and Lukowich. Pat Ryan finished in first spot, all alone with a record of 6–1. Werenich took out Howard 8–6 in one tie-breaker, and Lukowich downed Sparkes (9–4) that created a semifinal between Lukowich and Werenich, which Lukowich won by a score of 7–2. It was Lukowich all the way in the final, and the Calgary foursome won the men's trials 6–3.

In the women's division, Linda Moore led the way, finishing the round robin with a record of 6–1. Connie Laliberte finished second with a record of 5–2 while three teams—Pat Sanders, Kathy Fahlman, and Colleen Jones—finished tied for third with a record of 4–3. In the first tie-breaker, Sanders defeated Jones (7–0), and in the second tie-breaker, Sanders downed Fahlman (9–2) to advance to the semi against Laliberte, which Laliberte won 6–4. In a tightly fought final, Moore advanced over Laliberte by a score of 7–5.

The Linda Moore team won the 1987 Women's Canadian Olympic Curling Trials and earned a spot in the 1988 Olympics. The Moore team came through the selection camps and was created by the camp coaches. The lead player, Penny Ryan, was added to the team by the coaches. From the left, Linda Moore, Lindsay Sparkes, Debbie Jones-Walker and Penny Ryan.

The Ed Lukowich team won the men's division of the 1987 Curling Trials and represented Canada at the 1988 Winter Games. Lukowich and his mates won the right to participate in the Olympic Trials by winning the 1986 Brier and World Men's Championship. The team from the left Ed Lukowich, John Ferguson, Neil Houston and Brent Syme.

In the end, the media and the people who did not like the camp idea for selecting teams from the trials were hoping the traditionally selected teams would kick the crap out of the camp teams. However, that really didn't happen. On the men's side, Lukowich was a team that came through the Brier, but Ryan and Werenich finished second and third and were teams that found their way to the trials through the camps. It was similar in the women's division, with the Linda Moore team advancing to the trials from the camps, as did Laliberte while Sanders arrived at the trials via the Hearts. See Appendix #1 on for the details of the 1987 trials.

I had one final exchange with the Wrench before the trials were officially over. During the closing dinner, I ran into Paul Savage and we discussed some of the things that had taken place over the past number of weeks. Without divulging exactly what had officially taken place, I tried to explain the entire matter was not as it seemed, and everything had got totally out of hand. Savage suggested that Eddie really wasn't a bad guy, and the next time I was in Toronto, the three of us should get together and have a chat.

In the middle of our conversation, the Wrench wandered up and asked Savage if he needed any help. We both laughed because we thought he was kidding... but he wasn't. I came back with a comment that suggested the next time I was in Toronto, the three of us should get together for lunch. Werenich let it be known very quickly, in no uncertain terms, that he did not have any time for me and that he was getting involved with the CCA at the executive level, at which time I would find myself out of a job. I'm not sure exactly what I said, except I think I thanked him for the time and consideration and wished him all the best for the future, and then I walked away. To the best of my memory, those were the last words the Wrench and I ever exchanged. Over the next number of years, I ran into him more than once and always offered greetings, but he never responded.

CHAPTER 22

The Final Charge to the Olympics

ON JUNE 15, 1987, the NTPC met to discuss what had taken place since January 1, 1987, as to where things were and where they were going. Following is a summary of that meeting:

Team Selection

Five teams in both men's and women's divisions had already been selected prior to January 1st. Four were chosen from the selection camps and one from the 1986 Canadian championship.

The winner and runner-up teams from the Brier and Hearts were automatic selections. These were:

Women	*Men*
Pat Sanders	*Russ Howard*
Kathie Ellwood	*Bernie Sparkes*

The rationale behind the selection of the third teams was to pick individual curlers who had outstanding performance at the 1987 national championships. This method of selection gave every player an opportunity to qualify for the Olympic Trials. But this approach in the end did not really provide an individual player who performed in an outstanding fashion a path to the Trials even though his or her team did not perform all that well. The final selection involved full teams in each case. The Hearts selection was the Saskatchewan team skipped by Kathy Fahlman, and at the Brier, it was the Quebec team skipped by Kevin Adams.

The lead, second and third on the Fahlman team were exceptionally high in individual performance percentages. Fahlman did not perform as well as her team, but she already had been selected from the camps. On the men's side, after excluding all the curlers who had already qualified for the Trials, the four members of the Adams team all had the highest performance percentages at the Brier for their position. Based on this, the National Team Program Committee selected the entire Adams team to compete at the Trials.

Unfortunately, by not selecting third-place Mark Noseworthy, a great deal of controversy arose. Even though the intention had never been to automatically choose the third-place team, the Newfoundland team and many of their supporters felt that they should have been chosen. Subsequently, the CCA management committee directed the NTPC members to include Mark Noseworthy and third Randy Ferbey with the camps alternates since two more curlers had to be selected to replace Russ and Glen Howard, who had already qualified through the camps. The unanimous decision by the NTPC was the selection of Kirk Ziola and Mark Olson as the final two Trials competitors.

The Chris More team had to replace three members since Kathy Fahlman, Pat Sanders, and Louise Herlinveaux had qualified through the camps and then again at the Hearts. Cathy Shaw, Chris Gervais, and Sheila Kavanagh were selected from the camps alternate list to the Chris More team.

In both the Brier and Hearts, no curlers on the third-place team qualified for the Trials. The reason, as stated before, was that the selection was based on outstanding individual performance and allowed every curler not on the first or runner-up teams an equal opportunity. In spite of the fact that much controversy arose from this issue, many still strongly support the national team programs committee's final selections. In retrospect, another method should have been used to avoid this controversy, such as automatic inclusion to the trials of both winner and runner-up in both the 1986 and 1987 national championships.

Controversial Issues

Two further issues caused widespread interest and controversy with regard to our program. These were related to fitness and the contracts.

Initially, the fitness issue sparked great interest amongst curlers in general. The camp athletes were generally in support of some fitness requirements. However, the media eventually created the impression that this was an all-important aspect of the program, and the curlers would have to train a great deal. In point of fact, the program was designed to have each curler attain a very minimal physical requirement. The objective was to improve each curler's maximum physical requirement. The objective was to improve each curler's maximum potential as an athlete and also to make the general public more aware that many of the top curlers include physical training as part of their program. Unfortunately, a small minority were very vocal, while the comments and opinions of the majority of the curlers that attended the camps were never sought by the media. The media representation of the fitness issue will not be positive when it comes to promoting curling as a sport worthy of Olympic inclusion.

Contracts were issued to all trials competitors two months prior to the Trials. Controversy arose again, a good portion of it due to the lack of understanding of parts of the agreement by some of the athletes. In some cases, the media presented completely erroneous information, such as stating our Olympic teams were not going to be allowed to retain bonspiel winnings. The contracts were withdrawn, and a simple release agreement was signed by every athlete in the trials. Only the two Olympic teams had to sign an actual contract. In retrospect, this was the procedure that should initially have been followed.

Trials

The trials proved to be a very successful event. The host committee did an outstanding job, and the curling was fantastic. Ice conditions were excellent, and the only disappointment was the low attendance.

The results of the trials were as follows. In the women's section, three teams were tied for third. In the tie breakers, the Pat Sanders team first defeated Colleen Jones and then Kathy Fahlman. In the semi-final, Connie Laliberte won over Fahlman, and the final saw Linda Moore defeat Laliberte on last rock. In the men's section, four teams were tied for second. In the tie breakers, it was Lukowich over Sparkes and Werenich over Howard. In the tie-breakers, it was Lukowich over Sparkes and Werenich over Howard. The semi-final saw Lukowich defeat Werenich, and in the final Lukowich, scored a five-ender in the eighth, to win over the round-robin winner Pat Ryan.

Team Schedule and Training

Earle Morris and Garry DeBlonde met with the Moore and Lukowich teams to discuss contracts, team schedules, fitness training and mental preparation programs. The following is the progress to date:

Team Schedule — Intensive training schedules have been set up by the teams and national coach. A ten-day cross Canada tour sponsored by Labatt will probably start off the season. This tour is now scheduled for October 2nd to October 11th. The teams will play in the top Canadian bonspiels on the average of every two weeks until the first part of December. Both teams will compete in Europe in mid-January. The Lukowich team has indicated they will compete in Tankard playdowns if the Alberta playdowns do not conflict with the opening of the Olympics. This conflict does presently exist, but the Alberta Men's Curling Council is looking into the possibility of altering the dates. The Moore team will not be entered into the playdowns leading to the Scotties.

Fitness — The majority of the Olympic curlers have attended a fitness evaluation session. The national coach has met with the Lukowich team regarding this, and they are very receptive to the program. The Moore team will be taking their tests on June 9th and Dr. Quinney will shortly thereafter be setting up programs for them.

Mental Preparation Programs — Vera Pezer and the National Coach have already met with the Lukowich team and Penny Ryan. Vera will supply imagery, relaxation, and concentration audio tapes and will also issue selected readings on mental preparation. She will be meeting with the Moore team on June 20th to discuss their program.

Fifth Player — The following are the Olympic team members:

Men	*Women*
Ed Lukowich	*Linda Moore*
John Ferguson	*Lindsay Sparkes*
Neil Houston	*Debbie Jones*
Brent Syme	*Penny Ryan*
Wayne Hart	*Patti Vande*

The Lukowich team strongly lobbied for Wayne Hart as their fifth man since he curled with them regularly, had won cash spiels as part of the team, and they were completely familiar with him and his capabilities.

The Moore team wished to have Patti Vande as their fifth. Patti was an alternate chosen from the camps. The NTPC members have agreed with these choices.

Canadian Championship Teams — Part of the national coaches' responsibilities are training of both the National junior teams leading to the 1988 world championships and also assisting the current Canadian women's curling champions.

Planning through their club coaches has been initiated with both junior teams. A complete program will be completed by September.

High-Performance Coaches Seminar — A one-day coaches seminar is planned for mid-October in Halifax. Approximately 10 to 12 top-level coaches and apprentice coaches will be invited to participate. This will include some of the Olympic camp coaches and others such as Dave Sullivan and Dan Martel, who are coaching the current Canadian junior champions.

Elite Curlers Camp — A two-and-a-half-day camp for the top curlers has been scheduled for mid-October following the high-performance coaches seminar. The curlers invited will be of national-championship caliber, and the criteria for invitation will be the same as those for Olympic camps. Four men and four women will be invited from each of the following provinces: Newfoundland, PEI, Nova Scotia, New Brunswick, and Quebec. Also invited will be the 1987 junior men's and 1987 junior women's Canadian champions. Participating coaches will be those attending the coaches seminar. A second camp will be scheduled for Western Canada in 1988. Sport Canada will supply funding for coaches travel, accommodation and per diem and also for curlers accommodations and per diem.

Long-Range Plan — High-Performance Coaches' Development — The existing Curl Canada programs have produced many coaches at Levels I, II and some at level III. However, little has been done for the development of high-performance coaches, that is, those who would have experience at national and international events. Currently, only myself and Garry DeBlonde have worked with teams at world events. Now with four world championships, it becomes more critical to train people to coach at world events. It is important to send people with knowledge and expertise to assist teams, and it does little just to send a manager or someone with no experience. As such, the NTPC has recommended the establishment of a long-range plan incorporating the following elements:

- *Establish a core of high-performance coaches across Canada that would quickly move to level III*
- *Have a yearly high-performance coaches seminar*
- *Encourage provinces to send their high-performance coaches to the Brier and Scotties. The national coach would work with them at these events to further their knowledge and for evaluation purposes.*
- *Coaches to apprentice at international championships*

High Performance Coaches Seminar

Objective:

- *To establish a core of committed high-performance coaches across Canada*
- *To provide ongoing training opportunities for the top Canadian coaches*
- *As part of the long-range plan for high-performance coaches; development, a high-performance coaches; a seminar is being planned for the season pending CCA/CLCA ratification. Sport Canada will supply funding for coaches, travel, accommodation, and per diem. Key elements of the seminar are:*

- *10 to 12 top-level coaches and apprentice coaches to be invited to participate*
- *some of the invited coaches will be those who assisted at the Olympic camps*
- *Dave Sullivan and Dan Martl, our Canadian junior champions' coaches, will be invited to attend*
- *location — Halifax*
- *one-day seminar*
- *date — Friday, October 3rd (tentative)*
- *seminar content:*
  - *Fault analysis (videos, feedback, analysis technique)*
  - *Practice planning*
  - *Peaking concept*
  - *Fitness training*
  - *Mental preparation program*

Elite Curler Camp

Objective

To provide for our top curlers an opportunity for high-level development.

Participant feedback at the 1986 Olympic camps indicated a need to hold camps for the top competitive curlers. The Curl Canada programs have provided excellent opportunities for developing curlers and for juniors aspiring to Canadian championships. However, programs for our top Canadian athletes have been lacking. To respond to this need, a two-and-a-half-day camp for the top curlers has been scheduled for October following the high-performance coaches seminar. The curlers invited will be of national-championship caliber, and the criteria for invitation will be the same as those for the Olympic camps. Four men and four women will be invited from each of the following provinces: Newfoundland, PEI, Nova Scotia, New Brunswick, and Quebec. These provincial curling associations will be asked to supply names of athletes attending. Also invited will be the 1987 junior men's and women's Canadian champions. Participating coaches will be those attending the coaches seminar. A second camp will be scheduled for western Canada in 1988. Sport Canada will supply funding for curlers accommodations and per diem.

The following indicates program content for the camp:

- *Fault analysis*
- *Delivery discussion*
- *Strategy*
- *Drills*
- *Video*
- *Fitness*
- *Imagery*
- *Mental preparation*

In the year leading up to the Olympics, a few things happened, but the teams primarily prepared for the games and the review of that process was well documented in an article in *Curling Canada Magazine* written by Larry Wood:

> *To play down or not to playdown, that is the question. It is also the choice for Canada's Olympic curling standard bearers. And even they disagree.*
>
> *Come the sixth day of January when the Labatt Tankard zone playdowns commence in Calgary, former world champion Ed Lukowich and his gang will be right in the thick of the chase, as usual. But not so Linda Moore and Co. in their home North Vancouver precinct.*
>
> *"We talked about it following the Trials," recalls the 1985 world women's championship skip, "and we felt the best way we could prepare for the Olympics didn't include the Hearts playdowns. So we'll be taking the year off."*
>
> *Why the divergence of strategy? "We're not used to playing a lot of games before the playdowns," says Linda. "I think probably Ed and his team are more used to that. I'm not saying which*

is right. But we went a similar route in 1986 when we had a bye to the Scotties and although we didn't win it, I felt the team played well enough. We finished the round-robin at 10–1. And I think the way we prepared without the playdowns that year is good for us."

Lukowich is of a different mind. The more action the better, the way he sees it. And his rigorous schedule, on paper at least, will certainly tax his team to the hilt. "Maybe it's a little heavier than usual," he admits, "but I don't think it will bother us. For certain, we figure we'll be competition honed by the time the Olympics roll around."

Both teams have already begun fitness and training programs. In addition, both kicked off the new season in early October with a cross-country, eight-city tour co-sponsored by Labatt and Canadian Airlines. Matches were played against local hotshots in each centre — St. John's, Halifax, Chicoutimi, Sudbury, Saskatoon, Toronto, Brandon, Vancouver — with the winning teams each collecting $1,000.

For Lukowich and his team of John Ferguson, Neil Houston, Brent Syme and fifth player Wayne Hart, the subsequent schedule was to extend through seven competitions prior to Christmas.

"We considered going to Europe and decided against it prior to January," says Fast Eddy. "The European trip in the fall is too time consuming. We figured we could get better competition combined with less travelling by staying in Canada."

Still, travelling there was to be. The team was to follow its eight-city tour with challenges at the Kelowna Carspiel in mid-October, then the Vernon Carspiel, the Calgary Cashspiel, a cashspiel at Hamilton, the Nipawin Carspiel, the four-team TSN Skin's Game at Thunder Bay, Dec. 4–5, and Saskatoon's Bessborough Classic.

The day after the Calgary zones playoffs conclude, Luke and friends are drawn in a bonspiel at Grindelwald, Switzerland. Two days after the completion of that, the Southern Alberta regional Tankard goes in Calgary. Last on the preparatory list, hopefully, will be the provincial Tankard early in February.

"They've moved it ahead from its usual mid-month dates to accommodate the Olympics," says Lukowich. "Sure, it accommodates our team, too. But I think it's a sensible move, anyway. When the Games are in progress, precious little else is going to be given much public attention."

The Moore team, which includes old mates Lindsay Sparkes and Debbie Jones along with Edmonton-based lead Penny Ryan, will also compete at the Kelowna cashspiel. Then it will be on to the Toronto Royals, Saskatoon and Moncton in November.

"We've set aside December for practice," says Moore. "And we're going to play in two events, plus at least four exhibitions, in Europe, Jan. 9–25."

The bonspiels are at Berne, Switzerland and Lahr, Germany. Moore says another factor in her decision to skip the Hearts chase is the possibility of mental letdown.

"If we were to play poorly in the playdowns, I'm sure how the disappointment would affect us mentally at the Olympics.

"The way everything is going, the plans, the training, the fitness situation, our meetings with national team coaches, we feel pretty good about it. We've set some specific goals, with the help of the coaches and I don't think any of us will miss the Hearts at all."

Lukowich admitted his team had been outfitted with training programs.

"Actually, I think we've always maintained a reasonable level of fitness," he says. "But I'm not going to argue with it."

Neither is he contesting the Olympic team contract about which he had some harsh words prior to the Canadian trials last April.

"We're formulating a contract which I understand is standard for Olympic competition. It details duties of participants, suppliers, conduct codes, uses of drugs, things like that. It's necessary in a situation like we have, in which all the Olympic sports are in a wrestling match over funding from Sport Canada.

"We're fairly satisfied with the arrangements. We have a lot of our costs covered. It won't be a money-making proposition, that's for sure, but it's adequate."

Moore pleaded no comment to questions concerning contract other than to say, "I've never considered it an issue so I'm not concerned about it."

The Canadian teams each will compete with seven others in Olympic demo round-robin event at Calgary's Max Bell Arena with the top three finishers in each segment advancing to sudden death playoff.

In addition, the Calgary organizing committee has announced all demo sport participants will march in opening and closing ceremonies with their medal-sport counterparts and that medal presentation ceremonies will be identical to those for other Olympic sports.

"Maybe that indicates the Olympic people are looking with favor on admitting our game and the other demonstration events for the future," says Lukowich.

"They should. There aren't really enough sports in the Winter Olympics schedule as it stands now."

Over the next twelve months, there were many anxious moments, and all curling felt its way along with the process of becoming first a proper demonstration sport in 1988 and, hopefully, a full medal sport in future Winter Games. But along the way, the lack of understanding of protocol in dealing with the IOC cost curling some precious points when more emphasis was placed on how the sport would appear to the IOC and the world rather than making the back-room deals required for acceptance. No one in curling really understood how the IOC worked, and even when advised by people like Jack Lynch, the ICF, and CCA did not heed the advice. The key item ignored by the ICF was the fundamental IOC medal requirement calling for twenty-five member nations on three continents. The message sent to curling officials was incorrect when it was suggested that lobbying the IOC members and putting on a good demonstration would be all that was necessary.

Nevertheless, Ray Kingsmith and I, along with all the others involved in putting on the show in Calgary, did our jobs well as curling, in the early part of the 1988 Games, grabbed its share of media and public attention. However, we did our jobs too well, as the high profile created for curling as a demonstration sport did not receive a favourable nod from one of the key people, IOC Director of Sport Walter Troeger of Germany, who made it clear he wasn't pleased with the status of curling in Calgary and a demo sport would never again enjoy such a notable position. As a matter of fact, it wasn't long after Troeger's declaration that the IOC made a statement that indicated the 1992 Games in Albertville, France, would be the end of demonstration sports at the Winter Olympics.

To add to the confusion, a ticket fiasco created by OCO saw the strange scenario of numerous people wanting to get into Max Bell with no tickets available, yet the arena was nearly empty. By the third day of curling, OCO agreed that after the first end of the game had been completed, approximately 500 patrons could be allowed in the building to occupy some of the empty seats. I will still remember seeing hundreds of curling fans lining up around Max Bell Arena in the freezing February weather, and finally a few of them being allowed in once the games started. No one ever provided a reason for the confusion or the heart of the problem, but some close to the situation suggested that curling only had about 2,000 tickets to distribute, and most of them were probably sitting in the desk draw of corporate sponsors' offices.

By the end of the Games, most of us close to the scene knew there were many problems, and the probability of curling becoming a full medal sport in 1992 was slight, but we thought there was still a glimmer of hope. There was little question that too much negative profile had been created for the sport of curling, going back to the Air Canada sponsorship dispute in 1983. In addition, the ICF did not lobby the right people at the IOC long before the 1988 Games, and to some degree the IOC had its nose out of joint when it was clear that curling thought it could become a medal sport by simply putting on a good demonstration in Calgary at the Games.

The other shock that happened was within days of the Games ending was that Ray Kingsmith was diagnosed with lung cancer. Those of us close to him knew he was seriously ill during the Games. I remember being next to him at the back of the arena one afternoon, and he was coughing up blood. On May 3, 1988, Ray passed away, and I was devastated. Ray was only sixty years old, and I was fifteen years behind at forty-five ... He was still like a father to me. It was a sad, sad time for so many reasons.

The IOC advised that a decision on all demo sports from the Calgary Games would be made from the Summer Games in Seoul, and on September 19, 1988, the following statement was made by Vitaly Smirnov, IOC program commission chairman, and Walter Troeger: "Curling will not be a medal-sport at Albertville in 1992 or included on the 1994 Games agenda in Lillehammer, Norway. It will, however, be a demonstration sport again at Albertville. Curling did not meet the basic criteria in Calgary which states that a sport must be practiced by at least 25 nations on at least three continents. Possibly in five or six years curling can start again to put in a medal sport request before the IOC."

During the media conference, Canadian Olympic Association member Dick Pound also passed on comments for digestion: "The ticket confusion in Calgary, when the event was sold out but nevertheless had many empty seats, had no bearing on the final IOC decision. The best way for curling to get IOC recognition is to qualify under the existing criteria which is available as an excuse for its failure to merit recognition."

In other words, the IOC decided it did not want to accept curling as an Olympic medal sport, and the ICF not having twenty-five member nations gave them a reason to reject it—but there was more at play.

And so, in the fall of 1988, the torch was passed to retiring COA technical director, Jack Lynch, and then-Austrian President Gunther Hummelt to gain the necessary twenty-five member nations and the required representation from three continents. It became obvious that the biggest mistake made by curling officials going into 1988 was to assume the IOC requirement that the sport have participation in at least twenty-five countries was not important. In the end, both Canadian teams did pretty well. On the women's side, the Linda Moore team won the gold medal, and on the men's side, the Lukowich team captured the bronze. The summary for curling in the 1988 Winter Games can be reviewed in Appendix II.

The Linda Moore team on the gold medal podium at the 1988 Olympic Games in Calgary. From the left Moore, Lindsay Sparkes, Debbie Jones-Walker, Penny Ryan and Patti Vande. *Photo courtesy of the Canadian Olympic Committee.*

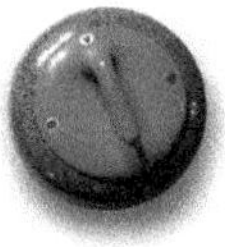

CHAPTER 23
The Next Steps After 1988

THERE WAS A bit of a calm after the 1988 Games as everyone tried to regroup and determine a path going forward. A meeting of the NTPC was held in early May and following are the minutes of that meeting:

1. 1992 Olympics – Albertville, France

- *Indications are positive that curling will again be a demonstration sport in 1992.*
- *A 3-year plan is required to cover the period from 1989 to 1992.*
    - *Plan dependent on if demonstration in 1991; or if medal in 1992; or if medal in 1991,*
    - *Camps and Trials were generally supported by the athletes and past plan with some suggested modifications.*

2. National Team Program Committee (NTPC) Mandate
Suggested NTPC responsibilities are as follows:

- *Develop 3 year plan leading to 1992 Olympics,*
- *Develop long range plans for national teams,*
- *Develop programs for national teams,*
- *Further develop elite camps,*

- *Develop programs to improve coaching,*
- *Recommend international coaches to assist national teams.*

The NTPC recommends that Linda Moore and Ed Lukowich become part of the committee as athlete representatives. A further recommendation is that the NTPC report to a Curl Canada Committee.

In addition the NTPC reviewed the entire three-year (1985–1988) Olympic program. Areas where changes are needed were listed and solutions suggested. Athlete feedback was a consideration with regard to program recommendations for the next Olympiad.

3. Areas Requiring Change

- *Player contracts. A simple letter of agreement may be all that is necessary.*
- *Fitness qualification: A very similar plan is recommended. Further clarification is necessary that is part of our program. This probably will not continue to be an issue.*
- *Trials selection team. The selection of an all-star team from the Brier and the Hearts was difficult to make and proved unpopular. Many curlers have suggested qualifying bonspiels for team selection. The NTPC's recommendation is to again have an eight team trials with team chosen as follows:*
    - *Four from qualifying camps,*
    - *1990 Canadian champion,*
    - *1991 Canadian champion plus the 1991 Canadian runner-up team,*
    - *One team from an eight-team qualifying bonspiel,*
    - *Practicalities of the eight-team qualifying spiel would be part of the three-year plan.*
- *Team not attending camps: Few curlers invited to the camps refused the invitation. However, two notable teams (Hackner-Burtnyk) did not*

attend since their entire team was not invited. The eight-team qualifying spiel would include teams of this caliber.

- *Selection to camps: The NTPC would provide definitive guidelines as to how provincial associations should select their athletes.*
- *Publicity: More care is to be taken to present our programs in a positive light.*
- *Funding for future camps and trials: Curl Canada Board will address this issue at the next meeting in June of 1988.*
- *Curler selection: A curler rating system based on competitive bonspiels should be structured.*
- *Camp sizes: Coaches duties at the camps were excessive. Planning to assist in this area is necessary.*
- *Trials timing: This will be part of the three-year plan.*

4. Coaching Development
To assist in coaching development (possibly master-apprentice situation) funds from Curl Canada should be obtained. A sum of $5,000/year is suggested.

5. National Teams
Curling should be able to better promote the sport by publicizing our four national teams. Also, our teams should be better supported financially. Sponsors can be solicited for this purpose. Also a portion of the $10,000 Olympic program surplus could be used.

6. Elite Camps
The 1988 camp will be held in Winnipeg in October. Four male and four female curlers will be invited from each of Southern Ontario, Northern Ontario, Manitoba and Saskatchewan. Also, the Canadian junior teams from Victoria and Edmonton will receive invitations.

7. Curling in Sport Canada Winter Unit
Very probably curling will be categorized as a Winter Unit Sport (currently it is in the development unit) which includes all Winter Olympic sports. This should give us better access to Olympic sport programs.

8. Canadian Champions Compete in World One Year Later
A questionnaire was sent to all female Canadian champions who competed at the World Women's level since 1979 and to all male Canadian champions who competed at the world men's level since 1980. The questionnaire posed pros and cons as to competing in the world championship three weeks after the Canadian championship as is currently done versus the pros and cons as to competing in the world championship one year later as is currently done at the junior level.

The majority of respondents indicated a preference for the same year concept as is in the current situation.

9. Recommendations

1. *That upon confirmation of our status as demonstration or medal after the Seoul Games, curling develop a three-year plan for the Olympics and our national teams.*

2. *That the National Team Program Committee continue to function and that Linda Moore and Ed Lukowich act as athlete representatives on that committee.*

3. *That the NTPC report to a Curl Canada committee which is to be established by the Board.*

4. *That a sum of $5,000 be made available from Curl Canada to assist in coaching development.*

5. *That the $10,000 Olympic program surplus be designated as seed money for the 1992 Olympics and for our national teams.*

6. *That avenues be explored to further assist and promote our national teams.*

The National Team Program Committee made another interesting decision. Because the trials and camp process had a lot of controversy attached to it, a consultant was hired by Curl Canada to survey the athletes who had been involved. These are the findings of the survey:

Summary and Analysis of the 1986 Olympic Curling Training Camps

I. INTRODUCTION

A. Background

In November of 1986, Curl Canada conducted two talent assessment camps. The purpose of the camps was to select four men's and four women's teams to complete the fields for the National Curling Trials to be held in April 1987. Following the three day camps, each participant was asked to complete an Olympic Program Evaluation form.

The overall purpose of this report is to offer a summary and an analysis of these evaluations. This information should prove helpful when it comes to designing an Olympic Selection Program for future Olympic efforts.

B. Methodology

Each questionnaire was read on at least three separate occasions. Eventually, all responses were recorded and totaled and all pertinent comments were categorized where possible. Where comments were favourable and obviously followed Curl Canada's reasoning, they were not included. Most of the comments that do appear are either somewhat critical or provide a unique slant on a particular issue. For these reasons, the reader should not assume that the comments included necessarily represent accurate proportions of curler opinion. The yes/no responses for each question are however, accurate in this regard.

For reasons of comparison the feedback from the male curlers and from the female curlers were analyzed separately.

II. RESULTS

A. Executive Summary

- *Both the male and female curlers overwhelmingly supported the stated program objectives.*
- *Both male and female curlers overwhelmingly supported the concept of multiple opportunities to qualify for the Trials.*
- *Almost all of the female curlers supported the concept of individual selection, while only about half of the male curlers supported it.*
- *Only a small majority of male and female curlers agreed with the system of selecting the camp rosters. A significant number were critical of the various provincial associations' publicity efforts and/or their actual nominations.*
- *The female curlers supported the concept of selection based on an individual's past performance more so than did the male curlers.*
- *There was much greater support for team invitations among the men than among the women. There was significant support in both groups for the concept of keeping partial team units (front end/back end) together.*
- *Both the male and female curlers supported the use of camps in the future. Male curlers showed significant support for at least supplementing these camps with two (East and West) qualifying bonspiels.*
- *Female curlers supported the invitation of juniors or recent junior graduates to future camps, more so than did the male curlers.*
- *Both male and female curlers overwhelmingly agreed that the activities at the camp were appropriate.*
- *Both the male and female curlers felt that the camps were generally well organized.*
- *A strong majority of both male and female curlers liked the length of the camps (3 days).*

- *The overwhelming majority of both the male and the female curlers found the camp coaches helpful and knowledgeable.*
- *A good majority of the male and female curlers agreed with the camp selection criteria. Both groups rated past proven performance as very important, shot-making at camp as moderately important and rated physical and psychological assessment as relatively unimportant.*
- *Many curlers from both groups felt that there should be more mini-games and game situations at camp. Many also felt that sweeping drills should be assessed and included in the evaluation.*
- *Many curlers from both groups felt that the accommodations should have been closer to the campsite and/or transportation between the two locations should have been provided.*

Curling and the Olympics were fairly quiet over the summer and into the fall of 1988. To the surprise of no one, the IOC announced in September, from the Summer Olympics in Seoul, South Korea, that curling would not be an Olympic medal sport in 1994 but would again be a demonstration in Albertville, France. The IOC kept its word, and the 1992 Games were the last time the Olympics allowed demonstration sports. During the same announcement, Lillehammer, Norway, was selected to host the 1994 Winter Games, so 1998 became the earliest date at which curling could get into the program and 1991—the year in which the host city for those Games would be selected—became the deadline for obtaining IOC acceptance.

On October 4, 1988, I sent a letter to Don MacLeod, who was now the CCA International Chairman, outlining what I thought were the challenges facing the quest for Olympic medal status. Following is that letter to MacLeod:

To: Don MacLeod, International Chairman
From: Warren Hansen

I'm writing this letter to you Don to stir some discussion and hopefully action at the October board meeting regarding what is or probably appropriately what isn't being done to ensure that curling at least has a good shot at gaining medal status for the 1998 Winter Games.

The entire Olympic movement held a great deal of significance to me because it was a combination of Ray Kingsmith and I that made the initial pitch and presentation in 1982 that eventually gained demonstration status for curling in 1988. The Calgary bid was to some degree botched by lack of experience, bad information and an insistence by a few people to swim against the current. However, 1988 should have been a great learning experience and I thought provided most of the answers as to what really was necessary for curling to become a medal sport. But again, it seemed to me the ICF was swimming against the current.

Following February of 1988 I felt some very clear messages came through:

1. Without 25 countries belonging to the ICF and in each case being properly recognized by each NOC it would be impossible for anything to happen. It would appear as though an honest effort is being made to gain the 25 countries but has anyone checked to see if the NOC's of those countries recognize and accept the sport?

2. Without question it was made obvious that one of the major hurdles to overcome was going to be the required lobby with the various NOC's around the world. To be more blunt it was obvious then and it still is now that no one within the curling fraternity has the background required to head the required lobby. However, the answer to the lobby challenge within the curling fraternity was solved when Jack Lynch showed up at the ICF door. For some strange reason the ICF did anything but jump at the opportunity to turn Lynch loose on behalf of world curling. Lynch has all the international contacts and respect to work well on curling's medal hopes. Without his efforts or by someone with similar credentials I really see little hope of ever gaining medal status.

3. It was obvious to the IOC in 1988 that the ICF was a weak body and didn't hide the fact that concerns existed. Along the same line there has been nothing done to remedy the situation. The solution could again be quickly improved by hiring Lynch and giving him the title of secretary-general which the IOC understands and respects. Again, with Lynch we have a man in the position who is recognized by the IOC.

4. It seems the ICF is showing little concern for the proper demonstration of the sport in 1992 at Albertville. If curling is going to be considered you can bet the IOC will take a very close look at it in Albertville. In addition CBC has already indicated to me an interest in televising a number of games.

Thanks.

Sincerely yours,

Warren Hansen
Director of Competitions, Media and Corporate Relations
c.c. CCA Board
Dave Parkes
Gerry Peckham
Shirley Morash

The ICF held a meeting in December 1988, and below is the report that ICF Olympic Chairman Harvey Mazinke presented to the membership:

ICF Olympic Committee, December 1988

I. Calgary's '88 Olympic Post Mortem

The ICF's bid for curling to become an Olympic medal sport was rejected as confirmed by our President's memorandum dated October 28, 1988. On November 5, 1988, Mr. Jack Lynch, Technical Director of the Canadian Olympic Association (COA) met with the executive members of the CCA to review the reasons curling's bid had not been successful and what might be done in the near future to reach that goal.

For the benefit of those who do not know Mr. Lynch, he has been a good friend of curling for some time and worked extremely hard towards the 1988

Olympics to help curling's demonstration event in Calgary. Just prior to our November meeting Jack held discussions with Mr. Dick Pound, a COA delegate and member of the executive committee. Mr. Lynch was anxious to pass onto us information that would be of value to curling in its quest for full Olympic medal status.

The first item Mr. Lynch gave us was a re-affirmation of the statement issued to the ICF by the Program Commission of the IOC that "the sport does comply with the standards laid out in the Olympic Charter. Specifically I refer to rule 44 of the Olympic Charter which deals with admission of sports which states, only sports widely practiced by women and/or men in at least 25 nations and three continents may be included in the program of the Olympic Winter Games." For further definition of "widely practiced," the Charter clarifies the IOC's position by stating that it means:

1. *National championships or cup competitions, regularly organized by the respective national federations;*

2. *International participation and organization of regional and/or world championships in the respective sports.*

Reviewing our status at the conclusion of the Calgary Games, it is apparent we did not comply with these requirements or perhaps pay enough attention to the importance of these items.

To add to our problems and for reasons unknown, there is news of a movement afoot by some members of the IOC to eliminate demonstration sports from all future programs. We are given that a motion to that effect has been put forward to the IOC for ratification at its December meetings.

Subject to the outcome of the IOC December meetings, we have been advised they are still looking to expand the Winter Games program to fill the two-week format, thereby still leaving the door open for us to demonstrate at Albertville, France for 1992 and/or Lillehammer, Norway in 1994.

With our opportunity to become a medal sport virtually eliminated for 1994 but still open for 1998 and if the ICF still keenly wishes to peruse becoming an Olympic medal sport, it is extremely important for us to put together a comprehensive strategy to be followed over the next few years to reach that objective. With the kind assistance of Mr. Lynch, I propose an outline for such a strategy in the foregoing.

II. FUTURE ICF OLYMPIC PROGRAM

While the impact of our demonstration at Calgary is still fresh in the minds of the IOC members, we have only a brief time to build on that momentum and eliminate our deficiencies to become a full-fledged member of the Olympic family. From our discussions with Mr. Lynch, to legitimize curling to medal status for the 1998 Winter Games, our efforts must be concluded prior to the IOC sessions in 1991. Although 1998 seems a long time away, 1991 is not. For compliance our strategy should include:

1. *The ICF should immediately apply to the General Association of International Sports Federations (GAISF).*

2. *The ICF should ensure all formal applications to demonstrate at Albertville have been filled with the IOC and host committees and continue lobbying both parties to have us included in the 1992 Winter Games Program.*

3. *The ICF should file similar applications for the 1994 Games to be held at Lillehammer, Norway. This application should be enhanced by the Norwegian men's team having won the gold in men's curling at the 1988 Calgary Games.*

4. *The ICF should expand every effort to meet the IOC's criteria for admission under their charter, specifically as has been laid out under rule 44.*

5. *The ICF executive committee through the president should establish a development committee immediately to provide the leadership and program direction to accomplish the required mission for curling to achieve medal status.*

6. *The ICF should place the IOC members on its mailing list of important information.*

7. *The ICF should ensure every one of its member countries has been recognized and is a member of its respective National Olympic Committee (NOC).*
8. *The ICF should confer with the IOC about the availability of development funding support such as:*
   - *Olympic Solidarity, an IOC sport fund;*
   - *Support funding from television revenue in Calgary.*

III. CONCLUSION

I'm sure we would all agree that for curling to become a truly major world sport there is a need to achieve entry into the Olympic Winter program. The ability of the ICF to reach this goal will be predicated on the determination of its members and the availability of funds to carry out the growth activities. In my view, it is only the limitations the members place on themselves that will determine the end result. I submit we're almost there now... let's "Go for Gold."

Respectively submitted,

Harvey Mazinke
Chair
ICF Olympic Committee
December 5, 1988

Development Committee

During the same meeting, a proposal was put forward for the formation of a development committee for developing a process to recruit the number of member nations necessary for curling to be considered for Olympic medal status.

I. Development Committee Program

1. *Establish contact with potential curling nations to introduce the game to.*

2. *Create and certify "Curling Development" teams to put on a sport builder demonstration. Members to include one team leader, all be qualified instructors and one qualified to make curling ice.*
3. *Oversee the organization and conduct of curling development clinics and/or exhibitions.*
4. *Source "Introductory Packages" of curling equipment for distribution to new curling nations.*
5. *Put together introductory training, informational and promotional aid packages for the organizer/administrators, player/instructors and icemaker.*

II. Introduction of Curling to a New Country

1. *Establish contact in the target country with an influential and interested person who knows that game (e.g. Canadian, Swiss, American, etc., businessman, embassy or consulate staff member, or resident who is a bonified curler). Recruit this individual as an "ICF Attaché" in that country.*

2. *Arrange a three-way meeting between ICF Attaché, the target Olympic committee (NOC) and an ICF team leader to sell the idea of a curling exhibition/clinic and prepare a basic plan including dates and budget for that event.*
3. *Implement the plan with the following division of responsibilities:*
   - *Host NOC*
     - *obtain ice and time available,*
     - *recruit 32 (plus or minus) athletes,*
     - *arrange hospitality and transportation.*
   - *ICF*
     - *put together curling development team,*
     - *obtain an "introductory package" of curling equipment,*
     - *put together training aid package,*
     - *arrange international travel.*

- *ICF Attaché*
  - *Recruit four reasonable competent curlers in the target country,*
  - *Negotiate arrangements for meals and accommodations for the curling development team.*

By the summer of 1989, the international development committee was formed, with Gunther Hummelt as the chair with Franz Tanner from Switzerland and Jack Lynch as committee members. Later that year, the ICF joined the Global Association of International Sports Federations (GAISF). This move promoted a request for a name change, since both canoeing and carting used the initials ICF. Curling complied and thereafter was identified as the World Curling Federation (WCF).

Austrian Gunther Hummelt became the driving force behind the World Curling Federation's efforts to get 25 nations as members following the 1988 Olympics in Calgary.

The newly formed development committee set out with three specific goals, to be reached prior to the 1991 session (General Assembly) of the IOC, when the host city for the 1988 Olympic Winter Games would be selected:

- Bring the WCF membership up to twenty-five or more countries.
- Revise the World Curling Championship format to ensure that three continents will always be represented.
- Lobby the program commission and executive board of the IOC and all the cities bidding to host the 1998 Games to be favourable toward curling.

The committee first attacked the second objective, and at the 1989 semi-annual meeting of the WCF, the initial proposals for a system of zonal qualification for the world championships were tabled. Keeping to the ten-team format, any proposal to guarantee one entry to the Pacific would automatically reduce either the North American or European entry by one. Hence, the debate was long and complex. It culminated in Winnipeg a year-and-a-half and three semi-annual meetings later when the current system was passed. It gave seven or eight entries to Europe, one or two entries to America, and a solitary entry to the Pacific (today, Europe has eight teams, Asia three, and the Americas two). The system was in place in time to provide the Pacific with entries in both the men's and women's demonstration events in Albertville.

In 1990, Gunther Hummelt, now the WCF president, went to work with a vengeance on the recruitment of new curling countries. He personally did all the spadework to bring Czechoslovakia, Hungary, Bulgaria, and Belgium into the fold and negotiated furiously with Romania, Yugoslavia, Argentina, Turkey, and Russia, among others. He also made some overtures to South Korea. Franz Tanner had contacts in Andorra and Liechtenstein, while WCF board member Pat Bannerman had Icelandic friends interested in curling. Jack Lynch made some inroads into Mexico.

The basic strategy that was laid out in 1988 was to find an influential "attaché" resident in the target country, who can remain on site to coordinate the introduction of the game, and guide an existing sports federation (e.g., the Confederation of Winter Sports in Mexico) toward the addition of a curling branch. A novice clinic followed, given by people like Keith Wendorf or Roger Schmidt from Germany to thirty-two or more new curlers, and the curling stones (usually two or three sets of sixteen) are left with the new national curling group on a renewable loan basis. Czechoslovakia joined the WCF in December 1990, entered the European Championships that same year, won its first international match the following year, and then started hosting a major international bonspiel in Prague.

In addition, New Zealand, which had been affiliated with the Royal Caledonian Curling Club for years but had never joined the WCF, was brought into the fold.

At the WCF annual meeting in Winnipeg in March 1991, the addition of New Zealand, Andorra, Liechtenstein, Iceland, and Mexico brought the WCF membership to twenty-five countries, counting Scotland, England, and Wales as only one: Great Britain. A group from the Virgin Islands applied in the summer of 1991, and Russia later became a member.

The main daunting task faced by a sport seeking Olympic status is to convince the IOC to accept it. The IOC set minimum guidelines to be met before it will consider the addition of a sport to the program of the Games, but acceptance in 1992 meant surviving a free vote of its ninety-odd individual members. And all applications get filtered through the program commission, as previously discussed. Once the program commission gives a sport its blessing, it goes before the executive board and then the general membership.

During the late eighties, the program commission was under tremendous pressure to keep the Olympic Games from getting too big. The committee was comprised of about half-dozen IOC members, supplemented with an appointee each from the International Federations, the National Olympic Committees, and the Athletes Commission.

After finally reaching the twenty-five-country, three-continent participation target in 1991, the WCF had the harrowing and unique distinction of seeing its application for Olympic medal status twice rejected by the program commission, only to have the recommendation reversed each time by the executive board.

During the IOC meetings held in Birmingham, England, in June 1991, the WCF was again hopeful that a positive announcement might be forthcoming regarding the acceptance of curling in the 1998 Winter Olympics as a full medal sport.

In March 1991, the program commission met in Barcelona. Attempts were made to circulate the WCF application to the members, but no personal interventions were possible. The commission, chaired at the time by Russian Vitaly Smirnov, came out with one conclusion that curling isn't really a sport but a pastime requiring little if any athletic skill. At the executive board, this conclusion was shot down in flames by former Olympic swimmer Dick Pound, son of a past president of the Montreal Thistle Club and a sometime curler himself. Pound was first vice president of the IOC at the time, and his arguments carried the day. The file was returned to the program commission for further study.

Five of the six bidding cities for the 1998 Winter Olympics did, in fact, support the inclusion of curling in the program. The city awarded the Games—Nagano, Japan—was one of the five cities that looked favourably upon curling. While the IOC did not give curling the required sanction, the possibility of curling becoming a medal sport for 1998 still very much existed. The IOC suggested if the Nagano Organizing Committee was prepared to take a positive position on curling along with the Japanese Olympic Committee, the IOC would give the matter further consideration and probably render a decision in September 1991.

In September, the IOC advised that the Nagano Organizing Committee was a different group than the bid committee and would not be in place until later in November 1991. So, it was obvious that it would not be possible for the Nagano committee and the Japanese Olympic Committee (JOC) to pass a verdict until at least November. However, Gunther Hummelt reported that the JOC and the Nagano Committee seemed to favour curling's inclusion.

The next IOC executive meeting was scheduled for December, but sports for 1998 did not meet the agenda. Many thought that the decision would come forth from the IOC at the meeting just prior to the 1992 Winter Games in February... but it did not.

CHAPTER 24

Revenge for the Wrench

FOLLOWING THE TRIALS in 1987, not much was heard from the Wrench until after the Winter Games in 1988. Werenich and Savage continued to play together, but with Savage on the tee head. The duo bounced right back into the heat of things and defeated defending world champion Russ Howard at the Ontario Tankard to advance to the Brier in Quebec. Werenich was fairly quiet at the Brier, but as usual, he did add a little excitement. It had been announced early in the year that both Savage and Werenich would be inducted into the Canadian Curling Hall of Fame at the Brier. However, Werenich composed a note to CCA President Harvey Mazinke that stated in no uncertain terms that he did not want to be inducted into the hall of fame or to be involved with anything the CCA was associated with. Despite the request, the selection committee still named Werenich to the Hall. During the CCA AGM on Thursday morning at the Chicoutimi Brier, Savage stepped forward to accept the award, but there was no sign of the Wrench.

The one other little incident involving the Wrench wasn't serious, but it is funny. Savage skipped the team to a third-place finish at the Brier, which meant the team would be on the winner's riser during the closing ceremonies to receive medals and awards. After the medal presentation, a lengthy entertainment package was presented at ice level. During the entertainment period, I noticed Werenich left the riser and disappeared. I got on one of the two-way radios and asked one of the officiating supervisors, Bob Decker, to search out the Wrench.

A few minutes later, Decker's response came through loud and clear: "He is in the dressing room, in his shorts, having a Blue and watching the closing on television. Do you want him back on the ice?"

My simple one-word answer: "No!"

During the fall of 1988 and the spring of 1989, little was heard from Werenich except for the odd barb in the media or some occasional off-the-wall comment. Most of his criticism was levelled at me and ice maker Don Lewis, who drew blame for screwing up the Brier ice and making it too straight. (Little did anyone know at the time, but it was mostly the rocks... not the ice.) It appeared in most of his comments that got back to me that I was to blame for the existence of officiating and every bad call ever made by an official. It seems the biggest issue that Werenich had with me was I represented the CCA and its authority as the governing body of the sport, for which he had little or no regard.

Hence, in February 1990, the final chapter in the issue between myself and Ed Werenich fell in place. Werenich won the Ontario Tankard, which gave him the right to represent Ontario at the Brier in Sault Ste. Marie, Ontario. During the entire event in Sault Ste. Marie, Werenich was a model curler on the ice, although he was still making wild statements to the media at every opportunity, but he did leave me alone. However, during the week, we met face-to-face a few times, and I said hello to him, but he never responded.

For the tenth consecutive year, I was scheduled to be the men's team leader at the world championship. I watched closely all week, but after Werenich clinched first place in the round robin and a bye to the final, I knew there was a potential problem in the making. On Friday afternoon, I met with the CCA board of directors and, in no uncertain terms, stated my concerns if Werenich won, mainly because of the issues Werenich had with me. The matter was discussed in length, and in the end, the board gave President Ed Steeves the green light to deal with the situation as he deemed necessary if Werenich was the eventual winner. I was more than uneasy, but what could I do?

In the second end of the final, New Brunswick third Charlie Sullivan missed a guard that could have in fact put his team up by two points. After Sullivan missed the guard, Werenich followed with a phenomenal shot that jumped Ontario in front 3–1. In reality… it was over! I, as a result, had the next two hours to think about what I was going to do and how to handle the impending potential disaster. I decided I would take it head-on and in the team meeting following the final, put the situation right on the table and get it over with. I felt third John Kawaja wouldn't be a problem, and both Pat Perroud and Ian Tetley had been members of Al Hackner's team when I worked with them in 1985 at the Silver Broom in Glasgow. However, I was soon to find out that the Wrench had other ideas and was thinking ahead of the curve.

I had made arrangements with Jeff Timson, the Labatt media director, that immediately following the closing ceremonies, the winning team would be taken to the away end of the arena for the waiting media and, from there, straight to the dressing room for the team meeting. Partway through the closing ceremonies, I got a call on my two-way radio from one of the supervising officials advising me that Timson had changed the plans. The Werenich team wives had to catch a flight at five p.m., so the team would be allowed to meet them in the dressing room for a few minutes before the media interviews. It all sounded harmless enough to me, and I thought that maybe this would be a way of starting a new wave of cooperation with Werenich. However, it was during this period that Werenich made a deal with his team regarding travel to the world championship in Sweden. Whether all the team members were in full agreement remains to be seen, but they went along with Werenich rather than create waves. The deal was that he was going to walk out to the throng of reporters and make the following statement: "I will negotiate with the CCA to have them remove Warren Hansen as the team leader of the men's team going to Sweden." While all of this was happening, I was standing 100 feet away. It was only seconds before the media were all over me. The first question was, "Did you hear what he said?"

"No," I replied. "What did he say?"

"He will only go to the world championship if the CCA removes you as team leader," was the reply. "And what do you think of that?"

Having been involved with the media for the past fifteen years, I knew the situation would constitute suicide if I reacted incorrectly. I immediately thought of CCA President Ed Steeves and General Manager Dave Parkes, who were sitting in the VIP lounge, waiting for me to summon them to the team meeting with the Werenich team. As soon as I found Parkes and Steeves, I told them what had taken place and resigned the position of team leader on the spot. I simply indicated I was out of the picture because of what happened, and it would be up to Steeves and Parkes to determine what was going to happen from this point forward regarding the Werenich team. Both agreed with my decision, and I headed back to the waiting reporters, where I planned to make as little comment as possible, knowing fair well that this was a situation where they would love to play one party against the other. I listened carefully to what each one had to say about Werenich's comments as I watched him out of the corner of my eye, leaning against the boards at the away end of the arena, spouting off to anyone who would listen. Some of the things he was saying about me, according to the reporters, were absolutely outrageous, but what could I do except to say two things: "I don't know what he is talking about, and I don't have a problem with him, but obviously he has a problem with me."

When the smoke cleared, Parkes and Steeves went into the dressing room to attempt to tame the roaring lion. I went to the VIP lounge and waited for Parkes and Steeves to return. I fully expected Steeves to listen to Werenich and then tell him he would get back to him on Monday after he talked to the balance of the board. However, when the two returned thirty minutes later, that wasn't the case. When I asked Steeves what happened, he indicated everything was fine and Werenich would go to Sweden without a team leader. I was shocked and numb from the entire experience and still wasn't sure I fully understood what had been said.

I flew to Toronto that evening and caught the red-eye back to Vancouver, arriving at around five a.m. I asked the cab driver to stop on the way home, and I bought a copy of the *Vancouver Province* to see what the sports editor, Kent Gilchrist, had written. While Kent, a long-time friend, had been fair, he told it all and I realized what was before my eyes had hit every newspaper in Canada. It wasn't funny... Werenich had made a number of claims against me that simply weren't true. The following is the summary.

- "It's well documented the runs he [Hansen] has taken at me..." (A ridiculous statement with absolutely nothing to back it up.)
- "Werenich said Hansen threatened to sue him in a CCA trade publication a few years ago. 'He didn't mention my name in the article,' Werenich said, 'but I know what he was talking about.'" (Again, without question, an unsubstantiated statement. The story in question didn't mention anything about anyone suing anyone.)

Ed Steeves was President of the CCA in 1990 when Ed Werenich won his second Brier. Werenich made a number of demands on Steeves, at the conclusion of the Brier, that were deemed as Werenich's conditions to be met before he would participate in the world men's championship.

- "Hansen and Werenich have had disagreements since the 1983 Canadian final when they battled over a sweeping rule." (I probably haven't said ten words to Werenich in my entire life, never mind a battle discussing rules.)
- "We feel Warren has targeted certain teams on Brier ice and has tried to intimidate certain teams. If they're here for the first time, they're not sure what Warren Hansen is all about and they can be intimidated and I don't like that," said Werenich. "He has no right to do that. Whether I'm the guy to change it or our players' association is, somebody has to."

The entire matter is best summarized by the following quote: "This isn't merely Ed

Werenich against Warren Hansen, it's Ed Werenich against the establishment. The Wrench has had several squabbles with the CCA. Hansen represents everything he dislikes about the governing body. The scandal in the Soo goes far beyond the Man Who Would Be Coach."

Nevertheless, it seemed that Ed Steeves simply wanted the entire matter to just go away. If the board of directors or Steeves himself wasn't being named, it was all right in their minds. A number of provincial/territorial associations showed their displeasure, but Steeves only seemed to take it as a personal affront to his decision. The most cutting letter came from the Northern Alberta Curling Association (NACA).

NACA Letter

Dr. Ed Steeves
President
Canadian Curling Association

Dear Mr. Steeves:

The Northern Alberta Curling Association wishes to express its extreme displeasure with the decision to remove Warren Hansen as coach of Canada's team to the World Curling Championship.

The issue is not Warren Hansen himself. The issue is the fact that Ed Werenich was successful in "blackmailing" the CCA.

The image that has been left with the public at large is that the CCA lacks fortitude, lacks leadership, lacks concern for all curlers, etc. It reinforces in the minds of many that the CCA is weak, can be manipulated and is headed by a group of old men interested in only the trappings that go with the executive suite and not in the betterment of the sport of curling.

The precedent set by succumbing to Werenich's "blackmail" will open future expectations of likewise ridiculous demands, e.g., remove that official, I don't like CBC, I won't play on that sheet, etc.

If the Werenich team is not prepared to represent Canada as per previously agreed to terms then let them stay home. We are sure that either the Sullivan team or the Harnden team, or for that matter any other Brier competing team would gladly wear Canada's colors.

For the good of the sport, to maintain respect for the CCA and to support our curlers wishes the Northern Alberta Curling Association demands the reinstatement of Warren Hansen as coach of Canada's team to the men's world curling championship.

If the Werenich team does not agree to go, so be it. Find someone else.

Respectfully submitted,

Stephen G. Pelech
President

The letter really got Steeves going, which I found interesting. It was fine for Werenich to slam me in every newspaper in Canada, but for an association to write a letter that directly condemned Steeves seemed to be an entirely different matter. I found it strange because Steeves and I got along well, but we suddenly were as far apart as the north and south poles. He expressed very little sympathy for my situation. Garry DeBlonde was scheduled to go to Sweden with the women's team as the team leader, and for whatever reason, Steeves replaced DeBlonde with me, so I was there and had a ringside seat to watch Werenich continue his outrageous behaviour, but Steeves continued to turn a deaf ear and a blind eye to the entire situation. Werenich won the men's worlds in a convincing way, so how could anyone argue with the situation?

After returning from Sweden, I thought after a couple of weeks things would cool down, but that wasn't the case. Toward the end of April, I spoke with Parkes and expressed my displeasure with the situation, and I felt the CCA board had simply hung me out to dry. Parkes sympathized with my concerns but suggested the only thing to do at this time would probably be to implement a policy that would prevent Werenich or anyone else from getting away with the same type of nonsense in the future. That sounded great, but somehow, at this stage of the game, it wasn't enough. The CCA board had allowed Werenich to bully them, going way back to the Werenich issue at the opening dinner in Victoria in 1984. How was some new legislation going to change anything?

So, I set out on a mission to tabulate not only all the details of the current Werenich episode, but also of his track record of causing the association, Garry DeBlonde, and yours truly grief and pain going back to the early eighties. My main concern was to attempt to convince the entire board of the CCA of the magnitude and seriousness of the situation. When the document was completed, it totalled over fifty pages and provided a complete history of everything that had taken place, going back to 1981. I produced a copy for every member of the CCA board, along with CEO Dave Parkes.

I believed that the curling populace overall did not favour Werenich, yet there was a nucleus of loyal supporters, especially in Ontario. And at the same time, the recently developed national coaches' group was shaking in its collective boots. That very group of people, the national coaches, held a meeting in Calgary on May 11, 1990. They were most concerned with the situation where Werenich demanded that an appointed national coach be removed and CCA authority, in the way of Ed Steeves, agreed to the demand. The following note sent to the CCA board summed up their joint position.

Note from National Coaches

May 13, 1990

Dear C.C.A. Board Member,

Those of us who have served Curl-Canada as international coaches were dismayed by the incident after the 1990 Brier where the winning team managed to convince the C.C.A. that the assigned international coach should be removed for the World Championship. That the matter was handled in a very high profile, public way was particularly upsetting. It made us realize that, without the support of the C.C.A. the same thing could happen to any of us. In our genuine efforts to serve curling as volunteers we are at the mercy of the teams we serve and we risk public embarrassment.

It is very worrisome to be involved in a sport where the legislative body is unable or unwilling to control individual athletes and therefore does not support its volunteers.

We urge the C.C.A. to develop guidelines which explain the role of the international coach and enforce those guidelines so that the above situation will not be repeated.

Sincerely,

Keith Reilly	*Ron Anton*
Gerry Peckham	*Jim Waite*
Jim Ursel	*Andre Ferland*
Vera Pezer	*Garry DeBlonde*

During the CCA annual meeting in Ottawa, June 14–17, Parkes and I, along with CCA lawyer Stewart McAlpine, worked diligently to develop detailed wording on two policy proposals that would ensure there would never be a repeat of the Werenich fiasco. The first policy was written to stipulate that a coach appointed to a world team by the CCA board would be a permanent fixture. That is, if the team didn't like the coach, the team would be replaced, not the coach. The second piece of legislation was a little more complex but was a long overdue disciplinary policy. In a nutshell, it defined the various situations that could place a player in a position of being disciplined, with the ultimate penalty being suspension. On the top of the list of violations that could lead to disciplinary action was public criticism of a CCA coach, official, staff member, or board member.

The board meeting, the first of a new amalgamated old CCA and CLCA, was a long and arduous affair. It appeared from the word go that President Ed Steeves did not really want to have anything to do with a policy that had teeth in it. Why? I think he, as well as anyone, knew how volatile the likes of a Werenich could be, and he felt he could be pressured into enforcing the new disciplinary policy. Nevertheless, at eleven p.m. on June 15, 1990, the board gave its approval of both policies, and Steeves wasn't happy. Through a divide-and-conquer approach, he managed to call a special in-camera meeting of the executive the following day to make one final attempt to sidetrack the new policies. The attempt was in vain, and on the morning of June 17, the CCA membership voted in favour of both new policies.

The next morning, I called Ian MacLaine at Canadian Press (CP) in Toronto to give him all the information. He wrote a story that must have made Steeves a little nervous since it indicated the policies had been developed as a result of the 1990 Brier scene with Werenich. This was, of course, true, yet Steeves took the position that it was simply the fact that curling was coming of age and needed to put some new required policies in place.

I felt it would only be days, maybe hours, before some reporter would contact Werenich for his opinion, and the cat would be out of the bag again, but nothing happened. In early July, I contacted MacLaine and asked him to do a story on Werenich for the *Curling Canada Magazine*. On Wednesday, July 11, MacLaine went to Werenich's home for the interview. The following day, the copy arrived on my fax and I couldn't believe what I was reading. Basically, Werenich suggested the entire matter following the Brier was a tongue-in-cheek scam... done in fun?

I immediately went to my VCR and inserted a tape from a TSN program with Pat Marsden interviewing Werenich exactly one week after the Brier in Sault Ste. Marie. Marsden's opening comments were, "Now, Wrench... were you really serious about all those comments made at the Soo?" Werenich's reply, "Absolutely."

Werenich Summary

I think it is necessary for me to clarify a few things with regard to the entire situation with Ed Werenich. Ed wasn't alone when it came to curlers who were opposed to what took place leading into and following the 1988 Olympics. Curling in those days, at the top level, was almost like a cult, and many of the people who were enjoying success were not too anxious to change anything. Deep down inside, Ed Werenich probably didn't want curling to be considered as an Olympic sport because it would change everything for him. He liked it the way it was. I will emphasize that he was not alone—he was just more vocal, and because of the success he enjoyed during those years, he was in a position to offer loud opinions about what he really didn't like. I do not fault Ed Werenich to the degree that I fault members of the Canadian Curling Association board, who repeatedly allowed themselves to be bullied by Werenich. The action of the CCA board from those days is not much different to how many other sport volunteer boards have dealt with various issues over the years. Anyone who thinks that the fuss created around the camps and trials prior to the 1988 Games and then the 1990 World Men's Curling Championships fiasco went unnoticed by the COA and the IOC are very naive. It was all covered in every media outlet in Canada, and I'm sure the Olympic poobahs had a chat amongst themselves and quietly decided that Mr. Samaranch and his friends did not care to take a risk of having to face similar challenges with curling's athletes.

I tried desperately at the meetings in June to get Steeves and the CCA board to do something with Werenich, but other than pass the two new pieces of disciplinary legislation for the future, there was no desire to do anything further. I weighed the entire situation, and as a result, at the end of June 1990, resigned from all of my duties with the NTPC and the national coaching system. I think a huge factor was the lack of desire by CCA board members to enforce any sort of legislation that involved an athlete that was obvious. Was this going to change going forward? Doubtful. My job with the CCA was now totally centred around events, and that is where I narrowed my focus. I continued to do whatever I could to influence the bid for Olympic medal status, but I was finished with the high-performance aspect of curling in Canada.

Garry DeBlonde felt he had also been put through enough, and as a result, resigned as technical director in the latter part of July and returned to Winnipeg. In September 1990, Gerry Peckham became the new technical director.

I will discuss it further in a future chapter, but this was pretty much the end of the NTPC, as the committee was not involved with determining the curling teams to represent Canada at the second demonstration in 1992 at Albertville.

CHAPTER 25
Albertville—That Was Really Pralognan-la-Vanoise

BY EARLY 1991, it was clear that curling would again be a demonstration sport at the 1992 Olympics in Albertville, France, but it was also clear what happened in Albertville would have little if any impact on the possibility of curling ever becoming a full medal sport. Prior to the Scott Tournament of Hearts in Saskatoon, it was announced that Canada's representatives at the 1992 Olympics in Albertville would be the winners of the Scotties in Saskatoon and the Brier in Hamilton.

Alberta's Kevin Martin made his first appearance at the Brier and came away the winner. Similarly, BC's Julie Skinner (Sutton) won the Hearts. Both teams were the image that curling wanted to portray in Albertville, and Skinner and Martin were both former Canadian junior champions. Skinner already had Elaine Dagg-Jackson in place as her teams coach, and Jules Owchar was the mentor for the Martin team. The CCA technical director, Gerry Peckham, was named as the team leader, and two people from the old NTPC program, Ron Anton and Vera Pezer, were named as consultants to the two teams. Both teams were put into a special program to follow between May and February 1992, but, otherwise, there wasn't really anything special done with either team. Plans continued for Skinner to participate at the Hearts in Halifax as Team Canada after the Olympics while Martin put things in place to participate in the Alberta playdowns prior to the Olympics. Martin won Alberta and placed third at the 1992 Brier in Regina after returning from the Olympics. Meanwhile, Sutton made it to the final of the Hearts before falling to Manitoba's Connie Laliberte.

The NTPC had been dissolved in 1990, and I was no longer involved with the CCA high-performance program, so I really did not have a role with the two teams representing Canada at Albertville. However, I still ended up with a function at the 1992 Olympics. I had served in two different positions at the Calgary Games in 1988, which had, in fact, caused its own bit of confusion. I was accredited as a member of the Calgary Organizing Committee, but in addition, my old friend Frank Ratcliffe, who was the OCO communications director, also named me as the media attaché for curling at the 1988 Games. This sent everyone into a tailspin, and it was eventually sorted out because apparently no one in Olympic history had ever held two accreditations. So, maybe I was the first, but at the 1988 Olympics, I held a host committee accreditation and a media accreditation.

The venue where curling was a demonstration sport at the 1992 Olympic Winter Games at Prolagnan-la-Vanoise, France.

I had not planned on attending the 1992 Games in Albertville, but in October 1991, I was again contacted by Frank Ratcliffe, who asked if I would like to be the COA media attaché for curling in Albertville. I accepted, and as a result, I was also in for an experience that was going to be very different from what had taken place in Calgary. First and foremost, curling was being staged a long, long ways from Albertville. Curling was being held in Pralognan-la-Vanoise, which was anything but on the beaten path. Today, the population of Albertville is shown as around 20,000, while Pralognan-la-Vanoise shows a total of about 1,000 full-time residents. To sum it up, Pralognan is a ski village high in the French Alps, about a one-hour-plus drive from Albertville, with a stretch of the road in winter being one-way because it was so narrow. A strange building was built for curling that was like a modified curling club, and was built to house the special needs for the Olympics, including television coverage.

From the time I arrived in Pralognan, I only made it back into Albertville and the main media centre once. We all arrived in Pralognan on Thursday, and Sunday evening a trip was planned back to the main media centre with the two skips, Julie Skinner and Kevin Martin. It did not start well, as the driver did not know where he was going, and when he finally found the main media centre, there wasn't anywhere to park. We finally got there about thirty minutes late, and because of that, a lot of the Canadian media did not stick around, but some of the faithful supporters of curling, such as Larry Wood and Terry Jones, were present. We did not get back to Pralognan until about eleven p.m., so all in all, from start to finish, the trip took about seven hours, and it was the last time I was in Albertville until I departed Pralognan about one week later.

The bronze-medal winners (curling demonstration) from Canada on the podium at the 1992 Winter Olympics. From the left Elaine Dagg-Jackson, Karri Wilms, Melissa Soligo, Jodie Sutton and Julie Sutton-Skinner.

Team Canada skip, Kevin Martin, left and third Kevin Park, discuss their next shot at the 1992 Winter Games in Prolagnan-la-Vanoise, France.

There were a number of difficulties with curling in Pralognan, not the least of which was that few of the locals knew anything about curling, but were given the green light by the organizing committee to run the event. There were many conflicts with everything from how the draw was scheduled and how the ice was installed and maintained. The ice conditions were awful, and at one point, one sheet of ice was shut down for a time. Kevin Martin, who was also a trained ice technician, got involved in the preparation at one point to help with the entire situation until IOC officials told him to stop.

My job as the media attaché for the COA was anything but simple. I was the only person from the Canadian media in Pralognan, so anything that was going to be provided to the main media centre had to come from me. This was before the internet and email, and while there was a computer link between me and the main media centre, it was anything but fast. Following every Canadian game, I had to gather a number of interviews, then transcribe them and transfer them to the media centre in Albertville. At the same time, I was to answer any questions the Canadian media might have, and of course, there wasn't any television coverage until the playoffs. Anyway, we all got through it, and in the end, the women managed to win the bronze medal and the men lost the bronze final. Below is the summary that was carried in the 1992 edition of *Curling Canada Magazine.*

1992 Olympic Curling

Swiss Men Mine Gold

Thievery played a major role in Switzerland's charge to the men's gold medal in Winter Olympic Games demonstration competition at Pralognan-la-Vanoise, France.

Urs Dick and his team of Jurg Dick, Robert Hurlimann and Thomas Klay stole the 7–6 winner in an extra-end gold medal final against Norway's Tormod Andreassen. In the semi-finals leading to the gold-medal match, Dick stole three crucial points en route to an 8–4 victory over Canada's Kevin Martin of Edmonton.

Martin failed to reach the medals, losing 9–2 to Bud Somerville of the USA in the bronze medal game. Andreassen overcame an early 3–0 deficit to hammer the USA 8–3 in the other semi-final and held control throughout much of the premier showdown. Norway had earlier breezed undefeated through the Group A preliminary, downing Switzerland 11–3 en route. Martin was unbeaten in Group B.

In the end, Switzerland and Norway were 4–1, Canada and the USA 3–2, Hammy McMillan of Scotland, representing Great Britain, finished 2–2 while Dominique Dupont-Roc of France and Hugh Millikin of Australia were 1–3 and Dan-Ola Eriksson of Sweden was 0–4.

Golden Girls From Germany

Former world champion Andrea Schopp of Garmisch-Partenkirchen twice defeated defending world champion Dordi Nordby of Norway en route to the gold medal in Winter Olympic Games demonstration play at Pralognan-la-Vanoise.

Schopp, skipping Stephanie Mayr, Monika Wagner and Sabine Huth, broke up a 2–2 match with seven points in the seventh and eighth ends to wallop Nordby 9–2 in the gold medal final.

Each team had posted a 2–1 record in Group A preliminaries along with Jackie Lockhart of Scotland, representing Great Britain. It was Lockhart who dealt Schopp her only defeat of the competition, 6–4 in the second round of Group A. Thereafter Schopp hung tough by whipping Nordby, undefeated in her first two games, 7–3. In tie-breakers, Germany stole a 10th-end single to oust Lockhart 5–4 and Nordby finished off Lockhart 9–4.

In the semis, Schopp again needed a 10th-end single to dispose of former world champion Helena Blach of Denmark 6–5 while Nordby wallowed Julie Sutton of Canada 9–2. Sutton claimed the bronze medal by defeating Blach 9–3. Canada sailed through Group B without a defeat while Blach lost only to Sutton 12–2.

Germany finished 5–1, Canada 4–1, Norway 4–2 and Denmark 2–3. Among the also-rans, Anette Norberg of Sweden was 2–2, Lockhart was 2–4, Annick Mercier of France was 1–3 and Seguchi Mayumi of Japan finished 0–4.

CHAPTER 26
Another Unnecessary Distraction

ROB WILSON-ROGERS WAS the president of the Rogers Group, which represented Pepsi-Cola, and as a result, was the company's agent for the operation of the Pepsi Junior Men's and Women's Championships. In addition, Rob Wilson-Rogers had a number of other companies in the stable he was primarily managing from a sponsorship point of view, and one of the companies/brands was cigarette manufacture Craven "A" Inc. (a division of Rothmans).

The Government of Canada had been putting huge pressure on the involvement of tobacco companies in sport, going back to 1972, and it was probably the main reason Macdonald Tobacco ended its fifty-year relationship with the Brier back in 1979. In addition, Sport Canada was funding the CCA to the tune of around $400,000 per year, and there was little question that if the CCA allowed a tobacco company to be associated with the sport in any way, funding would be gone in a moment. Bill C151 had been passed years before, and it clearly stated that any amateur sport organization receiving funds from a tobacco company could not receive any financial support from Sport Canada. Besides, we were in the final stretch toward curling becoming an Olympic medal sport, and if that did not happen by July 1992, it was probably never going to happen. So having anything out there that suggested the largest curling nation in the world was considering involvement with a tobacco company would not be good.

Sometime in November 1991, a number of discussions took place between CCA CEO Dave Parkes, President Mary-Anne Nicholson, and Wilson-Rogers. In addition, Parkes had positioned Wilson-Rogers as a potential member of the CCA Marketing Development Committee, yet as the CCA person responsible for marketing, I was kept in the dark on this fact. Parkes was aware that things were possibly going to change with Labatt, yet nothing official had been brought to our attention.

Parkes and I were summoned to a meeting with Labatt in Ottawa in January 1992 that was a bit of a surprise. We met with John Hudson, who at the time was the director of marketing for Labatt, and his message to us was very clear. While he did not wish to go public with the announcement, he was giving us a heads-up that at the end of the 1994 Brier in Red Deer, Alberta, Labatt would not be renewing its sponsorship of the Brier. It wasn't a surprise because after the 1988 Olympics, Labatt had been cutting costs everywhere possible, and they were spending a significant amount on the Brier. I was not fully aware of what Parkes and Rob Wilson-Rogers were working on at the time, but I was soon to find out.

The letter below was sent to Parkes at the end of January.

Dear Mr. Parkes,

As indicated in my letter of November 21, 1991, we are interested in establishing a long-term relationship between our company and the Canadian Curling Association (CCA).

This letter outlines the sponsorship rights we wish to acquire and the nature of the commitment we are willing to make to the CCA. To ensure that any questions or issues are resolved early we have arranged to have our representatives available to your committee on February 8th. We trust that we will be able to reach an agreement in principle at that time. Our intention would be to review this agreement with our own board of directors on February 13th.

I have taken the liberty of structuring the agreement we seek in three parts: specifically; the sponsorship rights we seek, our mutual obligations and finally, our financial offer to the CCA.

Sponsorship Rights to be Granted Craven "A" Inc. by the CCA
It is our understanding that the CCA and its affiliated provincial/territorial associations are the sanctioning body for the National and Provincial Men, Women, Mixed and Seniors Championships (the "Championships"). Craven "A" Inc. wishes to acquire the following rights:

1. *The right to include 'Craven "A" Inc.' in the name of each event making up the Championships.*
2. *The ownership of the broadcast rights to Championships.*
3. *The exclusive right to on-ice broadcast visible signage at the championships.*
4. *The right to badge competitors participating at the Championships.*
5. *Dominant editorial and advertising space in CCA publications and event programs associated with the Championships.*
6. *The right to approve any and all of the 'Craven "A" Inc.' name in promotion and/or merchandising of the Championships.*
7. *The right to badge teams winning the Championships and representing Canada in the World Curling Championships.*

In recognition of your existing contract with Labatt Brewing Company, acceptable timing for Craven "A" Inc. acquiring these sponsorship rights would be:

1992–93 (October–March)
-National/Provincial Women's Championships
-National/Provincial Mixed Championships
-National/Provincial Seniors Championships

1994–95 (October–March)
-National/Provincial Men's Championships

Mutual Obligations of Craven "A" Inc. and the CCA

It is our understanding that a process for selecting Championship host cities exists and that the legal and business relations between the host organizer, sponsor and CCA are governed by a document referred to as a Tripartite Agreement. We would assume that a similar process would govern our sponsorship.

We believe our relationship should be such that the CCA is responsible for the operational management of the Championships and Craven "A" Inc. assume the proper role as sponsor of the events. To this end, our mutual obligations would be as follows:

1. *The CCA, with the approval of Craven "A" Inc., would retain their right to levy Championship assessments from host organizers.*

2. *The CCA, with the approval of Craven "A" Inc., would be responsible for the management of co-sponsors and suppliers to the Championships and would retain any income that may be obtained from such activities.*

3. *The CCA, with the approval of Craven "A" Inc., would be able to sell and retain the income from licensed merchandise promoting the Championships.*

4. *The CCA would be responsible for the management of the Championships and all costs associated with competitor travel, accommodation and per diem expenses, in addition to technical, media relations and hospitality expenses.*

5. *The CCA would be responsible for paying any and all provincial/territorial subsidies that may be required under this agreement.*

6. *Craven "A" Inc. would be responsible for paying for their advertising and promotion supporting their sponsorship, and any trophy, sponsor signage and player identification costs surrounding the Championships.*

7. *Craven "A" Inc. would use the broadcast advertising time secured from the networks broadcasting the Championships to assist the CCA in attracting and retaining co-sponsors and suppliers to the Championships.*

Craven "A" Inc.'s Offer to the CCA

Assuming that the CCA is willing to grant the foregoing to Craven "A" Inc., we are willing to offer to the CCA:

1. *A ten-year sponsorship commitment, the initial term of which would extend from April 1, 1992 to March 31, 2002.*
2. *A sponsorship fee of $10,000,000 payable over the initial term.*
3. *A first installment of $1,000,000 payable over the initial term.*
4. *The balance of the sponsorship fee paid in nine (9) equal installments of $1,000,000 each on or before January 15th in each year of a National Championship beginning in 1994 and ending in 2002.*
5. *A guarantee that should Craven "A" Inc. withdraw its sponsorship that the CCA would receive the equivalent of 1 ½ years of sponsorship or $1,500,000 over the termination period unless such termination occurred in the final two years of the initial term.*
6. *Notice of continuation of this agreement no later than April 1, 2000—such notice which would automatically renew this agreement on similar terms and conditions.*

This letter and offer does not constitute a formal agreement but is submitted to you for consideration by your committee.

We would like a decision by your committee by February 9, 1992 and we understand that final acceptance would be dependent on board approval and acceptance by the Member Associations on the philosophical issue of tobacco sponsorship.

We look forward to our discussions on February 8th and wish you every success in your deliberations.

Sincerely,

Vice President
Craven "A" Inc.

I was summoned to a meeting in Ottawa for February 7 and 8 to discuss the proposal with President Mary-Anne Nicholson, Vice President Stan Oleson, and Parkes. It did not take us long to get right into it. I expressed in the strongest possible terms that nothing should happen with the proposal until after the final meeting of the IOC Program Commission, which we thought was set for some time in late April. If curling was possibly to receive the nod to be an Olympic medal sport, an association with a tobacco company could not happen. All three agreed with me until later in the day, when Rob Wilson-Rogers walked into the room, and within minutes, he managed to move everything back to his agenda—an agenda that had some very deliberate time lines and with some well-thought-out reasoning. I don't think it was any coincidence that the proposal landed on our laps just twelve days before the Albertville Olympics, with a deadline of April 1, 1992, for acceptance. If curling did, in fact, get medal sport acceptance, Parkes would have little choice except to drop the tobacco idea, but if it was done before the announcement by the IOC... it was done.

In 1992 Dave Parkes was the CEO of the CCA and he headed the committee that wanted Craven "A" to become the title sponsor of all the CCA national championships with the exception of the juniors.

When I was summoned to the meeting in Ottawa for February 7, I was also advised that Craven "A" would be holding a media training session on Saturday, February 8, that was supposed to help the CCA people deal with questions about tobacco sponsorship. In the end, it was one of the most annoying, frustrating days of my life. It wasn't a media training session but, in fact, a day with some very definite plans to plant in our brains the message Rothmans wanted us to deliver on their behalf. The entire day was conducted as if the tobacco arrangement was a done deal, and they were simply giving us the final lesson on how to blow all of this by the member associations and media. Some very basic psychological manipulation techniques were used, such as eight of them versus four of us, complete with the good cop–bad cop approach. They knew I was a potential problem, so they recruited the other three seemingly compliant CCA people in the room to assist in badgering me. I flew home to Vancouver on Saturday night but called Parkes at his home on Sunday and expressed how disgusted I was with everything that had taken place on Saturday. I indicated I was not prepared to say anything positive to anyone about Rothmans because there wasn't anything you could say positive about them. They had acted like thugs, and frankly, they were trying to steal something and knew it.

On February 21, I was copied on a letter sent to Don Pettit of Scott Paper and John Hudson at Labatt that advised both sponsors of the discussions the CCA was having with a possible tobacco sponsor. I was not consulted on the letter, but I thought it was really bad taste and insulting to the two companies that had spent millions of dollars on curling over the past decade. I was also shocked to see that my name was no longer listed as a member of the committee that was investigating the sponsorship possibility. When I questioned Parkes on it later, he suggested I was removed from the committee because of my comments at the meeting on February 8, where I had made it clear I was not in support of the tobacco sponsorship. To say that I was upset would be an understatement. My job was to be the key person in the organization when it came to dealing with sponsorship and proposing what I felt was the best for the CCA. Obviously, my thoughts and concerns were going to be completely ignored. For now?

First and foremost, in addition to a deal being considered with a tobacco company, the amount was simply not enough money and wouldn't even replace the money currently being spent by Labatt and Scott. Then there was the Sport Canada funding. Sport Canada was funding the CCA to the tune of about $400,000 per year, which would be gone, and the organization would also be kicked out of the National Sport and Recreation Centre. Then there was the question of Olympic inclusion. If curling became an Olympic medal sport, its Sport Canada funding would quickly move up the ladder of the top five or six sports. This would initially mean at least a doubling in the funding, and with the tobacco sponsorship, this would all be lost. I had no idea what Parkes was thinking, and he really had no intention of trying to explain it to me. Perhaps he did not think he had to?

I flew to Halifax on January 26 for the Hearts and the women's policy meetings. (The old CLCA and old CCA were amalgamated in 1990 to the new CCA.) The women and men still held separate meetings at the respective championships, which were referred to as policy meetings. For a topic to be on the agenda of the AGM in June, it needed to be passed for acceptance by at least one of the policy meetings. On March 2, the president, Mary-Anne Nicholson, and Dave Parkes presented the details of the tobacco deal to the women's contingent from the provincial/territorial associations. At the conclusion of the presentation, the provincial/territorial delegates asked for my opinion on what Parkes and Nicholson had presented, but Nicholson let the delegates know very quickly that I would not be granted permission by the chair to speak. So, I was silenced, for now.

Mary Anne Nicholson was the President of the CCA in 1992 and she was in full support of Craven "A" becoming the title sponsor of the Brier and the Scotties which would of had a major impact on any possibility curling might of had to become an Olympic medal sport.

Four days later, at the women's policy meeting AGM, Marilyn Barraclough, who was a CLCA past president from Yellowknife, put a motion on the floor that I be allowed to speak to the tobacco sponsor. It was seconded by the delegation from Ontario. Nicholson and Parkes were in a position to do absolutely nothing because the motion was passed by the majority of the delegates. I stood up and started to answer questions, and the key question that turned the tide was a simple one. If the CCA was to accept the sponsorship proposal from Craven "A", would it impact the ability of the CCA to receive financial support from Sport Canada? I stood up and, in a very calculated way, laid everything on the table. Yes, it would impact the ability for the CCA to receive any support from Sport Canada. I added further that if curling was to ever have a chance of becoming an Olympic medal sport, having the largest curling nation in the world complete a sponsorship agreement with a tobacco company would not benefit that cause in any way, shape, or form. That was all the delegates needed to hear as they voted overwhelmingly to not accept the Craven "A" proposal. Parkes and Nicholson were beside themselves, but there was nothing they could do. The tobacco deal had one more chance, and that was to pass at the men's policy meeting at the Brier in Regina, but that was highly unlikely after the defeat at the women's policy meeting. It was clear the women did not have any stomach to cancel the agreement with Scott Paper, and if something happened at the meetings in Regina that the men somehow decided to vote in favour of the Rothmans agreement, it would, amongst other things, signal a clear split between men's and women's curling in Canada.

However, Rob Wilson-Rogers gave it one more shot as he barrelled forward with his presentation at the men's policy meeting on March 14, but again, the membership voted against the proposal. While one would have thought that was the end of it, the following article on March 14 in the *Regina Leader-Post* had some interesting quotes from the president, to say the least.

> ***CCA Receives Pitch from Rothmans***
> *By Murray McCormick*
>
> *The increasing popularity of curling may be reflected in a bid put forward by Rothmans International.*
>
> *Rothmans has offered the Canadian Curling Association $1 million a year for 10 years to sponsor four major championships. Under terms of the bid, Rothmans would become the sole sponsor of the men's, women's, mixed and senior (men's and women's) championships.*
>
> *Labatt has an agreement with the CCA that covers its sponsorship of men's curling through 1994—the '93 Brier will be in*

Ottawa, with the '94 event in Red Deer. Labatt currently pays the CCA $50,000 a year for those rights.

Scott Paper is signed for the 1993 ladies' championship in Brandon, and is financially committed for the 1994 tournament which is scheduled for Kitchener–Waterloo, Ontario.

The mixed and senior events are presently without sponsors.

The Rothmans bid was discussed during the CCA's policy meetings, which were held during Brier week.

"We're like any other business," CCA president Mary-Anne Nicholson said. "If we get a written deal we must approach our partners, which is what we are doing.

"Has a decision been made? Absolutely not. We have two of the best sponsors in the world in Scott Paper and Labatt. But as a responsible board of directors, we have to look at any offer."

Using a tobacco company as a major sponsor would present some problems for the CCA. Those companies are banned from advertising their products on television and radio.

"It would open up avenues for us to make more money," Nicholson said. "Maybe Labatt can or Scott can, too. We have an open mind."

The CCA has been accused of less than that. But Nicholson said, "The CCA is actually every provincial body in Canada. That's who we are, we get elected so we have to take some of it. That's OK, we have broad shoulders."

If you're going to be a CCA member, you need broad shoulders. The association is often the fall-guy for everything from taking too much money out of the Brier to making arbitrary decisions that aren't in the best interests of curling.

> *"We only have two vehicles, other than Sport Canada, that make any money for us – the Brier and the Scott," Nicholson said. "Most curlers know what we gain from here we put out to curlers. They know we have to make something to promote junior curling.*
>
> *"If we don't do that, we won't have curlers at this level."*

A couple of shocking things for sure. First, that after the rejection of the tobacco proposal by both policy meetings, it seemed the board, led by Nicholson, had not let it go. The other interesting item was the reference to a $50,000 rights fee provided by Labatt. What was not mentioned was the fact that Labatt admittedly spent around $1 million per year on curling in Canada, which included all the expense for operating the Brier. Meanwhile, Scott Paper spent well over $500,000 for the total operation of the Scotties. Yes, Rothmans were going to pay the CCA a $1-million-per-year rights fee. The association would still hold the responsibility of paying the costs of operating the Brier, Hearts, Mixed, and Seniors. By my calculation, at the time after all those costs were covered, even in a modest way, there would be little left of the $1 million. In addition, the approximate $400,000 per year received from Sport Canada would be gone, so it did not take a brilliant mind to do the math. What Nicholson and Parkes were looking at is still beyond my understanding today. The deal would have been a deficit even in the first year, never mind ten years later. And it would leave the bid for curling to be an Olympic medal sport anything but positive with the largest curling nation in the world making a deal with a tobacco company.

The idea of Rothmans becoming the sponsor of the Brier and Hearts was dead, and now a new plan was on the table. Parkes and I were advised by the board to work with Rothmans and Rob Wilson-Rogers to attempt to develop a possible curling professional tour that could involve Rothmans. The instructions were very clear. If it was possible to develop a concept that would be workable and would not jeopardize the CCA position with Sport Canada, then we were to bring it forward to the board for consideration. A couple of board members made it really clear that until the staff person responsible for sponsorship (myself) was able to bring something forward that would be worthy of consideration, the board should not have any further involvement.

On April 9, Rob Wilson-Rogers faxed me the potential details of an idea that would become the Canada Cup of Curling. A few days later, he called me to discuss the idea in detail for well over an hour. His final words to me suggested he did not know where this whole thing was going, but when he did, I would be the first one to know. The next day, I received more faxed info from Wilson-Rogers, but then he went silent.

On May 20, I received a fax from Parkes that was pretty much the last straw and caused me to phone Dave immediately. It asked for my input on a world invitational idea that was virtually the same information I had received from Rob Wilson-Rogers on April 9, with his famous last words that whatever transpired, I would be the first to know. I was further shocked to find that Wilson-Rogers had also spoken to the president and vice president and was attempting to arrange to make a presentation at the June board meeting. I'd had no idea that any discussions were taking place at all.

In the meantime, Labatt got a hold of this whole thing, making it even more confusing. Although John Hudson had told Dave Parkes and I in January that Labatt would be done with the Brier after the 1994 event, I was still working with Bill Vronsky at Labatt in an attempt to find a way to keep the brewer involved. Vronsky was not happy with what was going on between the CCA and Rothmans and had shown his displeasure directly to Rob Wilson-Rogers.

On June 1, I sent the attached letter to all board members of the CCA, suggesting the board had more good reasons to not consider dealing any further with tobacco sponsorship.

To: CCA Board and Senior Staff
From: Warren Hansen
Topic: International Invitational and Tobacco Sponsorship

In discussion with Bill Vronsky from Labatt on Thursday, May 28th it was brought to my attention that Rob Wilson-Rogers will be making a presentation on June 23rd at the board meeting on behalf of Rothmans. I will make my position very clear and well known… I DO NOT believe the CCA should be entertaining an involvement with a world invitational event with tobacco sponsorship.

TOBACCO SPONSORSHIP
Once and for all I think it needs to be made very clear that the sport of curling can't and shouldn't be associated with a tobacco manufacturer. The immediate and most obvious reasons are:

- *Without question Sport Canada will not condone the involvement of any sport that receives Sport Canada funding with, tobacco. So, it simply means that if curling directly or indirectly receives one cent from tobacco it will be the end of administration and salary grants, the association with the Coaching Association of Canada and residency in the National Sport and Recreation Centre (NSRC). CURLING CAN'T TOUCH TOBACCO TODAY, TOMORROW OR EVER WITHOUT A CHANGE IN GOVERNMENT POLICY!*
- *We do not know any of the details but it is obvious that a great number of the CCA member associations, if not all, would in turn lose all of their provincial/territorial government funding. To the best of my knowledge the impact of this situation has not been investigated at all and is unknown?*
- *There also has never been any investigation of the potential corporate isolation that could result from an association with tobacco. Common sense would tell you it would create problems with a company that is lifestyle orientated or whose target markets are anti-smoking. But we have no idea how extensive this problem could be. Obviously, it is a*

concern because we look across the North American sport mosaic there is no visual presence of tobacco with any amateur sport of any consequence and the same situation exists with professional sport. If tobacco is such a good deal why aren't sports with more to offer than curling such as hockey, skiing and figure skating, to mention a few, not involved?

- *The matter of the anti-smoking lobby and potential concern of these special interest groups is a total unknown. Would we care to have the Cancer Society handing out anti-smoking literature at the entrance to each of our events?*

Then there is the matter of substance tobacco. How could we possibly consider making a deal with these people knowing the facts that are available today. The dictionary says nicotine is a poisonous water soluble alkaloid, found in tobacco leaves and used ordinarily in an aqueous solution of sulfate, as an insecticide. IT IS A DRUG AND A POISON!

There is no such thing as a moderate smoker! People who smoke are addicted! Any company who kills 48,000 of its best customers per year has to continually find new patrons. Who are the new customers going to be? There is little question that all tobacco promotion and influence will be aimed at the youth in the country. How many people do you know that smoke that didn't start until they were over the age of 20? Does the CCA wish to be part of this deadly game?

On June 27th the CCA will recognize the achievements of a curling executive who has made an outstanding contribution to the game of curling. The award is presented in the name of Ray Kingsmith, a person who gave more to curling than anyone I have ever known. Ray passed away at the age of 60 from lung cancer as a result of smoking. I still remember standing outside of Max Bell Arena during the 1988 Olympics with him as he coughed up blood and his comment, "is this what it took to make me quit." Six weeks later he was dead. During the same ceremony curling will also recognize Bill Good Sr. by inducting him into the Curling Hall of Fame. Bill won't be able to be in Ottawa on June 27th because he can't be without oxygen assisted breathing for more than a few minutes as a result of smoking.

THE FACTS

- *In Canada by 1995 it is expected 48,000 Canadians annually will die a death attributed to smoking. It is predicted that 500,000 will die a smoking related death in the Nineties (still today about 40,000 people die a year a smoking related death).*
- *It is predicted that tobacco will account for 26 percent of all deaths in 1995 (today it is still 17 percent).*
- *It is estimated that by 1995 14,000 Canadian men between the ages of 35 to 69 will die annually from tobacco use – about 39 percent of all male deaths in this age group.*
- *85% of lung cancer today is related to smoking.*
- *Lung cancer is the #1 cause of cancer deaths in men and it is #2 cause of cancer death in women.*
- *Second hand smoke can cause lung cancer in non-smokers.*

Does the Canadian Curling Association want to be partly responsible for making these statistics and predictions come true?

Based on the facts presented I feel there is little need for the CCA to spend more valuable staff and board time dealing with this issue.

I would strongly recommend all discussions with regard to tobacco sponsorships be discontinued and the presentation by Rothmans to the board on June 23rd should be cancelled.

If you have any questions or comments on the above PLEASE give me a call.

Thank you.

Sincerely yours,

Warren Hansen
Director of Competitions, Media and Corporate Relations

One might have thought that both Parkes and Nicholson would have got the message and cancelled the June 23 meeting, but not so. Just two days later, the memo below was sent out by Nicholson.

Memo To: Warren Hansen
From: Mary-Anne Nicholson, President
Copy To: CCA Board of Directors and Senior Staff
Subject: June 1 letter on International Invitational and Tobacco Sponsorship

I would like to bring to your attention that two Policy Meetings instructed the CCA Board of Directors to investigate all possibilities of curling sponsorships. Each policy meeting added restrictions to this mandate.

In the case of the women's policy meeting, they made it clear that at this point in time they were very happy with Scott Paper Ltd. sponsoring their event. The majority of the Provincial Representatives stated that the social aspect of tobacco and alcohol was equal in their opinion. They also stated that they did not want the sport funding to be in jeopardy, either at the federal or provincial level.

In the case of the men's policy meeting, they stated they wished us to first of all negotiate with Labatt if possible. They stated that if we could find a way in which we could keep the tobacco sponsorship involved without interfering with provincial or federal funding, we were to pursue same.

Further to this, the Board of Directors in attendance at the Brier discussed the possibility of an international invitational event similar to golf, tennis and equestrian—all of which receive tobacco sponsorship. Following this, two letters were written to Craven "A" Inc. by me (April 1 and April 8), which by the way, you received a copy of. We have received a request from Craven "A" Inc. representatives to make a presentation to the Board of Directors which we have booked for Tuesday, June 23 at 1:00 pm. I assume their presentation will be an answer to these two letters.

Warren, you have made your opinions known on numerous occasions regarding the tobacco industry. I would like to point out that the statistics on alcohol rival those of tobacco. They are not so well publicized but they are equally devastating. I can assure you that each of our Board of Directors would probably be able to relate, either in their immediate family or close friends, devastating consequences from both of these legal substances.

Ray Kingsmith and I were friends for forty years. I don't doubt that smoking was a contributing factor to his death, but I know that Ray's lungs were damaged many years ago through working conditions. We live in a country that allows freedom of choice. May I remind you that Ray had iron will when he wanted to use it.

Sincerely,

Mary-Anne Nicholson
President

Rob Wilson-Rogers made his pitch on June 23, but it did not really go far as the majority of the board voted against the idea. I assumed to a large degree it was because of my recommendation to not accept the proposal. I believe this was because it had been made clear by the early part of April that any proposal for sponsorship being considered required my recommendation. So, the tobacco deal died, but again, how much damage did it do to the image of curling in Canada? It was very public in Canada, as a number of media outlets covered it. Did it go unnoticed by Sport Canada and the Canadian Olympic Association? I doubt it. A few weeks later, at a program commission meeting of the IOC where curling was on the agenda, a Canadian skiing star Ken Read spoke soundly against curling gaining Olympic medal status. Was the smoking deal, along with everything else, enough for him to not want curling in the Olympic family? Who knows?

This is, again, one of those moments, like with the Hexagon deal, where you have to ask yourself, what were normally sensible, sane people thinking? Was it again some very slick operators able to put a shine on the whole tobacco industry that made it look so attractive on the surface it was hard to ignore? It made no sense from the moment I ever heard about it in 1992, and today, it makes even less sense. If this deal had gone through, the sport of curling in Canada would have suffered a blow from which it would have never recovered. Amongst other things, I doubt that Olympic medal status would ever have happened. My relationship with Dave Parkes was shattered because of the entire situation. Dave and I worked together at the CCA for another fifteen years, but it was never the same, and we were in constant conflict.

CHAPTER 27
The Japanese Connection

IN THE WINTER of 1986, I was contacted by a man from the Canadian Embassy in Tokyo by the name of Bob Merner regarding the possibility of doing some sort of a curling instruction tour of Tokyo. Bob suggested that curling was just getting rolling in the Tokyo area, and they needed some help. From that point, discussions started to take place between the embassy, the Canadian government, and CP Air regarding a possible tour to Japan in the fall of 1986. Bob put me in touch with a Japanese curler by the name of Hiroshi Kobayashi, and over the next months, communication between Bob, Hiroshi, and Hugh MacDonald at CP Air started to see things fall into place.

Hiroshi wanted us to bring a curling team along and requested the recently crowned Scott Tournament of Hearts champions, the Marilyn Bodogh team. I approached Hugh MacDonald at CP, and it did not take long for him to get back to me and confirm that CP would fly the five of us to Tokyo return. Hiroshi did not elaborate but told me clearly that upon arrival in Japan, everything would be taken care of.

Hiroshi Kobayashi, Warren Hansen and Bob Merner during Hansen's trip to Japan in October of 1986.

In the mid-October, I departed from Vancouver with Marilyn Bodogh, her team, and their husbands. When we arrived in Japan, we were met by Hiroshi and Bob Merner, who whisked us away to a hotel in downtown Tokyo. It was a gorgeous property, a Prince Hotel. I did recall that Prince did have a hotel in Toronto. Little did I know it was a Japanese chain, and I also knew little about the owner. Also, attached to the hotel was an arena that had five sheets of curling ice installed, which looked like a major event in Canada was about to be played there. What I could not understand was, who was in fact paying for all of this? We stayed at two different properties during our time in Japan, and each had an arena attached.

At some point in the first couple of days in Tokyo, I met this elder gentleman introduced as the Tokyo Curling Association president. Curling had been taking place in the northern island of Hokkaido for a few years, but there wasn't a Japanese Curling Association as such, so the group in Tokyo formed its own organization. However, the thing I did not understand about this gentleman, who was Kunio Nando, is that he did not know anything about curling, so why was he the president of the association?

Warren Hansen with Kunio Nando in Japan in 1986. Nando played a major role in leading curling to Olympic medal status at the 1998 Winter Games in Nagano, Japan.

During a discussion with the Canadian embassy people, some of the dots were connected. Nando was a well-known sports personality in Japan. He was a speed skater in the 1936 Olympics and had at one point been the president of the Japanese Speed Skating Association. Hiroshi Kobayashi's brother Sadao was a member of the Waseda University skate club, where he met Nando and somehow introduced him to Hiroshi. There were some other interesting connections. The Tsutsomi family owned many things in Japan, including the Seibu Railway and the Prince Hotels. The man now running the corporation was Yoshiaki Tsutsomi, who was also very prominent in the Japanese sporting community. Tsutsomi owned the Seibu Lions baseball team, a hockey team, golf courses, and was also very involved with the JOC. Between 1987 and 1990, Tsutsomi was rated as the richest man in the world, with a worth of about $18 billion. There was a connection between Nando and Tsutsomi in the fact that Mr. Nando's son was Mr. Tsutsomi's secretary. So, Nando probably was president of the Tokyo Curling Association for two reasons. One, he was connected to Tsutsomi, and two, he was heavily embedded into the Japanese sport system, and curling was a relatively unknown in those circles.

It was now clear why we were staying in the Prince Hotels and who was paying for our rooms, as well as the professional curling ice installation in each arena. Hiroshi had put this whole thing together very carefully, and his aim was to grow Japanese curling. With curling being a demonstration sport in Calgary, he also had the vision of curling being an Olympic medal sport. Our trip to Tokyo was a success, and many things were accomplished, which included teaching a number of people the basics, and all of us having the opportunity of playing in a bonspiel that was staged complete with pipers that made the whole presentation look like a mini-world championship.

The '86 venture was such a success that a trip for 1987 was in the planning stages before we left Japan. I returned in 1987, and this time, it was with the Canadian men's curling champion Russ Howard and his wife, Wendy, that made the journey to Tokyo with me. This trip was a little more diversified than the first venture, and amongst other things, we taught a number of people at Karuizawa, a small resort area to the west of Tokyo. Yes, you guessed it. While there, we stayed at the Karuizawa Prince Hotel. This was a very interesting stop on the trip, since when curling finally became part of the 1998 Olympics, it was Karuizawa that hosted curling.

Again, before we left Tokyo, a third trip was in the planning stages, but my involvement with the Calgary Games, along with my responsibilities to the CCA, made it next to impossible for me to continue to return to Japan. The last organized curling instruction clinic I ever did was in Karuizawa in the fall of 1987. It had been a fifteen-year run, dating back to my start with the Silver Broom School in October 1972.

Hiroshi travelled to Vancouver in the spring of 1988, and at his Canadian home in Whistler, I introduced him to Elaine Dagg and Glenn Jackson. I passed the torch to Elaine and Glenn, and from that point, Elaine became the main curling teacher in Japan. When the first Olympics happened for curling again in 1998, Elaine was the Japanese coach. Japan became a member of the then-ICF in 1985. At that time, curling was centred around the northern island of Hokkaido, but when the Tokyo Curling Association finally combined with the Japanese Association, Kunio Nando eventually became the president. In 2006, he was awarded the Elmer Freytag Award by the WCF for the work he did in getting curling into Nagano in 1998. Nando became a member of the World Curling Hall of Fame in 2012, when the WCF folded all the Freytag Award winners into the hall of fame. History now shows that he played a major role in curling eventually getting Olympic medal status, by being the man who connected the dots between curling, the Nagano Organizing Committee, and the IOC. All of this, of course, without question, involved the man who was behind the curtain: Yoshiaki Tsutsomi.

CHAPTER 28
The Final Sprint to Medal Status

FOLLOWING 1987, I no longer had a direct association with Hiroshi Kobayashi, yet I would talk to him on occasion and I would see him at the world curling championships. Hiroshi was also anxious to see curling become an Olympic medal sport, and that interest moved up a notch on June 15, 1991, when Nagano, Japan, was awarded the 1998 Winter Olympic Games.

Hiroshi called me in the latter part of May 1992 to advise that the program commission of the IOC would meet in Paris on June 16 to consider several applications for Olympic medal status. Two people from the Japanese Olympic Committee would be at the meeting and would be voting in favour of curling.

On June 18, I received a phone call from Hiroshi, who was pretty upset. His first question to me was, "Who is Mr. Ken Read?"

I replied, "He's a Canadian skier. Why do you ask?"

Hiroshi came right back with another question: "Why would he speak against curling?"

I was puzzled and started to dig further. I found out that Read was a member of the IOC's athlete commission and was sitting on the program commission as an athlete. He did speak against curling becoming a full medal sport. The following story, written by Read as told to James Christie, outlines why Read did what he did... sort of.

> ***Sport Verbatim***
> *By James Christie*
>
> *Up front it's appropriate to apologize for my thoughtless quote linking curling with darts and ballroom dancing. I know I wouldn't have liked it if my sport of skiing had been linked with roller derby and I should have taken that into consideration.*
>
> *Why I took the position I did with the subcommittee of the IOC's Program Commission was that I feel we must deal with a number of problems within the sports on the program gender equity, do the sports on the program already have an appropriate number of competitions, and there's always an issue of the size of the Games.*
>
> *Few people would argue that the Summer Games are too big. With the Winter Games many of the sports are outdoors and subject to vagaries of the weather. Even a one-day cancellation can throw a real monkey wrench into the schedule.*
>
> *We were asked to address a number of requests. Short-track speedskating wanted to include new distances, but not increase the quota of athletes. Free-style skiing was a medal sport at Albertville and the question was whether it was to stay on the schedule. Biathlon asked to include a new team event, but it was an artificial contest and so it was rejected.*
>
> *Ice hockey asked to have women's hockey. It adds to the size and complexity of the Games, but I was very much in favour of it because it addresses gender equality in the Olympics. Hockey is already an Olympic sport; it's not a new sport. Its inclusion will have a profound impact on women's sport.*
>
> *That brings us to curling... which would be a new medal sport and add to the program. I took the position of not supporting*

curling's inclusion. What's been represented back here is that my opposition nearly destroyed curling's chances. In fact, I was the third speaker of four on the committee who spoke against the inclusion of curling. It's wrong to suggest my opposition was the key point.

It's also important to note that we're only an advisory body ... I recognize there are many cases where the IOC does not accept the recommendation of the program commission.

There was a misunderstanding of my mandate at the meeting. I was there as a representative of the IOC athletes commission, not as a representative of Canada or of Western Canada. I represented both Olympic athletes and myself as an individual.

There was a surprise that a Canadian wasn't supporting a sport that has a wide following in Canada. But I wouldn't have been responding to my mandate if I supported curling just because I felt Canada would win a medal.

In summary, I believe the issue was blown out of proportion. I don't change my opinion because I don't think inclusion on the Olympic program is the be-all and end-all for a sport.

One of curling's strengths is its broad, grassroots appeal. Inclusion in the Olympics could bring elements (formalities) into the game that people in rural Alberta don't like.

Being in the Olympics has a tendency to make a sport very elite, and that would represent a loss to the sport.

If it had not been for Hiroshi calling me and asking about who Read was, Canada might have never known that he spoke against curling becoming a medal sport at the program commission. Hiroshi took some convincing that Canada, as a country, was still onside with curling's quest for medal status, that Read was acting on his own agenda, and that no one in Canada really understood why he was launching such a personal attack against a sport that was so strong in his native land. So, why did or would he do that? Who knows for sure, but there are a couple of good reasons. First and foremost would be the sharing of Olympic funds between the International Sporting Federations (ISFs). Following every Winter Games, each of the ISFs receives a share of funds from the Games. If curling were brought in, a new discipline would be introduced, which meant the pie would be split one more time. Read's sport of skiing would probably receive less funding if curling were accepted. I do not know Read, but indications from interviews and his overall persona would suggest that he was and probably still is very much a sport purist and a by-the-book kind of guy. Some of the hiccups within curling that became very public in Canada—including things like the Hexagon fiasco, the 1987 curling trials with the weight issue, and the willingness displayed by the CCA to accept tobacco as a sponsor of its largest events—could have all provided enough negative impact for Read to not feel comfortable accepting curling into the Olympic family.

The following story in the *Ottawa Citizen* on June 20 provides a summary of what took place at the meetings and that things were not looking very good for curling ever becoming a medal sport.

> ***Women's Ice Hockey a Good Bet For '98***
> *By Martin Cleary*
>
> *Women's ice hockey took a positive step this week toward becoming part of the 1998 Winter Olympics, but curling could be left in the hack.*
>
> *Freestyle skiing may be flying high for the 1994 Winter Olympics in Lillehammer, Norway, but ballet may have to wait another quadrennial.*
>
> *The program commission of the International Olympic Committee made these recommendations earlier this week after debating proposals from a variety of winter sports.*

The decisions are not final and must be discussed and voted on by the IOC's executive board. The earliest the executive board could address the recommendations is July 17–19 in Barcelona.

A women's ice hockey proposal was given a favorable reception by the program commission, although it fell short of meeting the major sport criteria—each sport must be widely practised in 25 countries on three continents.

It helped that ice hockey has been part of the Olympic family since 1920.

"Hockey didn't make any bones about the number of countries. They said they only had 20," said Calgary's Ken Read, an IOC program commission member. "They listed their registered players, but they didn't need (to meet) the strict criteria since ice hockey was on the calendar."

If the executive accepts the recommendation, women's hockey would be a medal sport in 1998 in Nagano, Japan, with a six-team tournament. By the 2002 Olympics, women's hockey would become a full team sport with eight countries.

Glynis Peters, manager of the Canadian Amateur Hockey Association female hockey program, was "happy and sad at the same time."

"That's great. I think we'll definitely be in for 1998," she said.

"But I was sad because there was a 50-50 chance of being in the 1994 Games."

The program commission rejected curling because it questioned the number of countries practicing the sport, and it couldn't resolve whether it was a high-performance or a recreation sport.

"Their documentation listed 23 countries, but Scotland, Wales and England form one national Olympic committee (Great

Britain), three were still not organized and ... I have deep reservations about how widely practiced the sport is in several other countries, like Mexico and Virgin Islands," Read said. "But the door is not closed."

Curling also was not well attended at the Winter Olympics in Albertville, France where it was a demonstration sport.

"We haven't been given formal notification of a negative recommendation from the program commission, but if that's the case, we'll be fairly disappointed," said Dave Parkes, Canadian Curling Association's general manager.

"We worked extensively to develop curling and meet the appropriate political steps. But we were well aware of some political pitfalls that lay ahead for us."

The program commission was impressed by how aerials skiing was organized at the 1992 Winter Olympics. But Read said ballet was "on a rocky road" and was put aside "for various reasons."

Tom Mc Illfaterick, managing director of Freestyle Canada, said the sport will still fight for ballet.

On June 22, 1992, Jack Lynch sent a memo to Canada's representatives to the IOC—Richard Pound, Carol Anne Letheren, and James Worrall—where he was questioning the message out of the Paris meeting that suggested women's hockey had been recommended for medal status while curling had not.

Lynch went on to point out that if the rumour was correct, it was very unfair for a number of reasons, which he stated as follows:

1. It makes a mockery of the argument—long raised by the ISU and IIHF—that curling is unacceptable because it will force organizing committees to provide additional ice arenas. (A six-team ice hockey round robin would require more ice time than two eight-team curling tournaments.)

2. A six-team ice hockey tournament will add more than 120 athletes to the Games, over three times as many as an eight-team women's curling competition would require.
3. The charter is unfair in allowing IFs that govern several different sports easier access to the program of the Games by defining them as "disciplines." (Women's ice hockey operates independently from the men's game, but has "insider" access to the IOC and less stringent worldwide practice requirements, simply because the latter is already on the program of the Games.)

He further pointed out that women's ice hockey had only held two world championships, only six teams had competed, and each time four of them were totally outclassed. Meanwhile, ten teams had been competing annually for the world women's curling championship, going back to 1979. It was suggested that it also flew in the face of the bidding cities for 1998, in particular Nagano, which had all given written approval of a women's curling competition.

While Lynch recognized that Pound, Letheren, and Worrall were not part of the executive committee, he felt they could have some influence to suggest the committee reject the recommendation of the program commission.

On July 7, I received a phone call from Hiroshi, and he suggested the JOC was very upset with the situation and the recommendation made by the program commission. He indicated that a meeting was being held between the JOC, the Nagano Organizing Committee, and the Japanese Curling Association (JCA) to determine a plan of attack regarding curling as a medal sport at the 1998 Games. Hiroshi reassured me a number of times that I should not worry, that everything would be worked out.

On July 9, the letter below went from Kunio Nando, president of the JCA, to Gunther Hummelt, president of the WCF.

Dear Mr. Hummelt,

An Organizing Committee meeting was held on July 6, 1992 in Tokyo. Discussed in the meeting were curling and women's ice hockey. As a result, final decisions on both topics were depended solely upon Mr. Eishiro Saito, chairman of the Organizing Committee. He consulted with the following four persons:

Mr. Yoshimura, Vice-Chairman of the OC,
Mr. Feruhaski, Vice-Chairman of the OC,
Mr. Hayaski, Executive Member of the OC,
Mr. Tsuda, Secretary General of the OC.

After their discussion they came to the following two conclusions:
(1) It is very difficult to accommodate women's ice hockey in the 1998 Winter Olympic Games.
(2) We should include curling in 1998, provided an existing ice arena outside Nagano City is available for the games. In addition, if the final decision could not be made at the IOC Executive meeting on July 17, 1992 in Barcelona, they'll ask the IOC Executive board to postpone their final decision. As you can easily guess, judging from what we've gone through so far, it is difficult for the Organizing Committee to present the IOC their decision.

We have therefore requested Mr. Furuhaski, President of the Japanese Olympic Committee, to write to Mr. Samaranch notifying him of the two conclusions as mentioned above. He agreed to do so and such a letter should have been sent by fax yesterday. The letter is also asking Mr. Samaranch to make necessary suggestions and recommendations to the executive board members.

Yes, it seems we are taking a long detour, but it is all necessary (please understand), partly because there are some people in Nagano City that are still against the Olympic games themselves (mainly because of an additional financial responsibility). That's why we had to follow this complicated procedure.

I gather you are going to Barcelona. Five organizing committee members are also going to attend the meeting (they're leaving on July 15, 1992).

They are:
Mr. Saito, President of the JOC
Mr. Tsukada, Mayor of Nagano City
Mr. Tsuda, Secretary General of the OC
Mr. Ogimura, Executive Member of the OC

They are going to stay at either one of the hotels below:
Hotel: Princess Sofia or the Royal

When I visited Nagano on July 3, 1992, I had a meeting with Mr. Soiehiro Yoshida. I asked hm to ask his friends in the IOC executive board, so they have a close cooperation with us.

Truly yours,

Kunio Nando
JCA President

On July 17, the program commission chair Vitaly Smirnov met with the executive committee on the IOC to put forth the recommendation of the acceptance of women's ice hockey but the rejection of curling for the third time. No one will ever know for sure what went on in the mind of President Juan Antonio Samaranch, except he stood up and suggested to Smirnov that he should reconsider the rejection of curling.

The Japanese lobby had apparently been very clear about Nagano wanting curling to be part of the 1998 program but would have trouble accommodating women's hockey. While no one will ever know for sure, the rumour mill said the Japanese lobby, with the blessing of Tsutsomi, suggested it would only be prepared to accommodate women's ice hockey at the 1998 Games if curling were also brought in as part of the medal program. Mr. Tsutsomi was still very much part of the scene, although he had to resign his position as the president of the JOC because of some irregularity by an underling. The IOC wanted women's hockey involved, and it was also easy to stomach the acceptance of curling since half of the participants would be women.

It was July 18, 1992, and an average Saturday morning, which found me by Jericho Beach, close to my Vancouver home, reading the morning *Vancouver Province.*

I was aware of the meeting of the IOC executive that had taken place in Barcelona, Spain, on the 17, at which time the future probably for all time of curling becoming an Olympic medal sport would be determined. However, I did not expect to hear the official results until the General Assembly meeting of the IOC on July 22. Nevertheless, I wasn't very hopeful because I knew the program commission was not going to recommend the acceptance of curling for the third time.

I came to the sports section and started to scan the second page when a headline caught my eye: "Canada's Medal Hopes Improve with New Events."

I zeroed in on the story, and the first item that jumped out was the inclusion of two more short track events for 1994. What I expected in the next paragraph was the usual "but curling didn't make it." I couldn't believe my eyes when the next paragraph read, "Curling was also granted full medal status and will be included by 2002—earlier if a rink is built for the Lillehammer Games or the 1998 Games in Nagano, Japan."

Emotion came over my whole body that was somewhere between disbelief and great joy. This was unbelievable! In the latter part of June, I knew the program commission had for the third time failed to provide a positive recommendation for curling as a medal sport. But it appeared that the plea by a number of people, and in particular, the JOC and the Nagano Organizing Committee had changed the view of the IOC executive committee. I immediately thought of Ray Kingsmith and how proud he would be of what had finally been accomplished from our humble beginnings way back in 1983. It was a tender moment as a tear came to my eye, knowing none of this would ever have happened without Ray and the initiative taken by him with the Calgary Organizing Committee a long time ago.

But the final official announcement from Barcelona and the 99th session of the IOC General Assembly stated as follows: "Men's and women's curling will be definitely included on the program of the Olympic Winter Games in 2002 and negotiations will be undertaken with the Nagano Organizing Committee to stage the sport in 1998 as well." Since the Nagano people, along with all the 1998 bidding cities, had promised to include curling even before they won the right to host the Games meant curling would be a medal sport in 1998. Of course, Nagano was going to make it happen because it was Japan who had made the final desperate plea to the executive committee of the IOC for curling to have medal status for 1998. While Nagano did not have the facilities required, the neighbouring City of Karuizawa was dying to host something Olympic and already had a curling facility. Interesting enough, on my second trip to Japan in 1987, Russ Howard and I directed a clinic at Karuizawa.

Many people claimed to have a role in curling becoming a medal sport, and the battle took place over a period of nine years. The key players from the curling world had originally been Ray Kingsmith and yours truly, who were the ones who initially convinced the 1988 Organizing Committee in Calgary to include curling as a demonstration sport. After the 1988 Games, Gunther Hummelt, Franz Tanner, and Jack Lynch picked up the torch and carried it to the finish line. Others helped the cause, particularly the three ICF/WCF presidents during that time—Clif Thompson, Philip Dawson, and Don Barcome—in addition to Gunther Hummelt. Kay Sugahara, who had connections in Japan, offered influence on the Nagano Organizing Committee for curling to be part of the 1998 Games.

CHAPTER 29
On to Nagano

FOLLOWING THE ANNOUNCEMENT in July 1992, that gave curling medal status, things went fairly quiet for a couple of years. Things moved along, and Japan officially agreed to include curling for 1998, and Karuizawa was named as the site.

The WCF decided that curling in the 1998 Olympics would involve eight men's and women's teams from the top eight nations in the world. In Canada, a number of discussions took place regarding holding a trials and how the teams participating would be determined and how many would be involved in the trials.

In my mind, it was important to go back and take a serious look at the camp situation from 1987, remembering that the majority of the curlers attending the camp liked the idea. However, after the fiasco created by the weight issue in 1987, there was a reluctance to address the camp idea because of the feared backlash. In place of the camps, the traditional approach was continued, where a skip put together a team with all four members being from the same city or region, and from that point attempted to be the best in the land. Eight teams (women and men) would compete for the right to represent Canada at the 1998 Games.

The Road to the 1997 Olympic Trials

MEN

WINNER OF	**SKIP**
1995 WCT Championship	Wayne Middaugh
1995 vs 1994 Labatt Brier champions playoff	Kerry Burtnyk
1996 Labatt Brier	Jeff Stoughton
1996 Canadian Club Cashspiel	Dave Smith
1996 Welton Beauchamp Classic	Mike Harris
1996 MT & T Mobility Classic	Ed Werenich
1996 Bessborough Classic	Brent MacDonald (2nd)
1996 WCT season points leader	Kevin Park/Doran Johnson
1997 Labatt Brier Winner	Kevin Martin
1996/97 WCT Championship Winner	Russ Howard

WOMEN

WINNER OF	**SKIP**
1994 vs 1995 Hearts playoff	Sandra Schmirler
1996 Hearts	Marilyn Bodogh
1996 Husky Autumn Gold	Shannon Kleibrink
1996 Welton Beauchamp	Sherry Scheirich
1996 MT & T Classic	Mary Mattatall
1996 SaskPower Ladies Classic	Anne Merklinger
1996/97 Women's Curling Tour	Cathy Borst (3rd)/Kelley Law (5th)
1997 Hearts	Alison Goring (2nd)
1997 CCA High Performance	Connie Laliberte

Brandon, Manitoba, was selected for the trials, but there were some other unique circumstances for the trials. It was the desire of the CCA to use the word "Olympic" in the title of the trials; however, it was quickly discovered that unless the Canadian Olympic Association (COA) was a partner in the operation, that would not be possible.

While that might have seemed simple enough, it wasn't because some of the CCA sponsors were competitors of the COA sponsors. And while the solutions to making it all a reality weren't easy, in the end, the event became a joint venture of the CCA, COA, and the Brandon host committee, and it became known as the 1997 Olympic Curling Trials. It was the first and only trials that Curling Canada partnered with the COA, and as a result, the only time in the twenty-two-year history of the trials that the word "Olympic" has been associated with the event.

There was also a considerable discussion regarding the timing of the trials. Some felt the spring of 1997 would have been the ideal time, while others felt a time closer to the Olympics would be more suitable. So, the final dates agreed on were November 22 to 30, 1997, which would give the winners about two months to get ready for the Olympics.

The Keystone Centre in Brandon is not a large arena, and when complimentary tickets and seat kills were completed, there might have been 4,500 tickets for public sale, but they were all scooped up almost a year ahead of the event.

The one more interesting team in the field was skipped by Ed Werenich, who was now fifty years old and amazingly still competing at an elite level, despite all the things that had gone on over the years. Most would have given him little chance, but I wasn't among them. I knew his resolve and how he could finally stick it in the CCA one last time if he were somehow able to make it through the trials and win the right to represent Canada at the 1998 Winter Games. When the round-robin preliminaries ended, Werenich managed to grab one of the three playoff spots by finishing in a second-place tie with Edmonton's Kevin Martin. However, Werenich's hopes were soon dashed, as Martin came out the victor in the semifinal by a score of 9–6. Martin went on against first-place finisher Mike Harris in the final but lost a last stone squeaker to the Toronto foursome by a score of 6–5. Skip Martin's miscue on a routine draw in the third end of the game allowed Harris to steal two to go up 3–0.

Men's Final

Mike Harris	*012 010 100 1	6
Kevin Martin	000 102 020 0	3

Men's Round-Robin Standings

Mike Harris	7	2
Kevin Martin	6	3
Ed Werenich	6	3
Kerry Burtnyk	5	4
Dave Smith	5	4
Jeff Stoughton	5	4
Brent MacDonald	4	5
Wayne Middaugh	3	6
Russ Howard	3	6
Kevin Park	1	8

On the women's side, Sandra Schmirler of Regina finished in first place with a record of 7–2. In second spot was Shannon Kleibrink of Calgary at 6–3, and in third spot with the same 6–3 record was Kelley Law of Richmond, BC. Kleibrink disposed of Law in the semifinals, which set the stage for the final showdown. The final was a classic, and everyone will always remember the seventh end, when Schmirler was trailing Kleibrink by a score of 4–3 but did have the hammer. After a lot of discussion, Schmirler decided to take the chance and play a cross-the-house double for three, which she made to go up in the game by two points. Kleibrink came back with a deuce in the eighth, but Schmirler put the game on ice with another three in the ninth. Schmirler ran Kleibrink out of stones in the tenth end, giving the Regina foursome a ticket to the Olympics in Nagano.

Women's Final

Shannon Kleibrink	000 103 020 X	6
Sandra Schmirler	*002 010 303 X	9

Women's Round-Robin Standings

Sandra Schmirler	7	2
Shannon Kleibrink	6	3
Kelley Law	6	3
Marilyn Bodogh	5	4
Cathy Borst	5	4
Anne Merklinger	5	4
Alison Goring	3	6
Connie Laliberte	3	6
Sherry Scheirich	3	6
Mary Mattatall	2	7

Without question, Schmirler was a known commodity, a three-time world champion who was expected to do well at the Olympics. However, Harris was virtually a newcomer on the international stage who had never played in the Brier, never mind won it. The story below, from *Extra End Magazine*, written by Larry Wood and yours truly provides the summary from Nagano.

> ***1998 Olympic Winter Games***
> *Olympic Men's and Women's Curling*
> *Played in Karuizawa, Japan, at Kazakoshi Park Arena*
> *February 9 to 15, 1998*
>
> *Sandra Schmirler's three-time world-champion team from Regina won a gold medal for Canada at the 1998 Olympic Winter Games in Karuizawa, Japan, winning eight of nine games and defeating Denmark 7–5 in the gold-silver final.*
>
> *Only two-time world champion Dordi Nordby of Norway beat the Canadian team in the eight-team women's shootout, stealing a point in the fifth end on her way to a 6–5 extra-end victory in Round 2 of the preliminary.*

While Canada soared from there, winning seven in a row, Nordby stumbled to an uncharacteristic 2–5 round-robin finish and failed to qualify for the medal round.

The race for the playoffs boiled down to the sixth round, where Canada faced the unbeaten Elisabeth Gustafson of Sweden and came away with a solid 7–5 victory. That win placed Canada first for medal purposes, while Sweden drew third-finishing Helena Blach Lavrsen of Denmark, who was riding a three-game winning streak.

In the semi-finals, Denmark stole deuces on the fifth and sixth ends and upended Sweden 7–5. Schmirler, with Jan Betker, Joan McCusker and Marcia Gudereit performing in high style in front, needed a shaky last-rock draw to defeat gutty two-time world junior champion Kirsty Hay of Scotland, representing Great Britain, 6–5.

Sweden walloped Great Britain 10–6 for the bronze medal.

Canada cracked three in the first end of the final and led 6–2 after six against a Danish team that, with its silver finish, earned its country's first medal at the Olympic Winter Games.

Denmark's final log was 6–3, while Sweden was 7–2 and Great Britain 4–5. Joining Norway at 2–5 were Mayumi Ohkutsu of Japan and Lisa Schoeneberg of the United States. Germany's Andrea Schopp, the gold medalist in Albertville, France, in 1992, finished dead last with one win in seven outings.

Canada's Mike Harris of Toronto, who appeared headed for a cakewalk gold medal at the 1998 Olympics, was struck by a fiendish flu bug and settled for silver after a 9–3 thrashing by Switzerland's Patrick Hurlimann in the climactic showdown.

Harris sailed through six rounds of the preliminary without a blemish, hammering Hurlimann 8–3 en route. Canada had already clinched first place for medal-round purposes when the team was beaten 10–8 in the last round by a Norwegian outfit skipped by Jan Thoresen in a match that featured a few defensive manoeuvres.

The game was Thoresen's lone skipping assignment of the week. Veteran Eigil Ramsfjell, a three-time world champion, directed Norway most of the way and the team finished 5–2, tied with Switzerland, but placed second by virtue of a 5–4 round-robin victory over Hurlimann.

Settling on Canada's opponent in the medal round called for a sorting-out process when Japan, the United States and defending world champion Sweden all finished with 3–4 records.

Japan's young Makoto Tsuruga was awarded a tie-breaker bye on the strength of round-robin conquests of both Tim Somerville of the United States and Peter Lindholm of Sweden, who lost his last four games.

The U.S. dumped Sweden 5–2, then Somerville executed a stunning double-touch takeout and roll with last rock and Japan lying buried to sideline Tsuruga 5–4.

Even with his temperature rising, Harris had no trouble whaling the U.S. 7–1 in the semis, while Hurlimann and his team of Patrick Lörtscher, Daniel Muller and Diego Perren avenged their earlier setback to Norway by shading Ramsfjell 8–7.

The gold-medal rout was a shocker, with Harris missing a routine shot and having to sit down between shots.

The 1988 Olympic gold medal winners from Canada from the left, alternate Atina Ford, lead Marcia Gudereit, second Joan McCusker, third Jan Betker and skip Sandra Schmirler.
Photo courtesy of the Canadian Olympic Committee.

The 1998 Olympic gold medalists from Switzerland, from the left, alternate Dominic Andres, lead Diego Perren, second Daniel Muller, third Patrick Loertscher and skip Patrick Hurlimann.
Photo courtesy of the Canadian Olympic Committee.

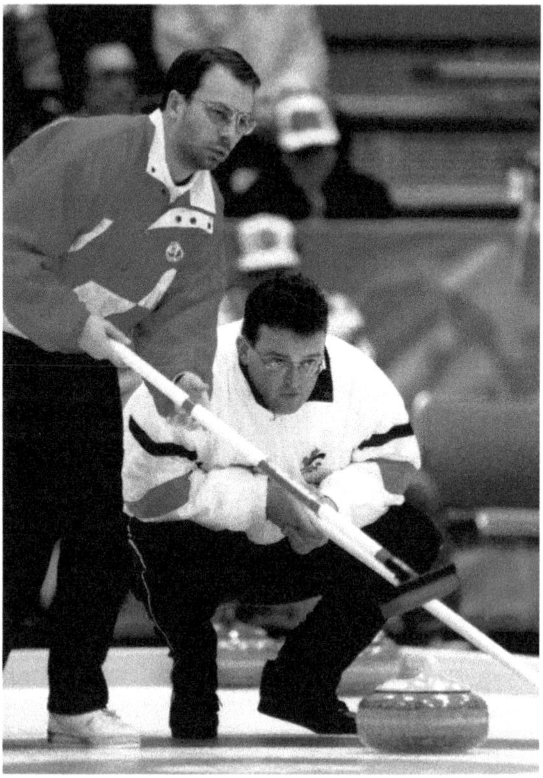

Switzerland's Patrick Hurliman prepares to sweep while Canada's Mike Harris watches the outcome closely during the men's final of the 1998 Winter Olympics. *Photo courtesy of the Canadian Olympic Committee.*

So, curling made it through its Olympic debut, and everything was a success. There was another thing that happened at the 1998 Games that worked very much in curling's favour. Poor snow and weather conditions caused several of the ski events that were scheduled for full coverage to be postponed or cancelled. Fortunately for curling, the television coverage slated, in many cases, for prime time, was switched from the ski hills to the curling venue, so a large segment of the worldwide television audience soon developed an appetite for curling. CBC Television's coverage did not go unnoticed, as the IOC developed a special medal that was presented to CBC for its outstanding coverage.

The pattern created for television from 1998 continued for the 2002 Winter Games in Salt Lake City, where again the television audience, particularly in the United States, learned to appreciate the sport of curling. And so, it continued with every Olympics since, as curling worked its way to the top of the Winter Olympic Games television list, along with the sports of hockey and figure skating.

Originally, curling was accepted as a medal sport on a contingent basis. Today, curling is recognized as a vital part of the Winter Olympic Games and continues to grow its audience around the world.

The arena at Karuizawa, Japan that was the site of curling at the 1998 Winter Olympic Games.

CHAPTER 30
After 1998 in Nagano

FOLLOWING THE 1998 Winter Olympics, many might have thought that curling continued as usual but not so. Things changed in the United States, Canada, and all over the world where curling was played. The changes varied, but for sure, things were very different.

In Canada, it became very evident in the years following the '98 Olympics that a new brand of curler had been created. The new brand of player was very much an athlete who trained and developed just like athletes in other sports, and the few very elite players began to separate themselves from all other aspects of the sport. This is not uncommon in most sports with a high-performance element, but it was foreign to curling, and in many cases, the upper elements of administration in the sport of curling in Canada today still haven't figured it out.

The top players also started to put other demands on the then-CCA, and when the response did not come back as desired, many of Canada's elite players broke away from the CCA in 2001. The new group declined to play in the Brier for two years, and in its place, they started what is known today as the Grand Slam of Curling. The Grand Slam has been around for nineteen years and is gaining strength. The combination of the Slam and the Olympics has left Canadian high-performance curlers with two Curling Canada events to play in, which on the men's side is the Brier and the women's the Scotties. The other event, the Canada Cup was introduced in 2002 and involves the top seven men's/women's teams in the nation.

Canada faces an ongoing challenge with regard to high performance structure. Canada has more top high-performance curlers than any other nation in the world, yet it clings to a system to determine it's Canadian champions that is almost 100 years old. Curling Canada is owned by the provincial/territorial associations (MAs), and as a result, there continues to be an insistence that the Canadian championships must have a representative from every province/territory. While the rules have been modified to allow some players to participate from a province/territory other than the one they reside the majority members of a team must still curl from the province/territory they live. A team participating in the Canadian Olympic Trials does not have to have the majority of its players reside in the same province/territory. However, the teams are established for a four-year period as a result of the Olympics, so the majority of teams are still created within the rules of the Brier/Scotties and they are able to compete in those events.

The system makes it almost impossible for the smaller provinces/territories to produce a team that is competitive enough to have a chance to win either the Brier or Scotties. Yet, many from the MAs still argue the method of determining a Canadian champion that involves a team from every province/territory must continue.

In my opinion, a true Canadian championship should only involve the top teams that have a chance of winning, regardless of which province/territory they come from.

Canada still produces many good teams, but possibly better units could be developed if the only requirement to be a member of a high performance team was Canadian citizenship.

Prior to 1998, curling had a presence in the United States, but it was to a very large degree obscure and played only in the northern states. When curling became an Olympic medal sport, two things happened for curling in the USA. First, it got the attention of the United States Olympic Committee (USOC) and the television network that carries the Olympics, NBC. USOC's involvement brought a funding injection into the USCA and assistance in areas involving physical and mental development. NBC's involvement started slow, but with each Olympics since 1998, the national Olympic rights holder in the USA has shown more and more curling, and as a result, the sport today holds a position of public awareness that is growing every year.

The combination of Olympics and world curling championships in 2018 had NBC air, on a combination of NBCSN and its Olympic network, well over 500 hours of curling. The new visibility has resulted in curling popping up all over the United States where it never existed before. In many cases, play is taking place on arena ice that is also being shared with hockey and skating. While these are not the best conditions, it *is* curling and it is growing. Curling in the USA received a further boost in 2018, when the men's team, skipped by John Shuster, won the Olympic gold medal. To some degree, this was another example of "miracle on ice," which was the reference made to the USA's Olympic hockey win in 1980. The nation where curling will become many times larger than it already is will be the USA, and it is all due to curling becoming an Olympic medal sport.

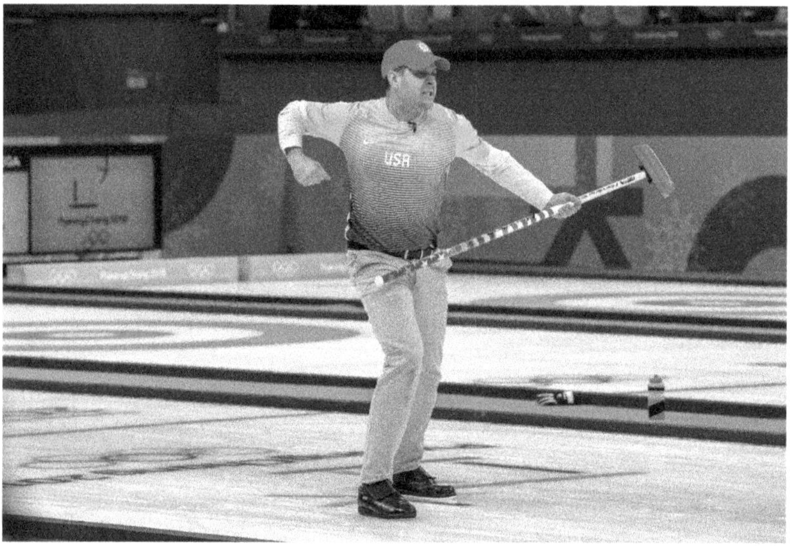

United States skip John Shuster on his way to winning the gold medal at the 2018 Winter Olympic Games. *Photo courtesy of World Curling Federation.*

I often use the Chaska Curling Center as a poster child example of where curling is and can be going in the USA. Chaska is a bedroom community of around 25,000 people about forty minutes southeast of Minneapolis–St. Paul, Minnesota. The curling centre is a City of Chaska/Parks and Recreation facility that was opened in December of 2015. The centre has six sheets of ice and approximately 1,000 members, one of the country's largest. Prior to the club being opened in 2015, no one in Chaska knew very much about curling. In addition to the very active membership, the club has also worked hard and recruited a large amount of corporate business, which plays a major role in keeping the facility up and running eleven months a year.

The Olympics has also led to the development and growth of curling worldwide. When the sport was officially accepted as a medal sport in 1992, there were only twenty-five member nations, and to be frank, that was a stretch. Today, the WCF has about sixty-seven members, including places such as Afghanistan, Bolivia, Brazil, Guyana, India, Kuwait, Saudi Arabia, Mexico, and Nigeria, to only mention a few.

Curling has also seen a considerable jump in popularity in Asia, and the nations producing the best results today are Japan and South Korea. Both nations have developed men's and women's teams that consistently rank in the top ten in the world.

I was involved in another project in 2001 that led to the creation of another variation of curling that I predict is going to have a major impact on the curling world in the next dozen or so years. A meeting between the WCF and CCA in the fall of 1999 started the development of a new event to world curling that became known as the Continental Cup. The discussions took place because following the 1998 Olympics, the IOC had approached the WCF and suggested it would be a good idea for them to have at least one event other than its traditional world championships because it was pretty much the only Olympic winter sport that did not have a world cup series. The WCF wasn't really in a position to develop a new event on its own and, therefore, asked if the CCA would do it with them.

I was the person fingered to develop the new idea, and my suggestion was to develop something that might resemble golf's Ryder Cup, which would probably be an event between North America (USA and Canada) and Europe or maybe the world. Everyone felt it was important to ensure the USA would be part of the project because of the potential growth, and to attempt to keep NBC television involved with curling. It wasn't lost on anyone in the room that most of the corporate dollars in the Olympics originated in the United States.

My working partner at the CCA, Neil Houston, worked with me on the project and we started to put together the idea. We determined the event needed to involve four segments, and both men and women would need to be part of all four fingers. Men's and women's team play was easy, as was probably skins. The other possible element was a game already being used at the Scotties and Brier in Canada called hot shots. Hot shots is a variation of the old Scottish game of points curling and could easily be modified to be a singles competition. That left a fourth element, and I suppose we could have gone with traditional mixed curling with a team constructed of two men and two women, but that would have just been another version of team play. So, I put on the thinking cap and a lot of imagination and came up with a game we called mixed doubles, which involved one man and one woman playing together in a unique game where only five rocks were played by each side and every end would start with two stationary stones in place—one as a guard out in front and the other positioned just behind the button. We tested the event, and everything seemed good, so the fourth leg of the Continental Cup competition format was determined to be mixed doubles. The first Continental Cup was held in Regina in the fall of 2002.

Mixed doubles caught on quickly, and in 2008, the WCF introduced a world championship and quickly, all sorts of nations that had in many cases never participated in a world championship sent a team. It has allowed nations that did not have enough good players to field four-person teams to send a team with a male and female that could be competitive. Things progressed so well that the WCF decided to submit mixed doubles to the IOC for consideration as an Olympic medal sport. In June 2015, the Program Commission of the IOC recommended to the executive committee that starting in 2018, mixed doubles be accepted as a full Olympic medal sport. At the 2018 Pyeongchang Olympics, mixed doubles was a full medal sport, with Kaitlyn Lawes and John Morris of Canada emerging as the gold-medal winners.

Canada's Kaitlyn Lawes and John Morris celebrate after winning the first-ever gold medal for mixed doubles curling at the 2018 Winter Olympic Games. *Photo courtesy of the World Curling Federation.*

I look to the future and see mixed doubles, men's doubles, and women's doubles being key factors in increasing curling participation around the world. The doubles game is quick, high scoring, very entertaining, and only requires two people, all of which should be appealing and assist in the worldwide growth of curling in the years ahead.

This has all been an interesting ride for me going back to the beginning in 1974. When I look at where curling was in the sport mosaic of Canada and the world then and now the change is breath taking. There is little question the acceptance of curling into the Olympic family in 1992 has impacted the sport in so many positive ways and there is more yet to come.

APPENDIX I
Curl Canada – Official Compiled History

(Canadian Curling Association 1982 — author unknown)

What is Curl Canada? How and when did it start? What does it do to justify its existence? How is it financed and how does it function? All of these questions are fairly straight forward and you might expect that the average Canadian curler should be able to supply most of the answers. Unfortunately, the opposite would be a more probable result. Your run of the mill curler would hazard to guess that Curl Canada is simply a new title for the Canadian Curling Association (formerly the Dominion Curling Association, DCA) but there has never been a significant change in its function or objectives. After all, Trans Canada Airlines became Air Canada, a few years ago [1965] and, by the same token, the name Curl Canada has a nice modern ring to it. Of course, this doesn't say much for the run of the mill curler. He would be quite wrong in his guess and it is high time that he learned a bit about this relatively new organization.

Actually, there is nothing very mysterious about Curl Canada. It is a joint venture of the Canadian Ladies Curling Association (CLCA) and the Canadian Curling Association (CCA); funded in part, originally, by these two associations and the Federal Government (Fitness and Amateur Sport). It is not involved in the day-to-day operations of

Canadian curling; including rules, national championships and such. Rather, its main efforts are devoted to training and development. It trains instructors, who in turn, conduct courses to improve the calibre of curling in Canada; both at club and school levels. It has conducted biomechanical studies to determine optimum methods of sweeping or of delivering a stone; vital parts of the game of curling. It has broadened its training base by conducting seminars on ice making and on the building and operation of curling clubs. In addition to preparing manuals and films for instructional purposes Curl Canada is involved in promoting and publicizing the grand old game of curling. In recent years its program has been expanded to include grants-in-aid to student athletes of both sexes; i.e., to young curlers who wish to continue both their educational and competitive curling careers. In short, Curl Canada devotes its efforts to promoting and improving the game of curling in Canada. If its future growth matches its impressive record to date, Canada's place in the curling world will be secure.

Curl Canada is a relatively new phenomenon but its birthday is vague and even its year of birth might be a subject of some argument. However, for lack of a better number let's say that it all started some time in 1974 and has been growing by leaps and bounds ever since. Of course, there has to be a reason for this ambiguity and when you review the steps which preceded its founding you can understand it. In some respects, the founding of Curl Canada was a bit like Columbus discovering America; the original goal was considerably different to the final result but things worked out pretty well, after all.

Perhaps the first indication of things to come was reported at the AGM of the CCA in 1971. At that time it was revealed that members of the executive had met with government officials at the Federal Fitness and Amateur Sports Centre in Ottawa. Consideration was given to moving the Association's office into the Sports Centre and employing a full-time executive director (financed by the Federal Government). Unfortunately, the amount of financial assistance available and the regulations involved in qualifying for the assistance were such that the executive decided to adopt a "wait and see" attitude and nothing was done with respect to moving. On the other hand, the meeting did produce some positive results. The Canadian Mixed Curling Championship was in jeopardy because of the withdrawal of its national sponsor and the government agreed to pay the travel expenses for the participants. In spite of these rather positive results there was some dissatisfaction expressed about the decision to "wait and see" and, as it turned out, the matter was resolved within a matter of months.

Strangely enough it was the Public Relations Committee of the Canadian Curling Association and the spark which ignited the whole thing was the desire to promote a National Curling Week. Efforts to do something of this type had fallen flat and it was decided that professional help was needed to get the program off the ground. Arrangements were made with a Toronto firm but, unfortunately, it had to withdraw its services before it got started. This was a great disappointment to Bill Leaman, the chairman of the Public Relations Committee in 1972, but in retrospect, it was a stroke of good luck. Mr. Leaman was forced to look around for a substitute and through a mutual friend, he got in touch with Norm Shannon, a public relations consultant located in Ottawa.

Undoubtedly, Norman Shannon had the ideal background for the job. He was a Public Relations officer for the Royal Canadian Legion. He had been involved in the planning and promotion of the Legion Curling Championship, the Legion track and field and coaching programs, the preparation of training films and other related activities. He lived in Ottawa, had a working relationship with the sports administration office and, fortunately, had a bit of spare time which he was willing to devote to the CCA's problems. Accordingly, he was asked to consider a total package which, in addition to a National Curling Week might include a collection of films and other instructional aids for curling promotion, improved liaison between the CCA and its member associations. In addition, there was a good possibility that the CCA would require an Ottawa agent to conduct business with the sports administration centre. Accordingly, Mr. Shannon was asked to be available for discussions with the CCA management committee in Edmonton in March 1973.

As a result of this meeting Norm Shannon was asked to prepare a comprehensive program covering the requirements set forth in Mr. Leaman's original request. In spite of the fact that he was quite competent in his field and was prepared to tackle the job his estimated fee for the preliminary survey work was surprisingly low; only $300.00. Whether this was responsible for several months of delay in his appointment to undertake phase one of the program is open to question. More likely, the delay was due to the appointment of a new chairman for the public relations committee. Herb Millham ofVancouver, B.C., would be the first to admit that his knowledge in this particular field was rudimentary apparently a rather common shortcoming for people assigned to this position. Fortunately, this was recognized and steps were taken to reduce if not to eliminate this problem. Herb Millham's stint as chairman lasted through 1977 providing badly needed continuity at a time when it was of utmost importance.

Eventually, Norm Shannon was retained and by the end of June 1973 things were progressing well. A new logo had been designed; a blue curling stone with a red maple leaf on its edge. This wasn't a static symbol: several vapour trials indicated the stone had been delivered with considerable velocity and was on its way to a firm double takeout or a similarly firm miss.

In spite of this there was something lacking and Herb Millham made a suggestion which made it right; the words "Curl Canada" were added to the logo, bracketing the red maple leaf. This was the origin of the name although, of course, it was similar to the terminology used in Sport Canada, Ski Canada, Racquets Canada and Air Canada. In addition to the work on the logo design the matter of newsletters, posters, wall charts, TV promos, etc. had been considered and costs were estimated. Training aids, films and coaching guides were investigated too, and it was suggested that the O'Keefe Sports Foundation should be approached for financial assistance for any training projects which could be designed.

Finally, by August 1973 Norm Shannon was able to present a detailed proposal which involved both a national curling week with numerous promotional aids and a continuing program to develop curling in Canada. However, he suggested that it would be a mistake to over-emphasize the national curling week. In fact, he recommended that National Curling Week should be delayed until 1974 and that action should be taken on the development program first.

There were several reasons for this recommendation. In his preliminary surveys he discovered that there was relatively little communication between the CCA and its provincial associations. To his surprise he discovered that there was no accurate list of clubs and addresses. Without communication it seemed that National Curling Week would be doomed to failure and that the prestige of the CCA would suffer.

It was obvious that the prestige of the CCA would be the core of the whole public relations program. The Association should be a service organization providing a tangible assistance to provincial associations and clubs; such things as coaching and development materials, training aids, films, posters, TV promos, background articles and program suggestions for National Curling Week. It was important that many of these things should be prepared prior to becoming involved in the national campaign.

Accordingly, he made the following suggestions:

1. Establish closer communications by updating the mailing list.

2. Survey the provincial associations to determine what training programs and aids are available.

3. Assess all this material and, from the best, devise a program to improve the calibre of curling at all levels. Proven ideas should be blended with new ideas to produce an up to date, effective program.

4. This program should be based on the assumption that Federal assistance will be available in certain areas.

5. A news letter should be published and distributed three times per year.

6. One of Sport Canada's major roles is to assist with transportation costs to national competitions.
7. A publicity program to make curlers and the general public more familiar with the activities of the CCA should be a priority item.
8. Although basic planning for National Curling Week is completed it should be postponed until December 1974, subject to approval at the 1974 annual meeting.

This proposal was discussed at a meeting of the management Committee in the fall of 1973 and was approved, including a proposed fee of $4,500.00 to cover the costs of the program in 1974. Although this fee was rather high in relationship to the Association's revenue it was hoped that most, if not all of it, could be recovered from the sports directorate. Several types of grants were available but some negotiations would be involved because of the nature of the curling association's overall strategy. Hopefully, Norm Shannon would become "Director of Program Development," or some other suitable title and would qualify for government assistance.

Regarding possible assistance in the training area it became apparent the O'Keefe Sports Foundation might provide a helping hand. Certainly, training was the foundation's primary interest and it seemed likely that an application for financial aid would receive sympathetic attention. In the meantime, negotiations with Sport Canada continued.

It would be fair to say that these negotiations were prolonged and not particularly productive. However, although this may have discouraged Heb Millham it didn't stop him. He and the CCA executive were convinced that they were on the right track and were determined to proceed with the program, with or without outside help. Affiliation fees were doubled and there was money to pay Shannon plus $3,000 to get a training program underway.

Of course, $3,000 was completely inadequate for the job. They visualized setting up clinics to train curlers to be qualified instructors and they, in turn, would set up clinics in their home clubs. Sixteen to eighteen clinics would be held in various centres across Canada and transportation costs and living expenses would make short work of the $3,000. In short, additional money would have to be found. Regarding professional help to conduct the clinics, this was a lesser problem. There were in fact, three curling schools available, providing experts with Brier experience. The Silver Broom Curling School had been in operation for several years, founded by Warren Hansen and Jim Pettapiece. In addition there was the DTU Curling School (Duguid, Turnbull, Ursuliak) and the Canadian Curling Alliance (Bryan Wood, Sam Richardson, Hec Gervais and Bob Pickering).

Why Warren Hansen was selected to take charge of the program isn't clear, but he was. Possibly it was because he had been involved in football coaching for seven years and had developed and trained minor league football coaches as well as players? Possibly it was because he was operating a successful curling school with Air Canada and was able to bring them to the table. Possibly it was because he happened to be curling as second for Hec Gervais in the 1974 Brier in London and because he was available for a meeting once the decision was made to proceed with the training program? At any rate, the first meeting between Herb Millham and Warren Hansen took place on Thursday morning during the 1974 Brier. It was a short meeting but it established the idea that the program would involve teaching instructors rather than teaching curlers. Arrangements were made for Warren Hansen to meet Norm Shannon in Ottawa at the first opportunity. With that, the meeting broke up. Warren had other things on his mind; like helping win the 1974 Brier, which he did. Then he was off to Berne, Switzerland and the Silver Broom competition but on the way, he stopped off in Ottawa for a day and discussed the basic plans with Norm Shannon.

Following those preliminary discussions Herb Millham requested Norm Shannon to prepare an application for the O'Keefe Foundation for a grant to carry out the training program. By the time Warren Hansen returned from Berne and met with Herb Millham to iron out some final details the application was being considered. There was one development which had been considered but not acted upon. The O'Keefe Foundation informed Norm Shannon that the

Canadian Ladies Curling Association (CLCA) had applied for a similar grant for training instructors for their junior program. Naturally, the Foundation suggested the CCA & CLCA should put together and apply for a grant to conduct a joint program. A meeting between the two associations in June 1974 produced agreement and they applied for a grant to carry out a joint program. To get things started, each Association deposited $2,500 to a joint account to defray preliminary expenses and to get the program off the ground.

Fortunately, the O'Keefe Sports Foundation acted quickly because there was a lot of work to be done if the program was to start in 1974. The joint application was submitted in late June; by mid-July an $18,000 grant was approved. Warren Hansen, and his company, International Curling Promotions Ltd. would direct the program. Don Duguid and Jim McConnell who had been working with the CLCA were retained as consultants on both the program and on the written material which was to be prepared by Warren Hansen.

Of course, that wasn't the end of the problem; in fact, it was only the start. There was a great amount of instructional material to be written up and not much time to do it. Arrangements had to be made to receive applications, curling facilities had to be reserved and a schedule prepared. All in all, it was a hectic two months but the first Curl Canada clinic to train instructors took place in Edmonton in late September 1974.

Over the next several months similar clinics were held in Vancouver, Montreal, Quebec City, London, Thunder Bay, Toronto, Winnipeg, Halifax, St. John's, Ottawa, Saskatoon, Saint John, Charlottetown, Moncton and Kelowna; sixteen cities in all. Each two day clinic involved twelve hours of instruction and a great deal of interest was generated considering the fact that time for preparation and for advertising the clinics was limited.

In all, 527 people enrolled in the first course; 263 women and 264 men. The majority were in the 30–40 age group but there were 17 potential instructors under 20 years of age and 12 who were over 60 years of age. Considering the amount of travelling involved it was surprising that the operation stayed within its budget. Receipts of $28,270 (including 527 registrants who paid $10 each) exceeded expenses by approximately $3,000.

Warren Hansen's airline agreement with Air Canada for the operation of the Silver Broom Schools provided a lot of financial relief on the cost of airfares to the various cities where clinics were operated.

Of course, there were some criticisms and these were duly noted. Probably the most vocal criticism developed at the first accreditation committee meeting in which standards were developed to conform with the Coaching Association of Canada's methods of evaluating or measuring the skills of any certified instructors. Warren Hansen refers to it as "the toughest three days of his life." All the committee members were expert curlers in their own right and not surprisingly, experts tend to disagree sometimes. However, the meeting accomplished what it set out to do. Level I Technical Curling was defined and passing standards were set. Of course, passing the course in itself didn't qualify the student to become an Instructor-Coach. Additional training was required including Level I Theory Course administered by the provincial sport branches and specified training activities. A follow-up meeting revised and polished the Level I manual and a more advanced course, Level II Technical, was defined and discussed. All in all, in spite of a rough start, things were underway and, with a year of learning experience behind him, improved guidelines and more time to get organized, Warren Hansen looked forward to better things in 1975.

In fact, 1975 was better. Twenty-three Curl Canada Level I clinics were held with nearly 1,000 participants. The whole country was involved, with the exception of Saskatchewan. Actually Saskatchewan, Southern Alberta and Ontario had been involved in development programs prior to the Curl Canada Clinics and had trained a number of qualified instructors. Some opposition to the program developed in certain areas, too; unfortunate because it tended to waste the effort and the money which was involved in the Curl Canada program. However, it was hoped that the dissenters would become involved in 1976; particularly, following the introduction of the Level II program.

Thanks to increase of budgeting by the CCA and CLCA ($5,000 each), the sale of the Novice Manual (put together by Hansen) and the generous grant from the O'Keefe foundation the clinic program remained solvent. Unfortunately, this pleasant condition was rather short lived. In June of 1976, the O'Keefe Foundation announced that it was withdrawing its support. Unfortunately, this coincided with a reduction in the contributions from the curling associations to $3,000 each. That looked like the end of the road for the clinics but Sport Canada came to the rescue with a $10,000 grant. This salvaged the program and, in fact, it has continued since 1977 without any financial support from either the CCA or the CLCA.

Since then the program has grown and diversified. In 1976 there were nineteen Level I clinics, five Level II clinics and two senior instructor seminars, with every curling association in Canada being involved in some phase of the program. Unfortunately, Level I theory clinics were not readily available in some areas and this resulted in delays in accreditation and certification. However, the fact that 2,000 persons took the Level I course in the first three years of operation signified the popularity of the program; possibly as many as 80,000 curlers benefited, in turn, from their efforts. When 115 persons enrolled for the Level II clinic it was obvious that it was something more than a passing fad.

In the meantime, there were activities on other fronts. The CCA and CLCA decided to avail themselves of the grants and facilities offered by Sport Canada and took steps to hire an executive director for Curl Canada and set-up offices in the National Sport and Recreation Centre (NSRC) in Vanier City (Ottawa). This decision was made in late 1975 and early in 1976 and advertisements were sent out to provincial secretaries for distribution to individual clubs. These efforts produced thirty-nine applications for the position of executive director and these were reviewed in March 1976 by a committee consisting of Dave Smith, President, CCA, Herb Millham, Vice-President, Janet Merry, President CLCA and Edith Corby, Vice-President, CLCA. Eight of the applicants were chosen to be interviewed and this meeting took place in Ottawa on June 6th. John MacLeod of Shearwater, Nova Scotia, was the unanimous choice of the group and this was confirmed by David Smith and Janet Merry on June 27/76. John began his official duties on September 1, 1976.

Of course, a new position and a new office brings problems. Fortunately, the principals had the foresight to set up an organization committee which must have been a great assistance to John in getting things steered in the right direction. At the same time, John had an excellent background for the job. He started out as a sports writer and after joining the Canadian Army in 1948 he continued to be involved in writing and sports with various Forces newspapers. In addition, he was a sports broadcaster with the Canadian Forces in Europe and on his return to Canada was supervisor of minor officials and statisticians for the Winnipeg Jets of the WHA in 1972 and 1973 and for the Nova Scotia Voyageurs of the AHL in the 1975–76 season. As if that wasn't enough, he had managed to curl whenever his army career took him; from Manitoba to Germany with a few intermediate stops on the way. All in all, it was a pretty good selection.

Things have moved along since the Ottawa office was established in 1976. The clinics have continued; not only Level I but Level II and Level III. Refresher courses have been established and manuals have been rewritten. Instructors have been trained to become coaches and the game has benefited. An ice technician program has been established with master instructors conducting clinics; very well attended clinics, we should add. Curl Canada has been offering assistance to the High School Athletic Associations and instructors have participated in at least one summer instructional camp organized by a provincial school athletic association. They have gotten into the finer points of the game, too. High speed films and biomechanical studies have revealed surprising details about the curling delivery and sweeping.

Getting into the office, the CCA decided to transfer its office from Winnipeg to Ottawa and this was done in the summer of 1979. Charles Scrymgeour assumed the position of general manager and executive director of Curl Canada while John MacLeod assumed the positions of secretary for the CCA and assistant to the executive director of Curl Canada. Warren Hansen remained as Technical Director. This reorganization took place as May 1, 1979 and the move occurred in late September 1979. Since that time his duties have been changed again; Garry DeBlonde has taken over the position of Technical Director of Curl Canada. Garry is well qualified for the job; he has been a Brier competitor on two occasions and has four Manitoba mixed curling championships and two Canadian mixed championship titles to his credit.

You might wonder what happened to National Curling Week; after all, it was the primary objective of the whole exercise when Norm Shannon was hired. Herb Millham reported at the Annual General Meeting in March 1975 that "many problems were encountered last year but it is hoped that these can be ironed out." That sums it up; more or less. National Curling Week never really got off the ground. However, the television and newspaper exposure of national and international events and the interest generated by good training in the fundamentals of the game has more than made up for the once per year publicity which was planned, originally. Curling in Canada seems to have a secure future, thanks to the far sighted officers of the CCA and the CLCA. Thanks also, to the O'Keefe Foundation and Sport Canada and to the provincial organization which gave the financial aid and organizational assistance. Finally, thanks to Herb Millham, Norm Shannon and Warren Hansen. Perhaps someone else could have completed what they accomplished but it is doubtful that anyone could have done it better.

APPENDIX II

Curling's Olympic History

Chamonix, France, 1924 (Demonstration Sport)

The Olympic Winter Games burst upon the sports consciousness of the world in 1924. But the first "winter" games was held in London in 1908, with four skating events the only discipline on the program.

At the instance of European nations, the demand for winter events grew, and the point was made. Thus, the first separate Winter Games was launched in 1924 at Chamonix, France.

While only five competitions were listed—ice hockey, figure skating, skiing, speed skating, and bobsledding—curling was not to be denied, and by the time the Games were over, the curling was recognized. The winning nation, Great Britain, was presented with gold medals for its members with all the fanfare, glory, and flag raising that greeted the winners in other sports events on that historic occasion.

Curling historians and modern Olympic purists will contend that curling participation at Chamonix was defined as a demonstration sport on the program, but the bible of curling, the Scottish-based Royal Caledonian Curling Club, has chronicled the event in its 1924–25 annual differently.

We are indebted for the excerpts from the "Official Report of the VIII Olympiad 1924" published by the British Olympic Association and from the RCCC annual for the following.

"On the occasion of the celebration of the VIII Olympiad at Chamonix, France from the 25th of January to the 5th of February, the Olympic Committee, in collaboration with the Federation Francaise des sports d'Hiver, invited the Royal Caledonian Curling Club to send a rink of four curlers with an equal number of reserves, W.K. Jackson, R. Welsh, T.B. Murray, L. Jackson, Col. Robertson-Aikman, J. McLeod, Major D.G. Astley and W. Brown."

Leaving London on the 23rd of January, the team travelled to Dover, Calais, Paris, and thence to Chamonix. On the opening-day parade to the site, the British curling team, with the Union Jack on the left arm, got a splendid reception.

At the Patinoice, curling was indulged, and the ice was found to be similar to that encountered under ordinary conditions in Scotland, though falling short of the ideal ice provided at the Haymarket Ice Rink.

For the international competition, the committee chose Willie Jackson, Robin Welsh, Tom Murray, and Lawrence Jackson to represent Great Britain, and they gave a splendid exhibition of curling; the accuracy of every shot merited the admiration of opponents and spectators alike.

(Sweden and France were the only other nations entered. Switzerland withdrew at the last moment.)

Sweden, while playing a sound game, was defeated 38–7. France found the same British team in great form and acknowledged defeat, 46–4. In earlier match, Sweden beat France 18–10.

When it became known that Great Britain had won the world curling championship, the Union Jack run to the top of the mast and while competitors and spectators stood at attention with heads uncovered, the military band played "God Save the King."

"The curlers were congratulated for gaining the maximum number of points and thus materially assisting Great Britain to occupy the third highest position among all the nations competing, the British players received Gold Medals and Diplomas."

(During the Games, an International Curling Congress was held at Chamonix; Canadian delegates were W.A. Hewitt and P.J. Mulqueen.)

Curling did not get an invitation to be part of the 1928 Winter Games in St. Moritz, but the reason why is unknown.

Lake Placid, New York, 1932 (Demonstration Sport)

Eight years later, at Lake Placid in 1932, Canada and the United States competed in a two-country demonstration, with each nation entering four teams from the provinces or states. Canada's final record in the inter-country competition was 12–4, Manitoba 4–0, Ontario and Quebec 3–1, and Northern Ontario 2–2. The American standings were Connecticut 2–2, New York and Massachusetts 1–3, and Michigan 0–4.

Calgary, Alberta, 1988 (Demonstration Sport)

Fifty-six years later, Calgary's Max Bell Arena was the next site of a competitive demonstration of curling at the Olympic Winter Games. The 1988 Winter Games featured men's and women's divisions with eight countries in each playing a round robin followed by a three-way playoff among the leaders to decide the medals. Canada, as the host country, automatically qualified, while the other seven teams were determined by final positioning at the 1987 world curling championships.

Standings After Round Robin:

Men		**Women**	
Switzerland	5–2	Sweden	5–2
Canada	5–2	Canada	5–2
USA	4–3	W. Germany	4–3
Norway	4–3	Norway	4–3
Sweden	4–3	USA	4–3
Denmark	3–4	Denmark	3–4
W. Germany	3–4	Switzerland	2–5
Great Britain	0–7	France	1–6

Final		**Final**	
Norway	10	Canada	7
Switzerland	2	Sweden	5
Semifinal		**Semifinal**	
Norway	8	Canada	6
Canada	5	Norway	5
Bronze Medal		**Bronze Medal**	
Canada		Norway	
Tiebreakers		**Tiebreakers**	
Norway	6	Norway	8
USA	3	W. Germany	4
Norway	6	Norway	10
Sweden	4	United States	7

Albertville, France, 1992 (Demonstration Sport)

Curling returned as a demonstration sport again in 1992 at Albertville, France, and was staged in the mountain village of Pralognan-La-Vanoise. The event again was comprised of eight men's and women's teams. This time, the teams were divided into two four-team pools for a round robin, with the top two teams from each division entering the semifinals. Following the sudden death semifinals, the two winners advanced to the final while the losers played in the bronze medal game.

France, as the host, earned a spot in both the men's and women's divisions while the other seven teams were determined by final positionings in the 1991 world curling championships.

Final Standings

Women

Round Robin

Group 1	Wins	Losses	Group 2	Wins	Losses
Canada	3	0	Norway	2	1
Denmark	2	1	Germany	2	1
Sweden	1	2	Great Britain	2	1
France	0	3	Japan	0	3

Finals

Germany	9
Norway	2

Bronze Medal

Canada	9
Denmark	3

Semifinals

Germany	6	Denmark	5
Norway	9	Canada	2

Tiebreakers

Germany	5	Great Britain	4
Norway	9	Great Britain	4

Playoffs	**Wins**	**Losses**
Germany (Gold)	3	0
Norway (Silver)	2	1
Canada (Bronze)	1	1
Denmark	0	2
Great Britain	0	2

Men

Round Robin

Group 1	Wins	Losses	Group 2	Win	Losses
Norway	3	0	Canada	3	0
Switzerland	2	1	United States	2	1
Great Britain	1	2	France	1	2
Australia	0	3	Sweden	0	3

Finals

Norway	6
Switzerland	7

Bronze Medal

Canada	2
United States	9

Semifinals

Canada	4	Switzerland	8
Norway	8	United States	3

Playoffs	**Wins**	**Losses**
Switzerland (Gold)	2	0
Norway (Silver)	1	1
United States (Bronze)	1	1
Canada	0	2

Nagano, Japan, 1998 (Olympic Medal Sport)

Men's Final

Canada (Mike Harris)	*001 000 20 X	3
Switzerland (Patrick Hurlimann)	020 223 00 X	9

Bronze Medal

Norway	9	United States	4

Semifinals

Switzerland	8	Norway	7
Canada	7	United States	1

Tiebreakers

United States	5	Sweden	2
United States	5	Japan	4

Final Standings

Playoffs	**Wins**	**Losses**
Switzerland (Patrick Hurlimann)	2	0
Canada (Mike Harris)	1	1
Norway (Eigil Ramsfjell)	1	1
United States (Tim Somerville)	2	2
Japan (Makoto Tsuruga)	0	1
Sweden (Peja Lindholm)	0	1

Round Robin

Canada (Mike Harris)	6	1
Switzerland (Patrick Hurlimann)	5	2
Norway (Eigil Ramsfjell)	5	2
United States (Tim Somerville)	3	4
Japan (Makoto Tsuruga)	3	4
Sweden (Peja Lindholm)	3	4
Great Britain (Douglas Dryburgh)	2	5
Germany (Andy Kapp)	1	6

Gold: Switzerland

Patrick Hurlimann, Patrick Lörtscher, Daniel Muller, Diego Perren

Silver: Canada

Mike Harris, Richard Hart, Collin Mitchell, George Karrys

Bronze: Norway

Eigil Ramsfjell, Jan Thoresen, Stig-Arne Gunnestad, Anthon Grimsmo

Women's Final

Denmark (Helena Blach Lavrsen)	020 000 201 5
Canada (Sandra Schmirler)	*300 111 010 7

Bronze Medal

Sweden	10	Great Britain	6

Semifinals

Canada	6	Great Britain	5
Denmark	7	Sweden	5

Final Standings

Playoffs	Wins	Losses
Canada (Sandra Schmirler)	2	0
Denmark (Helena Blach Lavrsen)	1	1
Sweden (Elisabet Gustafson)	1	1
Great Britain (Kirsty Hay)	0	2

Round Robin		
Canada (Sandra Schmirler)	6	1
Sweden (Elisabet Gustafson)	6	1
Denmark (Helena Blach Lavrsen)	5	2
Great Britain (Kirsty Hay)	4	3
Japan (Mayumi Ohkutsu)	2	5
Norway (Dordi Nordby)	2	5
United States (Lisa Schoeneberg)	2	5
Germany (Andrea Schopp)	1	6

Gold: Canada
Sandra Schmirler, Jan Betker, Joan McCusker, Marcia Gudereit

Silver: Denmark
Helena Blach Lavrsen, Margit Portner, Dorthe Holm, Trine Qvist

Bronze: Sweden
Elisabet Gustafson, Katarina Nyberg, Louise Marmont, Elisabeth Persson

Salt Lake City, Utah 2002

Men's Final

Canada (Kevin Martin)	*000 021 020 0 5
Norway (Pal Trulsen)	010 200 101 1 6

Bronze Medal

Switzerland	7	Sweden	3

Semifinals

Canada	6	Sweden	4
Norway	7	Switzerland	6

Final Standings

Playoffs	**Wins**	**Losses**
Norway (Pal Trulsen)	2	0
Canada (Kevin Martin)	1	1
Switzerland (Andreas Schwaller)	1	1
Sweden (Peja Lindholm)	0	2

Round Robin

Canada (Kevin Martin)	8	1
Norway (Pal Trulsen)	7	2
Switzerland (Andreas Schwaller)	6	3
Sweden (Peja Lindholm)	6	3
Finland (Markku Uusipaavalniemi)	5	4
Germany (Sebastian Stock)	4	5
Denmark (Ulrik Schmidt)	3	6
Great Britain (Hammy McMillan)	3	6
United States (Tim Somerville)	3	6
France (Dominique Dupont-Roc)	0	9

Gold: Norway

Pal Trulsen, Lars Vagberg, Flemming Davanger, Bent Anund Ramsfjell

Silver: Canada

Kevin Martin, Don Walchuk, Carter Rycroft, Don Bartlett

Bronze: Switzerland

Andreas Schwaller, Christof Schwaller, Markus Eggler, Damian Grichting

Women's Final

Switzerland (Luzia Ebnother)	000 100 011 0	3
Great Britain (Rhona Martin)	*000 020 100 1	4

Bronze Medal

Canada	9	United States	5

Semifinals

Great Britain	6	Sweden	4
Great Britain	9	Germany	5

Final Standings

Playoffs	Wins	Losses
Great Britain (Rhona Martin)	4	0
Switzerland (Luzia Ednother)	1	1
Canada (Kelley Law)	2	1
United States (Kari Erickson)	1	1
Germany (Natalie Nessler)	0	1
Sweden (Elisabet Gustafson)	0	1
Round Robin		
Canada (Kelley Law)	8	1
Switzerland (Luzia Ednother)	7	2
United States (Kari Erickson)	6	3
Germany (Natalie Nessler)	5	4
Sweden (Elisabet Gustafson)	5	4
Great Britain (Rhona Martin)	5	4
Norway (Dordi Nordby)	4	5
Japan (Akiko Katoh)	2	7
Denmark (Lene Bidstrup)	2	7
Russia (Olga Jarkova)	1	8

Gold: Great Britain

Rhona Martin, Debbie Knox, Fiona MacDonald, Janice Rankin

Silver: Denmark

Luzia Ebnother, Mirjam Ott, Tanya Frei, Laurence Bidaud

Bronze: Canada

Kelley Law, Julie Skinner, Georgina Wheatcroft, Diane Nelson

Pinerolo, Italy, 2006

Men's Final

Canada (Brad Gushue)	021 106 00X X	10
Finland (Markku Uusipaavalniemi)	*200 010 01X X	4

Bronze Medal

United States	8	Great Britain	6

Semifinals

Finland	4	Great Britain	3
Canada	11	United States	5

Final Standings

Playoffs	Wins	Losses
Canada (Brad Gushue)	2	0
Finland (Markku Uusipaavalniemi)	1	1
United States (Pete Fenson)	1	1
Great Britain (David Murdoch)	0	2

Round Robin		
Finland (Markku Uusipaavalniemi)	7	2
Canada (Brad Gushue)	6	3
United States (Pete Fenson)	6	3
Great Britain (David Murdoch)	6	3
Norway (Pal Trulsen)	5	4
Switzerland (Ralph Stockli)	5	4
Italy (Joel Retornaz)	4	5
Germany (Andreas Kapp)	3	6
Sweden (Peja Lindholm)	3	6
New Zealand (Sean Becker)	0	9

Gold: Canada

Brad Gushue, Mark Nichols, Russ Howard, Jamie Korab

Silver: Finland

Markku Uusipaavalniemi, Wille Makela, Kalle Kiiskinen, Teemu Salo

Bronze: United States

Pete Fenson, Shawn Rojeski, Joe Polo, John Shuster

Women's Final

Sweden (Anette Norberg)	*020 101 101 0 1	7
Switzerland (Mirjam Ott)	002 000 020 2 0	6

Bronze Medal

Canada	11	Norway	5

Semifinals

Sweden	5	Norway	4
Switzerland	7	Canada	5

Final Standings

Playoffs	Wins	Losses
Sweden (Anette Norberg)	2	0
Switzerland (Mirjam Ott)	1	1
Canada (Shannon Kleibrink)	1	1
Norway (Dordi Nordby)	0	2

Round Robin		
Sweden (Anette Norberg))	7	2
Switzerland (Mirjam Ott))	7	2
Canada (Shannon Kleibrink)	6	3
Norway (Dordi Nordby)	6	3

Great Britain (Rhona Martin)	5	4
Russia (Liudmila Privivkova)	5	4
Japan (Ayumi Onodera)	4	5
United States (Cassandra Johnson)	2	7
Denmark (Dorthe Holm)	2	7
Italy (Diana Gaspari)	1	8

Gold: Sweden
Anette Norberg, Eva Lund, Cathrine Lindahl, Anna Svard

Silver: Switzerland
Mirjam Ott, Binia Beeli, Valeria Spalty, Michele Moser

Bronze: Canada
Shannon Kleibrink, Amy Nixon, Glenys Bakker, Christine Keshen

Vancouver, Canada, 2010

Men's Final

Canada (Kevin Martin)	*010 110 201 X	6
Norway (Thomas Ulsrud)	000 002 010 X	3

Bronze Medal

Switzerland	5	Sweden	4

Semifinals

Canada	6	Sweden	3
Norway	7	Switzerland	5

Tie-breaker

Sweden	7	Great Britain	6

Final Standings

Playoffs	Wins	Losses
Canada (Kevin Martin)	2	0
Norway (Thomas Ulsrud)	1	1
Switzerland (Markus Eggler)	1	1
Sweden (Niklas Edin)	1	2
Great Britain (David Murdoch)	0	1

Round Robin		
Canada (Kevin Martin)	9	0
Norway (Thomas Ulsrud)	7	2
Switzerland (Markus Eggler)	6	3
Sweden (Niklas Edin)	5	4
Great Britain (David Murdoch)	5	4
Germany (Andy Kapp)	4	5
France (Thomas Dufour)	3	6
China (Fengchun Wang)	2	7
Denmark (Ulrik Schmidt)	2	7
United States (John Shuster)	2	7

Gold: Canada

Kevin Martin, John Morris, Marc Kennedy, Ben Hebert

Silver: Norway

Thomas Ulsrud, Torger Nergard, Christoffer Svae, Havard Vad Petersson

Bronze: Switzerland

Markus Eggler, Ralph Stockli, Jan Hauser, Simon Strubin

Women's Final

Canada (Cheryl Bernard)	★010 101 201 0 0	6
Sweden (Anette Norberg)	002 020 000 2 1	7

Bronze Medal

China	12	Switzerland	6

Semifinals

Canada	6	Switzerland	5
Sweden	9	China	4

Final Standings

Playoffs	**Wins**	**Losses**
Sweden (Anette Norberg)	2	0
Canada (Cheryl Bernard)	1	1
China (Bingyu Wang)	1	1
Switzerland (Mirjam Ott)	0	2

Round Robin		
Canada (Cheryl Bernard)	8	1
Sweden (Anette Norberg)	7	2
China (Bingyu Wang)	6	3
Switzerland (Mirjam Ott)	6	3
Denmark (Angelina Jensen)	4	5
Germany (Andrea Schopp)	3	6
Great Britain (Eve Muirhead)	3	6
Japan (Moe Meguro)	3	6
Russia (Liudmila Privivkova)	3	6
United States (Debbie McCormick)	2	7

Gold: Sweden

Anette Norberg, Eva Lund, Cathrine Lindahl, Anna Le Moine

Silver: Canada

Cheryl Bernard, Susan O'Connor, Carolyn Darbyshire, Cori Bartrel

Bronze: China
Bingyu Wang, Yin Liu, Quingshuang Yue, Yan Zhou

Sochi, Russia, 2014

Men's Final

Canada (Brad Jacobs)	*203 102 01X X	9
Great Britain (David Murdoch)	010 010 10X X	3

Bronze Medal

China	4	Sweden	6

Semifinals

Canada	10	China	6
Sweden	5	Great Britain	6

Tie-breaker

Norway	5	Great Britain	6

Final Standings

Playoffs	Wins	Losses
Canada (Brad Jacobs)	2	0
Norway (Thomas Ulsrud)	1	1
Great Britain (David Murdoch)	2	1
Sweden (Niklas Edin)	1	1
China (Rui Liu)	0	2
Norway (Thomas Ulsrud)	0	1

Round Robin		
Sweden (Niklas Edin)	8	1
Canada (Brad Jacobs)	7	2

China (Rui Liu)	7	2
Great Britain (David Murdoch)	5	4
Norway (Thomas Ulsrud)	5	4
Denmark (Rasmus Stjerne)	4	5
Russia (Andrey Drozdov)	3	6
Switzerland (Sven Michel)	3	6
United States (John Shuster)	2	7
Germany (John Jahr)	1	8

Gold: Canada

Brad Jacobs, Ryan Fry, E.J. Harnden, Ryan Harnden

Silver: Great Britain

David Murdoch, Greg Drummond, Scott Andrews, Michael Goodfellow

Bronze: Sweden

Niklas Edin, Sebastian Kraupp, Fredrik Lindberg, Viktor Kjäll

Women's Final

Sweden (Margaretha Sigfridsson)	010 020 000 X	3
Canada (Jennifer Jones)	*100 200 012 X	6

Bronze Medal

Great Britain	6
Switzerland	5

Semifinals

Great Britain	4	Canada	6
Sweden	7	Switzerland	5

Final Standings

Playoffs	Wins	Losses
Canada (Jennifer Jones)	2	0
Sweden (Margaretha Sigfridsson)	1	1
Great Britain (Eve Muirhead)	1	1
Switzerland (Mirjam Ott)	0	2

Round Robin		
Canada (Jennifer Jones)	9	0
Sweden (Margaretha Sigfridsson)	7	2
Switzerland (Mirjam Ott)	5	4
Great Britain (Eve Muirhead)	5	4
Japan (Ayumi Ogasawara)	4	5
Denmark (Lene Nielsen)	4	5
China (Bingyu Wang)	4	5
Korea (Ji-sun Kim)	3	6
Russia (Anna Sidorova)	3	6
United States (Erika Brown)	1	8

Gold: Canada

Jennifer Jones, Kaitlyn Lawes, Jill Officer, Dawn McEwen

Silver: Sweden

Margaretha Sigfridsson, Maria Prytz, Christina Bertrup, Maria Wennestrom

Bronze: Great Britain

Eve Muirhead, Anna Sloan, Vicki Adams, Claire Hamilton

Gangneung, South Korea, 2018

Men's Final

Sweden (Niklas Edin)	*020 020 102 X	7
United States (John Shuster)	002 102 050 X	10

Bronze Medal

Switzerland	7	Canada	6

Semifinals

Sweden	9	Switzerland	7
Canada	3	United States	5

Tie-breaker

Switzerland	9	Great Britain	5

Final Standings

Playoffs	Wins	Losses
United States (John Shuster)	2	0
Sweden (Niklas Edin)	1	1
Switzerland (Peter de Cruz)	2	1
Canada (Kevin Koe)	0	2
Great Britain (Kyle Smith)	0	1

Round Robin

United States (John Shuster)	7	2
Canada (Kevin Koe)	6	3
United States (John Shuster)	5	4
Switzerland (Peter de Cruz)	5	4
Great Britain (Kyle Smith)	5	4
Norway (Thomas Ulsrud)	4	5

South Korea (Chang Min Kim)	4	5
Japan (Yusuke Morozumi)	4	5
Italy (Joel Retornaz)	3	6
Denmark (Rasmus Stjerne)	2	7

Gold: United States

John Shuster, Tyler George, Matt Hamilton, John Landsteiner

Silver: Sweden

Niklas Edin, Oskar Eriksson, Rasmus Wanna, Christoffer Sundgren

Bronze: Switzerland

Benoit Schwarz, Claudio Patz, Peter de Cruz, Dominik Marki

Women's Final

Sweden (Anna Hasselborg)	002 110 301 X	8
South Korea (EunJung Kim)	★100 001 010 X	3

Bronze Medal

Great Britain	3	Japan	5

Semifinals

Sweden	10	Great Britain	5
South Korea	8	Japan	7

Final Standings

Playoffs	Wins	Losses
Sweden (Anna Hasselborg)	2	0
South Korea (EunJung Kim)	1	1
Japan (Satsuki Fujisawa)	1	1
Great Britain (Eve Muirhead)	0	2

Round Robin

South Korea (EunJung Kim)	8	1
Sweden (Anna Hasselborg)	7	2
Great Britain (Eve Muirhead)	6	3
Japan (Satsuki Fujisawa)	5	4
China (Bingyu Wang)	4	5
Canada (Rachel Homan)	4	5
Switzerland (Silvana Tirinzoni)	4	5
United States (Nina Roth)	4	5
OAR[1] (Victoria Moiseeva)	2	7
Denmark (Madeleine Dupont)	1	8

Gold: Sweden

Anna Hasselborg, Sara McManus, Agnes Knochenhauer, Sofia Mabergs

Silver: South Korea

Eun-jung Kim, Kyeong-ae Kim, Seon-yeong Kim, Yeong-mi Kim

Bronze: Japan

Satsuki Fujisawa, Chinami Yoshida, Yumi Suzuki, Yurika Yoshida

Mixed Doubles Final

Canada (Lawes/Morris)	*204 022 XX	10
Switzerland (Perret/Rios)	020 100 XX	3

Bronze Medal

OAR	8
Norway	4

Semifinals

Canada	8	Norway	4
OAR	5	Switzerland	7

1 Olympic athlete from Russia.

Tie-breaker

China	7	Norway	9

Final Standings

Playoffs	**Wins**	**Losses**
Canada (Lawes/Morris)	2	0
Switzerland (Perret/Rios)	1	1
Norway (Skaslien/Nedregotten)[2]	1	2
China (Wang/Ba)	0	1
OAR (Bryzgalova/Krushelnitckii)	X	X

Round Robin		
Canada (Lawes/Morris)	6	1
Switzerland (Perret/Rios)	5	2
OAR[3] (Bryzgalova/Krushelnitckii)	4	3
Norway (Skaslien/Nedregotten)	4	3
China (Wang/Ba)	4	3
South Korea (Jang/Lee)	2	5
United States (B. Hamilton/M. Hamilton)	2	5
Finland (Kauste/Rantamaki)	1	6

Olympic Champions Honour Roll

Men

Medal Sport

2018 United States John Shuster, Tyler George, Matt Hamilton, John Landsteiner

2014 Canada Brad Jacobs, John Morris, E.J. Harnden, Ryan Harnden

2 Norway was awarded the bronze medal when Aleksandr Krushelnitckii of the Olympic Athlete from Russia team was disqualified for violation of the anti-doping rule. The results obtained by the OAR team were disqualified.

3 Olympic Athlete from Russia.

2010 Canada Kevin Martin, John Morris, Marc Kennedy, Ben Hebert
2006 Canada Brad Gushue, Mark Nichols, Russ Howard, Jamie Korab
2002 Norway Pal Trulsen, Lars Vagberg, Flemming Davanger, Bent Anund Ramsfjell
1998 Switzerland Patrick Hurlimann, Patrick Lörtscher, Daniel Muller, Diego Perren

Demonstration Sport

1992 Switzerland Urs Dick, Jurg Dick, Robert Hurlimann, Thomas Klay.
1988 Norway Eigil Ramsfjell, Sjur Leon, Morten Sogaard, Bo Bakke.

Women

Medal Sport

2018 Sweden Anna Hasselborg, Sara McManus, Agnes Knochenhauer, Sofia Mabergs
2014 Canada Jennifer Jones, Kaitlyn Lawes, Jill Officer, Dawn McEwen
2010 Sweden Anette Norberg, Eva Lund, Cathrine Lindahl, Anna Le Moine
2006 Sweden Anette Norberg, Eva Lund, Cathrine Lindahl, Anna Svard
2002 Great Britain Rhona Martin, Debbie Knox, Fiona MacDonald, Janice Rankin
1998 Canada Sandra Schmirler, Jan Betker, Joan McCusker, Marcia Gudereit

Demonstration Sport

1992 Germany Andrea Schopp, Stephanie Mayr, Monika Wagner, Sabine Huth
1988 Canada Linda Moore, Lindsay Sparkes, Debbie Jones, Penny Ryan

Mixed Doubles

2018 Canada Kaitlyn Lawes/John Morris

CPSIA information can be obtained
at www.ICGtesting.com
Printed in the USA
BVHW052321080122
625755BV00003BB/21

9 781039 117907